Twenty-Four Hours a Day

Twenty-Four
Hours a Day

Center City, MN. 55012

First Published, 1954
Thirty-first Printing, 1982

Printed in the United States of America

FOREWORD

Twenty-Four Hours a Day is intended for members of Alcoholics Anonymous as a help in their program of living one day at a time. It is designed for those who want to start each day with a few minutes of thought, meditation, and prayer.

These daily readings contain most of the material used in the booklet "For Drunks Only" and other A.A. literature; also some passages from "the Big Book," *Alcoholics Anonymous*.

As a basis for the meditations in this book, the author has used many passages from the book, *God Calling* by Two Listeners, edited by A. J. Russell. Permission to use the universal spiritual thoughts expressed in this book, without using direct quotations, has been granted by Dodd, Mead & Co., New York City.

The author hopes that these daily readings may help members of Alcoholics Anonymous to find the power they need to stay sober each twenty-four hours. If we don't take that first drink today, we'll never take it, because it's always today.

Look to this day,
For it is life,
The very life of life.
In its brief course lie all
The realities and verities of existence,
The bliss of growth,
The splendor of action,
The glory of power—

For yesterday is but a dream,
And tomorrow is only a vision,
But today, well lived,
Makes every yesterday a dream
   of happiness
And every tomorrow a vision of hope.

Look well, therefore, to this day.

Sanskrit Proverb

JANUARY 1—A.A. Thought for the Day

When I came into A.A., was I a desperate person? Did I have a soul-sickness? Was I so sick of myself and my way of living that I couldn't stand looking at myself in a mirror? Was I ready for A.A.? Was I ready to try anything that would help me to get sober and to get over my soul-sickness? *Should I ever forget the condition I was in?*

Meditation for the Day

In the new year, I will live one day at a time. I will make each day one of preparation for better things ahead. I will not dwell on the past or the future, only on the present. I will bury every fear of the future, all thoughts of unkindness and bitterness, all my dislikes, my resentments, my sense of failure, my disappointments in others and in myself, my gloom and my despondency. I will leave all these things buried and go forward, in this new year, into a new life.

Prayer for the Day

I pray that God will guide me one day at a time in the new year. I pray that for each day, God will supply the wisdom and the strength that I need.

JANUARY 2—A.A. Thought for the Day

What makes A.A. work? The first thing is to have a revulsion against myself and my way of living. Then I must admit I was helpless, that alcohol had me licked and I couldn't do anything about it. The next thing is to honestly want to quit the old life. Then I must surrender my life to a Higher Power, put my drinking problem in His hands and leave it there. After these things are done, I should attend meetings regularly for fellowship and sharing. I should also try to help other alcoholics. *Am I doing these things?*

Meditation for the Day

You are so made that you can only carry the weight of twenty-four hours, no more. If you weigh yourself down with the years behind and the days ahead, your back breaks. God has promised to help you with the burdens of the day only. If you are foolish enough to gather again that burden of the past and carry it, then indeed you cannot expect God to help you bear it. So forget that which lies behind you and breathe in the blessing of each new day.

Prayer for the Day

I pray that I may realize that, for good or bad, past days have ended. I pray that I may face each new day, the coming twenty-four hours, with hope and courage.

JANUARY 3—A.A. Thought for the Day

When I came into A.A., I learned what an alcoholic was and then I applied this knowledge to myself to see if I was an alcoholic. When I was convinced that I was an alcoholic, I admitted it openly. Since then, have I been learning to live accordingly? Have I read the book, *Alcoholics Anonymous*? Have I applied the knowledge gained to myself? Have I admitted openly that I am an alcoholic? *Am I ready to admit it at any time when I can be of help?*

Meditation for the Day

I will be renewed. I will be remade. In this, I need God's help. His spirit shall flow through me and, in flowing through me, it shall sweep away all the bitter past. I will take heart. The way will open for me. Each day will unfold something good, as long as I am trying to live the way I believe God wants me to live.

Prayer for the Day

I pray that I may be taught, just as a child would be taught. I pray that I may never question God's plans, but accept them gladly.

JANUARY 4—A.A. Thought for the Day

Have I admitted I am an alcoholic? Have I swallowed my pride and admitted I was different from ordinary drinkers? Have I accepted the fact that I must spend the rest of my life without liquor? Have I any more reservations, any idea in the back of my mind that some day I'll be able to drink safely? Am I absolutely honest with myself and with other people? Have I taken an inventory of myself and admitted the wrong I have done? Have I come clean with my friends? *Have I tried to make it up to them for the way I have treated them?*

Meditation for the Day

I will believe that fundamentally all is well. Good things will happen to me. I believe that God cares for me and will provide for me. I will not try to plan ahead. I know that the way will unfold, step by step. I will leave tomorrow's burden to God, because He is the great burden-bearer. He only expects me to carry my one-day's share.

Prayer for the Day

I pray that I may not try to carry the burden of the universe on my shoulders. I pray that I may be satisfied to do my share each day.

JANUARY 5—A.A. Thought for the Day

Have I turned to a Higher Power for help? Do I believe that each man or woman I see in A.A. is a demonstration of the power of God to change a human being from a drunkard into a sober, useful citizen? Do I believe that this Higher Power can keep me from drinking? Am I living one day at a time? Do I ask God to give me the power to stay sober for each twenty-four hours? *Do I attend A.A. meetings regularly?*

Meditation for the Day

I believe that God's presence brings peace and that peace, like a quiet-flowing river, will cleanse all irritants away. In these quiet times, God will teach me how to rest my nerves. I will not be afraid. I will learn how to relax. When I am relaxed, God's strength will flow into me. I will be at peace.

Prayer for the Day

I pray for that peace which passes all understanding. I pray for that peace which the world can neither give nor take away.

JANUARY 6—A.A. Thought for the Day

Keeping sober is the most important thing in my life. The most important decision I ever made was my decision to give up drinking. I am convinced that my whole life depends on not taking that first drink. Nothing in the world is as important to me as my own sobriety. Everything I have, my whole life, depends on that one thing. *Can I afford ever to forget this, even for one minute?*

Meditation for the Day

I will discipline myself. I will do this disciplining now. I will turn out all useless thoughts. I know that the goodness of my life is a necessary foundation for its usefulness. I will welcome this training, for without it God cannot give me his power. I believe that this power is a mighty power when it is used in the right way.

Prayer for the Day

I pray that I may face and accept whatever discipline is necessary. I pray that I may be fit to receive God's power in my life.

JANUARY 7—A.A. Thought for the Day

When temptation comes, as it does sometimes to all of us, I will say to myself: "No, my whole life depends on not taking that drink and nothing in the world can make me do it." Besides, I have promised that Higher Power that I wouldn't do it. I know that God doesn't want me to drink and I won't break my promise to God. I've given up my right to drink and it's not my decision any longer. *Have I made the choice once and for all, so that there's no going back on it?*

Meditation for the Day

In silence comes God's meaning to the heart. I cannot judge when it enters the heart. I can only judge by results. God's word is spoken to the secret places of my heart and, in some hour of temptation, I find that word and realize its value for the first time. When I need it, I find it there. "Thy Father, who seeth in secret, shall reward thee openly."

Prayer for the Day

I pray that I may see God's meaning in my life. I pray that I may gladly accept what God has to teach me.

JANUARY 8—A.A. Thought for the Day

Everyone who comes into A.A. knows from bitter experience that he or she can't drink. I know that drinking has been the cause of all my major troubles or has made them worse. Now that I have found a way out, I will hang onto A.A. with both hands. Saint Paul once said that nothing in the world, neither powers nor principalities, life nor death, could separate him from the love of God. *Once I have given my drink problem to God, should anything in the world separate me from my sobriety?*

Meditation for the Day

I know that my new life will not be immune from difficulties, but I will have peace even in difficulties. I know that serenity is the result of faithful, trusting acceptance of God's will, even in the midst of difficulties. Saint Paul said: "Our light afflictions, which are but for a moment, work for us a far more exceeding and eternal weight of glory."

Prayer for the Day

I pray that I may welcome difficulties. I pray that they may test my strength and build my character.

JANUARY 9—A.A. Thought for the Day

When we were drinking, most of us had no real faith in anything. We may have said that we believed in God, but we didn't act as though we did. We never honestly asked God to help us and we never really accepted His help. To us, faith looked like helplessness. But when we came into A.A., we began to have faith in God. And we found out that faith gave us the strength we needed to overcome drinking. *Have I learned that there is strength in faith?*

Meditation for the Day

I will have faith, no matter what may befall me. I will be patient, even in the midst of troubles. I will not fear the strain of life, because I believe that God knows just what I can bear. I will look to the future with confidence. I know that God will not ask me to bear anything that could overcome or destroy me.

Prayer for the Day

I pray that I may put this day in the hands of God. I pray for faith, so that nothing will upset me or weaken my determination to stay sober.

JANUARY 10—A.A. Thought for the Day

When we were drinking, most of us were full of pride and selfishness. We believed we could handle our own affairs, even though we were making a mess of our lives. We were very stubborn and didn't like to take advice. We resented being told what to do. To us, humility looked like weakness. But when we came into A.A., we began to be humble. And we found out that humility gave us the power we needed to overcome drinking. *Have I learned that there is power in humility?*

Meditation for the Day

I will come to God in faith and He will give me a new way of life. This new way of life will alter my whole existence, the words I speak, the influence I have. They will spring from the life within me. I see how important is the work of a person who has this new way of life. The words and the example of such a person can have a wide influence for good in the world.

Prayer for the Day

I pray that I may learn the principles of the good life. I pray that I may meditate upon them and work at them, because they are eternal.

JANUARY 11—A.A. Thought for the Day

When we were drinking most of us never thought of helping others. We liked to buy drinks for people, because that made us feel like big shots. But we only used others for our own pleasure. To really go out and try to help somebody who needed help never occurred to us. To us, helping others looked like a sucker's game. But when we came into A.A., we began to try to help others. And we found out that helping others made us happy and also helped us to stay sober. *Have I learned that there is happiness in helping others?*

Meditation for the Day

I will pray only for strength and that God's will be done. I will use God's unlimited store of strength for my needs. I will seek God's will for me. I will strive for consciousness of God's presence, for He is the light of the world. I have become a pilgrim, who needs only marching orders and strength and guidance for this day.

Prayer for the Day

I pray that I may seek God's guidance day by day. I pray that I may strive to abide in God's presence.

JANUARY 12—A.A. Thought for the Day

The longer we're in A.A., the more natural this way of life seems. Our old drinking lives were a very unnatural way of living. Our present sober lives are the most natural way we could possibly live. During the early years of our drinking, our lives weren't so different from the lives of a lot of other people. But as we gradually became problem drinkers, our lives became more and more unnatural. *Do I realize now that the things I did were far from natural?*

Meditation for the Day

I will say thank you to God for everything, even the seeming trials and worries. I will strive to be grateful and humble. My whole attitude toward the Higher Power will be one of gratitude. I will be glad for the things I have received. I will pass on what God reveals to me. I believe that more truths will flow in, as I go along in the new way of life.

Prayer for the Day

I pray that I may be grateful for the things I have received and do not deserve. I pray that this gratitude will make me truly humble.

JANUARY 13—A.A. Thought for the Day

When we were drinking, we were living an unnatural life physically and mentally. We were punishing our bodies by loading them with alcohol. We didn't eat enough and we ate the wrong things. We didn't get enough sleep or the right kind of rest. We were ruining ourselves physically. We had an alcoholic obsession and we couldn't imagine life without alcohol. We kept imagining all kinds of crazy things about ourselves and about other people. We were ruining ourselves mentally. *Since I came into A.A., am I getting better physically and mentally?*

Meditation for the Day

I believe that my life is being refined like gold in a crucible. Gold does not stay in the crucible, only until it is refined. I will never despair or be despondent. I now have friends who long for me to conquer. If I should err or fail, it would cause pain and disappointment to them. I will keep trying to live a better life.

Prayer for the Day

I pray that I may always call on God's strength, while the gold of my life is being refined. I pray that I may see it through, with God's help.

JANUARY 14—A.A. Thought for the Day

When we first came into A.A., a sober life seemed strange. We wondered what life could possibly be like without ever taking a drink. At first, a sober life seemed unnatural. But the longer we're in A.A., the more natural this way of life seems. And now we know that the life we're living in A.A., the sobriety, the fellowship, the faith in God, and the trying to help each other, is the most natural way we could possibly live. *Do I believe it's the way God wants me to live?*

Meditation for the Day

I will learn to overcome myself, because every blow to selfishness is used to shape the real, eternal, unperishable me. As I overcome myself, I gain that power which God releases in my soul. And I too will be victorious. It is not the difficulties of life that I have to conquer, so much as my own selfishness.

Prayer for the Day

I pray that I may obey God and walk with Him and listen to Him. I pray that I may strive to overcome my own selfishness.

JANUARY 15—A.A. Thought for the Day

The A.A. program is a way of life. It's a way of living and we have to learn to live the program if we're going to stay sober. The twelve steps in the book are like guide posts. They point the direction in which we have to go. But all members of the group have to find their own best way to live the program. We don't all do it exactly alike. Whether by quiet times in the morning, meetings, working with others, or spreading the word, we have to learn to live the program. *Has the A.A. way become my regular, natural way of living?*

Meditation for the Day

I will relax and not get tense. I will have no fear, because everything will work out in the end. I will learn soul-balance and poise in a vacillating, changing world. I will claim God's power and use it because if I do not use it, it will be withdrawn. As long as I get back to God and replenish my strength after each task, no work can be too much.

Prayer for the Day

I pray that I may relax and that God's strength will be given to me. I pray that I may subject my will to God's will and be free from all tenseness.

JANUARY 16—A.A. Thought for the Day

The A.A. program is more a way of building a new life than just a way of getting over drinking, because in A.A. we don't just stop drinking. We did that plenty of times in the old days when we "went on the wagon." And, of course, we always started to drink again, because we were only waiting for the time when we could fall off. Once we've got sober through the A.A. program, we start going uphill. In our drinking days, we were going downhill, getting worse and worse. We either go down or up. *Am I going uphill, getting better and better?*

Meditation for the Day

I will try to obey God's will day in and day out, in the wilderness plains as well as on the mountaintops of experience. It is in the daily strivings that perseverence counts. I believe that God is Lord of little things, the Divine Controller of little happenings. I will persevere in this new way of life. I know that nothing in the day is too small to be part of God's scheme.

Prayer for the Day

I pray that the little stones which I put into the mosaic of my life may make a worthwhile pattern. I pray that I may persevere and so find harmony and beauty.

JANUARY 17—A.A. Thought for the Day

It doesn't do much good to come to meetings only once in a while and sit around, hoping to get something out of the program. That's all right at first, but it won't help us very long. Sooner or later we have to get into action by coming to meetings regularly, by giving a personal witness of our experience with alcohol, and by trying to help other alcoholics. Building a new life takes all the energy that we used to spend on drinking. *Am I spending at least as much time and effort on the new life that I'm trying to build in A.A.?*

Meditation for the Day

With God's help, I will build a protective screen around myself which will keep out all evil thoughts. I will fashion it out of my attitude toward God and my attitude toward other people. When one worrying or impatient thought enters my mind, I will put it out at once. I know that love and trust are the solvents for the worry and frets of life. I will use them to form a protective screen around me.

Prayer for the Day

I pray that frets and impatience and worry may not corrode my protective screen against all evil thoughts. I pray that I may banish all these from my life.

JANUARY 18—A.A. Thought for the Day

The new life can't be built in a day. We have to take the program slowly, a little at a time. Our subconscious minds have to be re-educated. We have to learn to think differently. We have to get used to sober thinking instead of alcoholic thinking. Anyone who tries it, knows that the old alcoholic thinking is apt to come back on us when we least expect it. Building a new life is a slow process, but it can be done if we really follow the A.A. program. *Am I building a new life on the foundation of sobriety?*

Meditation for the Day

I will pray daily for faith, for it is God's gift. On faith alone depends the answer to my prayers. God gives it to me in response to my prayers, because it is a necessary weapon for me to possess for the overcoming of all adverse conditions and the accomplishment of all good in my life. Therefore, I will work at strengthening my faith.

Prayer for the Day

I pray that I may so think and live as to feed my faith in God. I pray that my faith may grow because with faith God's power becomes available to me.

JANUARY 19—A.A. Thought for the Day

On the foundation of sobriety, we can build a life of honesty, unselfishness, faith in God, and love of our fellow human beings. We'll never fully reach these goals, but the adventure of building that kind of a life is so much better than the merry-go-round of our old drinking life that there's no comparison. We come into A.A. to get sober, but if we stay long enough we learn a new way of living. We become honest with ourselves and with other people. We learn to think more about others and less about ourselves. And we learn to rely on the constant help of a Higher Power. *Am I living the way of honesty, unselfishness, and faith?*

Meditation for the Day

I believe that God had already seen my heart's needs before I cried to Him, before I was conscious of those needs myself. I believe that God was already preparing the answer. God does not have to be petitioned with sighs and tears and much speaking, before he reluctantly looses the desired help. He has already anticipated my every want and need. I will try to see this, as His plans unfold in my life.

Prayer for the Day

I pray that I may understand my real wants and needs. I pray that my understanding of those needs and wants may help to bring the answer to them.

JANUARY 20—A.A. Thought for the Day

In A.A., we're all through with lying, hangovers, remorse, and wasting money. When we were drinking, we were only half alive. Now that we're trying to live decent, honest, unselfish lives, we're really alive. Life has a new meaning for us, so that we can really enjoy it. We feel that we're some use in the world. We're on the right side of the fence, instead of on the wrong side. We can look the world in the face instead of hiding in alleys. We come into A.A. to get sober and if we stay long enough, we learn a new way of living. *Am I convinced that no matter how much fun I got out of drinking, that life never was as good as the life I can build in A.A.?*

Meditation for the Day

I want to be at one with the Divine Spirit of the universe. I will set my deepest affections on things spiritual, not on things material. As a man thinketh, so is he. So I will think of and desire that which will help, not hinder, my spiritual growth. I will try to be at one with God. No human aspiration can reach higher than this.

Prayer for the Day

I pray that I may think love, and love will surround me. I pray that I may think health, and health will come to me.

JANUARY 21—A.A. Thought for the Day

To grasp the A.A. program, we have to think things out. Saint Paul said: "They are transformed by the renewing of their minds." We have to learn to think straight. We have to change from alcoholic thinking to sober thinking. We must build up a new way of looking at things. Before we came into A.A., we wanted an artificial life of excitement and everything that goes with drinking. That kind of a life looked normal to us then. But as we look back now, that life looks the exact opposite of normal. In fact, it looks most abnormal. We must re-educate our minds. *Am I changing from an abnormal thinker to a normal thinker?*

Meditation for the Day

I will take the most crowded day without fear. I believe that God is with me and controlling all. I will let confidence be the motif running through all the crowded day. I will not get worried, because I know that God is my helper. Underneath are the everlasting arms. I will rest in them, even though the day be full of things crowding in upon me.

Prayer for the Day

I pray that I may be calm and let nothing upset me. I pray that I may not let material things control me and choke out spiritual things.

JANUARY 22—A.A. Thought for the Day

In the beginning, you want to get sober, but you're helpless, so you turn to a Power greater than yourself and by trusting in that Power, you get the strength to stop drinking. From then on, you want to keep sober, and that's a matter of re-educating your mind. After a while, you get so that you really enjoy simple, healthy, normal living. You really get a kick out of life without the artificial stimulus of alcohol. All you have to do is to look around at the members of any A.A. group and you will see how their outlook has changed. *Is my outlook on life changing?*

Meditation for the Day

I will never forget to say thank you to God, even on the greyest days. My attitude will be one of humility and gratitude. Saying thank you to God is a daily practice that is absolutely necessary. If a day is not one of thankfulness, the practice has to be repeated until it becomes so. Gratitude is a necessity for those who seek to live a better life.

Prayer for the Day

I pray that gratitude will bring humility. I pray that humility will bring me to live a better life.

JANUARY 23—A.A. Thought for the Day

Alcoholics are people whose drinking got them into a "blind alley." They haven't been able to learn anything from their drinking experiences. They are always making the same mistakes and suffering the same consequences over and over again. They refuse to admit they're alcoholic. They still think they can handle the stuff. They won't swallow their pride and admit that they're different from ordinary drinkers. They won't face the fact that they must spend the rest of their lives without liquor. They can't visualize life without ever taking a drink. *Am I out of this blind alley?*

Meditation for the Day

I believe that God has all power. It is His to give and His to withhold. But He will not withhold it from the person who dwells near Him, because then it passes insensibly from God to that person. It is breathed in by the person who lives in God's presence. I will learn to live in God's presence and then I will have those things which I desire of Him: strength, power and joy. God's power is available to all who need it and are willing to accept it.

Prayer for the Day

I pray that I may get myself out of the way, so that God's power may flow in. I pray that I may surrender myself to that power.

JANUARY 24—A.A. Thought for the Day

Alcoholics who are living in a blind alley refuse to be really honest with themselves or with other people. They're running away from life and won't face things as they are. They won't give up their resentments. They're too sensitive and too easily hurt. They refuse to try to be unselfish. They still want everything for themselves. And no matter how many disastrous experiences they have had with drinking, they still do it over and over again. There's only one way to get out of that blind alley way of living and that's to change your thinking. *Have I changed my thinking?*

Meditation for the Day

I know that the vision and power which I receive from God are limitless, as far as spiritual things are concerned. But in temporal and material things, I must submit to limitations. I know that I cannot see the road ahead. I must go just one step at a time, because God does not grant me a longer view. I am in uncharted waters, limited by my temporal and spatial life, but unlimited in my spiritual life.

Prayer for the Day

I pray that, in spite of my material limitations, I may follow God's way. I pray that I may learn that trying to do His will is perfect freedom.

JANUARY 25—A.A. Thought for the Day

We used to depend on drinking for a lot of things. We depended on drinking to help us enjoy things. It gave us a "kick." It broke down our shyness and helped us to have a "good time." We depended on drinking to help us when we felt low physically. If we had a toothache or just a hangover, we felt better after a few drinks. We depended on drinking to help us when we felt low mentally. If we'd had a tough day at work or if we'd had a fight with our husband or wife, or if things just seemed against us, we felt better under the influence of alcohol. For us alcoholics, it got so that we depended on drinking for almost everything. *Have I got over that dependence on drinking?*

Meditation for the Day

I believe that complete surrender of my life to God is the foundation of serenity. God has prepared for us many mansions. I do not look upon that promise as referring only to the after-life. I do not look upon this life as something to be struggled through, in order to get the rewards of the next life. I believe that the Kingdom of God is within us and we can enjoy "eternal life" here and now.

Prayer for the Day

I pray that I may try to do God's will. I pray that such understanding, insight, and vision shall be mine, as shall make my life eternal, here and now.

JANUARY 26—A.A. Thought for the Day

As we became alcoholics, the bad effects of drinking came more and more to outweigh the good effects. But the strange part of it is that, no matter what drinking did to us, loss of our health, our jobs, our money and our homes, we still stuck to it and depended on it. Our dependence on drinking became an obsession. In A.A., we find a new outlook on life. We learn how to change from alcoholic thinking to sober thinking. And we find out that we can no longer depend on drinking for anything. We depend on a Higher Power instead. *Have I entirely given up that dependence on drinking?*

Meditation for the Day

I will try to keep my life calm and unruffled. This is my great task, to find peace and acquire serenity. I must not harbor disturbing thoughts. No matter what fears, worries and resentments I may have, I must try to think of constructive things, until calmness comes. Only when I am calm can I act as a channel for God's spirit.

Prayer for the Day

I pray that I may build up instead of tearing down. I pray that I may be constructive and not destructive.

JANUARY 27—A.A. Thought for the Day

Alcoholics carry an awful load around with them. What a load lying puts on your shoulders! Drinking makes liars out of all of us alcoholics. In order to get the liquor we want, we have to lie all the time. We have to lie about where we've been and what we've been doing. When you are lying you are only half alive, because of the fear of being found out. When you come into A.A., and get honest with yourself and with other people, that terrible load of lying falls off your shoulders. *Have I got rid of that load of lying?*

Meditation for the Day

I believe that in the spiritual world, as in the material world, there is no empty space. As fears and worries and resentments depart out of my life, the things of the spirit come in to take their places. Calm comes after a storm. As soon as I am rid of fears and hates and selfishness, God's love and peace and calm can come in.

Prayer for the Day

I pray that I may rid myself of all fears and resentments, so that peace and serenity may take their place. I pray that I may sweep my life clean of evil, so that good may come in.

JANUARY 28—A.A. Thought for the Day

What a load hangovers put on your shoulders! What terrible physical punishment we've all been through. The pounding headaches and jumpy nerves, the shakes and the jitters, the hot and cold sweats! When you come into A.A. and stop drinking, that terrible load of hangovers falls off your shoulders. What a load remorse puts on your shoulders! That terrible mental punishment we've all been through. Ashamed of the things you've said and done. Afraid to face people because of what they might think of you. Afraid of the consequences of what you did when you were drunk. What an awful beating the mind takes! When you come into A.A., that terrible load of remorse falls off your shoulders. *Have I got rid of these loads of hangovers and remorse?*

Meditation for the Day

When you seek to follow the way of the spirit, it frequently means a complete reversal of the way of the world which you had previously followed. But it is a reversal that leads to happiness and peace. Do the aims and ambitions that a person usually strives for bring peace? Do the world's awards bring heart-rest and happiness? Or do they turn to ashes in the mouth?

Prayer for the Day

I pray that I may not be weary, disillusioned, or disappointed. I pray that I may not put my trust in the ways of the world, but in the way of the spirit.

JANUARY 29—A.A. Thought for the Day

What a load wasting money puts on your shoulders! They say that members of A.A. have paid the highest initiation fee of any club members in the world, because we've wasted so much money on liquor. We'll never be able to figure out how much it was. We not only wasted our own money, but also the money we should have spent on our families. When you come into A.A., that terrible load of wasted money falls off your shoulders. We alcoholics were getting round-shouldered from carrying all those loads that drinking put on our shoulders. But when we come into A.A., we get a wonderful feeling of release and freedom. *Can I throw back my shoulders and look the whole world in the face again?*

Meditation for the Day

I believe that the future is in the hands of God. He knows better than I what the future holds for me. I am not at the mercy of fate or buffeted about by life. I am being led in a very definite way, as I try to rebuild my life. I am the builder, but God is the architect. It is mine to build as best I can, under His guidance.

Prayer for the Day

I pray that I may depend on God, since He has planned my life. I pray that I may live my life as I believe God wants me to live it.

JANUARY 30—A.A. Thought for the Day

A drinking life isn't a happy life. Drinking cuts you off from other people and from God. One of the worst things about drinking is the loneliness. And one of the best things about A.A. is the fellowship. Drinking cuts you off from other people, at least from the people who really matter to you, your family, your co-workers, and your real friends. No matter how much you love them, you build up a wall between you and them by your drinking. You're cut off from any real companionship with them. As a result, you're terribly lonely. *Have I got rid of my loneliness?*

Meditation for the Day

I will sometimes go aside into a quiet place of retreat with God. In that place, I will find restoration and healing and power. I will plan quiet times now and then, times when I will commune with God and arise rested and refreshed to carry on the work which God has given me to do. I know that God will never give me a load greater than I can bear. It is in serenity and peace that all true success lies.

Prayer for the Day

I pray that I may strengthen my inner life, so that I may find serenity. I pray that my soul may be restored in quietness and peace.

JANUARY 31—A.A. Thought for the Day

Drinking cuts you off from God. No matter how you were brought up, no matter what your religion is, no matter if you say you believe in God, nevertheless you build up a wall between you and God by your drinking. You know you're not living the way God wants you to. As a result, you have that terrible remorse. When you come into A.A., you begin to get right with other people and with God. A sober life is a happy life, because by giving up drinking, we've got rid of our loneliness and remorse. *Do I have real fellowship with other people and with God?*

Meditation for the Day

I believe that all sacrifice and all suffering is of value to me. When I am in pain, I am being tested. Can I trust God, no matter how low I feel? Can I say, "Thy will be done," no matter how much I am defeated? If I can, my faith is real and practical. It works in bad times as well as in good times. The Divine Will is working in a way that is beyond my finite mind to understand, but I can still trust in it.

Prayer for the Day

I pray that I may take my suffering in my stride. I pray that I may accept pain and defeat as part of God's plan for my spiritual growth.

FEB. 1—A.A. Thought for the Day

When we think about having a drink, we're thinking of the kick we get out of drinking, the pleasure, the escape from boredom, the feeling of self-importance, and the companionship of other drinkers. What we don't think of is the letdown, the hangover, the remorse, the waste of money, and the facing of another day. In other words, when we think about that first drink, we're thinking of all the assets of drinking and none of the liabilities. What has drinking really got that we haven't got in A.A.? *Do I believe that the liabilities of drinking outweigh the assets?*

Meditation for the Day

I will start a new life each day. I will put the old mistakes away and start anew each day. God always offers me a fresh start. I will not be burdened or anxious. If God's forgiveness were only for the righteous and those who had not sinned, where would be its need? I believe that God forgives us all of our sins, if we are honestly trying to live today the way He wants us to live. God forgives us much and we should be very grateful.

Prayer for the Day

I pray that my life may not be spoiled by worry and fear and selfishness. I pray that I may have a glad, thankful, and humble heart.

FEB. 2—A.A. Thought for the Day

We got a kick out of the first few drinks, before we got stupefied by alcohol. For a while, the world seemed to look brighter. But how about the letdown, the terrible depression that comes the morning after? In A.A., we get a real kick: not a false feeling of exhilaration, but a real feeling of satisfaction with ourselves, self-respect, and a feeling of friendliness toward the world. We got a sort of pleasure from drinking. For a while we thought we were happy. But it's only an illusion. The hangover the next day is the opposite of pleasure. *In A.A., am I getting real pleasure and serenity and peace?*

Meditation for the Day

I will practice love, because lack of love will block the way. I will try to see good in all people, those I like and also those who fret me and go against the grain. They are all children of God. I will try to give love; otherwise, how can I dwell in God's spirit whence nothing unloving can come? I will try to get along with all people, because the more love I give away, the more I will have.

Prayer for the Day

I pray that I may do all I can to love others, in spite of their many faults. I pray that as I love, so will I be loved.

FEB. 3—A.A. Thought for the Day

By drinking, we escaped from boredom for a while. We almost forgot our troubles. But when we sobered up, our troubles were twice as bad. Drinking had only made them worse. In A.A., we really escape boredom. Nobody's bored at an A.A. meeting. We stick around after it's over and we hate to leave. Drinking gave us a temporary feeling of importance. When we're drinking, we kid ourselves into thinking we are somebody. We tell tall stories to build ourselves up. In A.A., we don't want that kind of self-importance. We have real self-respect and honesty and humility. *Have I found something much better and more satisfactory than drinking?*

Meditation for the Day

I believe that my faith and God's power can accomplish anything in human relationships. There is no limit to what these two things can do in this field. Only believe, and anything can happen. Saint Paul said, "I can do all things through Him who strengtheneth me." All walls that divide you from other human beings can fall by your faith and God's power. These are the two essentials. Everyone can be moved by these.

Prayer for the Day

I pray that I may try to strengthen my faith day by day. I pray that I may rely more and more on God's power.

FEB. 4—A.A. Thought for the Day

Treating others to drinks gave us a kind of satisfaction. We liked to say, "Have a drink on me." But we were not really doing the other people a favor. We were only helping them to get drunk, especially if they happened to be alcoholic. In A.A., we really try to help other alcoholics. We build them up instead of tearing them down. Drinking created a sort of fellowship. But it really was a false fellowship, because it was based on selfishness. We used our drinking companions for our own pleasure. In A.A., we have real fellowship, based on unselfishness and a desire to help each other. And we make real friends, not fair weather friends. *With sobriety, have I got everything that drinking's got, without the headaches?*

Meditation for the Day

I know that God cannot teach anyone who is trusting in a crutch. I will throw away the crutch of alcohol and walk in God's power and spirit. God's power will so invigorate me that I shall indeed walk on to victory. There is never any limit to God's power. I will go step by step, one day at a time. God's will shall be revealed to me as I go forward.

Prayer for the Day

I pray that I may have more and more dependence on God. I pray that I may throw away my alcoholic crutch and let God's power take its place.

FEB. 5—A.A. Thought for the Day

One thing we learn in A.A. is to take a long view of drinking instead of a short view. When we were drinking we thought more about the pleasure or release that a drink would give us than we did about the consequences which would result from our taking that drink. Liquor looks good from the short view. When we look in a package store window, we see liquor dressed up in its best wrappings, with fancy labels and decorations. They look swell. *But have I learned that what's inside those beautiful bottles is just plain poison to me?*

Meditation for the Day

I believe that life is a school in which I must learn spiritual things. I must trust in God and He will teach me. I must listen to God and He will speak through my mind. I must commune with Him in spite of all opposition and every obstacle. There will be days when I will hear no voice in my mind and when there will come no intimate heart-to-heart communion. But if I persist, and make a life habit of schooling myself in spiritual things, God will reveal Himself to me in many ways.

Prayer for the Day

I pray that I may regularly go to school in things of the spirit. I pray that I may grow spiritually, by making a practice of these things.

FEB. 6—A.A. Thought for the Day

On a dark night, the bright lights of the corner tavern look mighty inviting. Inside, there seems to be warmth and good cheer. But we don't stop to think that if we go in there we'll probably end up drunk, with our money spent and an awful hangover. A long mahogany bar in the tropical moonlight looks like a very gay place. But you should see the place the next morning. The chairs are piled on the tables and the place stinks of stale beer and cigarette stubs. And often we are there too, trying to cure the shakes by gulping down straight whiskey. *Can I look straight through the night before and see the morning after?*

Meditation for the Day

God finds, amid the crowd, a few people who follow Him, just to be near Him, just to dwell in His presence. A longing in the Eternal Heart may be satisfied by these few people. I will let God know that I seek just to dwell in His presence, to be near Him, not so much for teaching or a message, as just for Him. It may be that the longing of the human heart to be loved for itself is something caught from the Great Divine Heart.

Prayer for the Day

I pray that I may have a listening ear, so that God may speak to me. I pray that I may have a waiting heart, so that God may come to me.

FEB. 7—A.A. Thought for the Day

A night club crowded with men and women all dressed up in evening clothes looks like a very gay place. But you should see the men's room of that night club the next morning. What a mess! People have been sick all over the place and does it smell! The glamour of the night before is all gone and only the stink of the morning after is left. In A.A., we learn to take a long view of drinking instead of a short view. We learn to think less about the pleasure of the moment and more about the consequences. *Has the night before become less important to me and the morning after more important?*

Meditation for the Day

Only a few more steps and then God's power shall be seen and known in my life. I am now walking in darkness, surrounded by the limitations of space and time. But even in this darkness, I can have faith and can be a light to guide feet that are afraid. I believe that God's power will break through the darkness and my prayers will pierce even to the ears of God Himself. But only a cry from the heart, a trusting cry, ever pierces that darkness and reaches to the divine ear of God.

Prayer for the Day

I pray that the divine power of God will help my human weakness. I pray that my prayer may reach through the darkness to the ear of God.

FEB. 8—A.A. Thought for the Day

When the morning sun comes up on a nice bright day and we jump out of bed, we're thankful to God that we feel well and happy instead of sick and disgusted. Serenity and happiness have become much more important to us than the excitement of drinking, which lifts us up for a short while, but lets us way down in the end. Of course, all of us alcoholics had a lot of fun with drinking. We might as well admit it. We can look back on a lot of good times, before we became alcoholics. But the time comes for all of us alcoholics when drinking ceases to be fun and becomes trouble. *Have I learned that drinking can never again be anything but trouble for me?*

Meditation for the Day

I must rely on God. I must trust Him to the limit. I must depend on the Divine Power in all human relationships. I will wait and trust and hope, until God shows me the way. I will wait for guidance on each important decision. I will meet the test of waiting until a thing seems right before I do it. Every work for God must meet this test of time. The guidance will come, if I wait for it.

Prayer for the Day

I pray that I may meet the test of waiting for God's guidance. I pray that I will not go off on my own.

FEB. 9—A.A. Thought for the Day

In the past, we kept right on drinking in spite of all the trouble we got into. We were foolish enough to believe that drinking could still be fun in spite of everything that happened to us. When we came into A.A., we found a lot of people who, like ourselves, had had fun with drinking, but who now admitted that liquor had become nothing but trouble for them. And when we found that this thing had happened to a lot of other people besides ourselves, we realized that perhaps we weren't such queer birds after all. *Have I learned to admit that for me drinking has ceased to be fun and has become nothing but trouble?*

Meditation for the Day

The life-line, the line of rescue, is the line from the soul to God. On one end of the life-line is our faith and on the other end is God's power. It can be a strong line and no soul can be overwhelmed who is linked to God by it. I will trust in this life-line and never be afraid. God will save me from doing wrong and from the cares and troubles of life. I will look to God for help and trust Him for aid when I am emotionally upset.

Prayer for the Day

I pray that no lack of trust or fearfulness will make me disloyal to God. I pray that I may keep a strong hold on the life-line of faith.

FEB. 10—A.A. Thought for the Day

Since I realized that I had become an alcoholic and could never have any more fun with liquor and since I knew that from then on liquor would always get me into trouble, common sense told me that the only thing left for me was a life of sobriety. But I learned another thing in A.A., the most important thing anyone can ever learn: that I could call on a Higher Power to help me keep away from liquor; that I could work with that Divine Principle in the universe; and that God would help me to live a sober, useful, happy life. So now I no longer care about the fact that I can never have any more fun with drinking. *Have I learned that I am much happier without it?*

Meditation for the Day

Like a tree, I must be pruned of a lot of dead branches before I will be ready to bear good fruit. Think of changed people as trees which have been stripped of their old branches, pruned, cut, and bare. But through the dark, seemingly dead branches flows silently, secretly, the new sap, until with the sun of spring, comes new life. There are new leaves, buds, blossoms, and fruit, many times better because of the pruning. I am in the hands of a Master Gardener, who makes no mistakes in His pruning.

Prayer for the Day

I pray that I may cut away the dead branches of my life. I pray that I may not mind the pruning, since it helps me to bear good fruit later.

FEB. 11—A.A. Thought for the Day

If we're going to stay sober, we've got to learn to want something else more than we want to drink. When we first came into A.A., we couldn't imagine wanting anything else so much or more than drinking. So we had to stop drinking on faith, on faith that some day we really would want something else more than drinking. But after we've been in A.A. for a while, we learn that a sober life can really be enjoyed. We learn how nice it is to get along well with our family, how nice it is to do our work well—whether at home or outside— how nice it is to try to help others. *Have I found that when I keep sober, everything goes well for me?*

Meditation for the Day

There is almost no work in life so hard as waiting. And yet God wants me to wait. All motion is more easy than calm waiting, and yet I must wait until God shows me His will. So many people have marred their work and hindered the growth of their spiritual lives by too much activity. If I wait patiently, preparing myself always, I will be some day at the place where I would be. And much toil and activity could not have accomplished the journey so soon.

Prayer for the Day

I pray that I may wait patiently. I pray that I may trust God and keep preparing myself for a better life.

FEB. 12—A.A. Thought for the Day

As we look back on all those troubles we used to have when we were drinking, the hospitals, the jails, we wonder how we could have wanted that kind of a life. As we look back on it now, we see our drinking life as it really was and we're glad we're out of it. So after a few months in A.A., we find that we can honestly say that we want something else more than drinking. We've learned by experience that a sober life is really enjoyable and we wouldn't go back to the old drunken way of living for anything in the world. *Do I want to keep sober a lot more than I want to get drunk?*

Meditation for the Day

My spiritual life depends on an inner consciousness of God. I must be led in all things by my consciousness of God and I must trust Him in all things. My consciousness of God will always bring peace to me. I will have no fear, because a good future lies before me as long as I keep my consciousness of God. If in every single happening, event and plan I am conscious of God, then no matter what happens, I will be safe in God's hands.

Prayer for the Day

I pray that I may always have this consciousness of God. I pray for a new and better life through this God consciousness.

FEB. 13—A.A. Thought for the Day

Sometimes we can't help thinking: Why can't we ever drink again? We know it's because we're alcoholics, but why did we have to get that way? The answer is that at some time in our drinking careers, we passed what is called our "tolerance point." When we passed this point, we passed from a condition in which we could tolerate alcohol to a condition in which we could not tolerate it at all. After that, if we took one drink, we would sooner or later end up drunk. *When I think of liquor now, do I think of it as something which I can never tolerate again?*

Meditation for the Day

In a race, it is when the goal is in sight that heart and nerves and muscles and courage are strained almost to the breaking point. So with us. The goal of the spiritual life is in sight. All we need is the final effort. The saddest records are made by people who ran well, with brave, stout hearts, until the sight of the goal and then some weakness or self-indulgence held them back. They never knew how near the goal they were or how near they were to victory.

Prayer for the Day

I pray that I may press on until the goal is reached. I pray that I may not give up in the final stretch.

FEB. 14—A.A. Thought for the Day

After that first drink, we had a single track mind. It was like a railroad train. The first drink started it off and it kept going on the single track until it got to the end of the line, drunkenness. We alcoholics knew this was the inevitable result when we took the first drink, but still we couldn't keep away from liquor. Our will-power was gone. We had become helpless and hopeless before the power of alcohol. It's not the second drink or the tenth drink that does the damage. It's the first drink. *Will I ever take that first drink again?*

Meditation for the Day

I must keep a time apart with God every day. Gradually I will be transformed mentally and spiritually. It is not the praying so much as just being in God's presence. The strengthening and curative powers of this I cannot understand, because such knowledge is beyond human understanding, but I can experience them. The poor, sick world would be cured if every day each soul waited before God for the inspiration to live aright. My greatest spiritual growth occurs in this time apart with God.

Prayer for the Day

I pray that I may faithfully keep a quiet time apart with God. I pray that I may grow spiritually each day.

FEB. 15—A.A. Thought for the Day

If alcoholism were just a physical allergy, like asthma or hay fever, it would be easy for us, by taking a skin test with alcohol, to find out whether or not we're alcoholics. But alcoholism is not just a physical allergy. It's also a mental allergy or obsession. After we've become alcoholics, we can still tolerate alcohol physically for quite a while, although we suffer a little more after each binge and each time it takes a little longer to get over the hangovers. *Do I realize that since I have become an alcoholic, I cannot tolerate alcohol mentally at all?*

Meditation for the Day

The world doesn't need super men or women, but super-natural people. People who will turn the self out of their lives and let Divine Power work through them. Let inspiration take the place of aspiration. Seek to grow spiritually, rather than to acquire fame and riches. Our chief ambition should be to be used by God. The Divine Force is sufficient for all the spiritual work in the world. God only needs the instruments for His use. His instruments can remake the world.

Prayer for the Day

I pray that I may be an instrument of the Divine Power. I pray that I may do my share in remaking the world.

FEB. 16—A.A. Thought for the Day

One drink started a train of thought which became an obsession, and from then on, we couldn't stop drinking. We developed a mental compulsion to keep drinking until we got good and drunk. People generally make two mistakes about alcoholism. One mistake is that it can be cured by physical treatment only. The other mistake is that it can be cured by will-power only. Most alcoholics have tried both of these ways and have found that they don't work. But we members of A.A. have found a way to arrest alcoholism. *Have I got over my obsession by following the A.A. program?*

Meditation for the Day

I will try to be unruffled, no matter what happens. I will keep my emotions in check, although others about me are letting theirs go. I will keep calm in the face of disturbance, keep that deep, inner calm through all the experiences of the day. In the rush of work and worry, the deep, inner silence is necessary to keep me on an even keel. I must learn to take the calm with me into the most hurried days.

Prayer for the Day

I pray that I may be still and commune with God. I pray that I may learn patience, humility, and peace.

FEB. 17—A.A. Thought for the Day

Alcohol is poison to the alcoholic. Poison is not too strong a word, because alcoholism leads eventually to the death of the alcoholic. It may be a quick death or a slow death. When we go by package stores and see various kinds of liquor all dressed up in fancy packages to make it look attractive, we should always make it a point to say to ourselves so we'll never forget it: "That stuff's all poison to me." And it is. Alcohol poisoned our lives for a long time. *Do I know that since I'm an alcoholic all liquor is poison to me?*

Meditation for the Day

I must somehow find the means of coming nearer to God. That is what really matters. I must somehow seek the true bread of life, which is communion with Him. I must grasp for the truth at the center of all worship. This central truth is all that matters. All forms of worship have this communion with God as their purpose and goal.

Prayer for the Day

I pray that I may meet God in quiet communion. I pray that I may partake of the soul-food which God has provided for me.

FEB. 18—A.A. Thought for the Day

After I became an alcoholic, alcohol poisoned my love for my family and friends, it poisoned my ambition, it poisoned my self-respect. It poisoned my whole life, until I met A.A. My life is happier now than it has been for a long time. I don't want to commit suicide. So with the help of God and A.A., I'm not going to take any more of that alcoholic poison into my system. And I'm going to keep training my mind never even to think of liquor again in any way except as a poison. *Do I believe that liquor will poison my life if I ever touch it again?*

Meditation for the Day

I will link up my frail nature with the limitless Divine Power. I will link my life with the Divine Force for Good in the world. It is not the passionate appeal that gains the Divine attention as much as the quiet placing of the difficulty and worry in the Divine Hands. So I will trust God like a child who places its tangled skein of wool in the hands of a loving mother to unravel. We please God more by our unquestioning confidence than by imploring Him for help.

Prayer for the Day

I pray that I may put all my difficulties in God's hands and leave them there. I pray that I may fully trust God to take care of them.

FEB. 19—A.A. Thought for the Day

Many things we do in A.A. are in preparation for that crucial moment when, walking down the street on a nice sunshiny day, we see a nice cool cocktail lounge and the idea of having a drink pops into our minds. If we've trained our minds so that we're well prepared for that crucial moment, we won't take that first drink. In other words, if we've done our A.A. homework well, we won't slip when temptation comes. *In preparation for that crucial moment when I'll be tempted, will I keep in mind the fact that liquor is my enemy?*

Meditation for the Day

How many of the world's prayers have gone unanswered because those who prayed did not endure to the end? They thought it was too late, that they must act for themselves, that God was not going to guide them. "He that endureth to the end, the same shall be saved." Can I endure to the very end? If so, I shall be saved. I will try to endure with courage. If I endure, God will unlock those secret spiritual treasures which are hidden from those who do not endure to the end.

Prayer for the Day

I pray that I may follow God's guidance, so that spiritual success shall be mine. I pray that I may never doubt the power of God and so take things into my own hands.

FEB. 20—A.A. Thought for the Day

Liquor used to be my friend. I used to have a lot of fun drinking. Practically all the fun I had was connected with drinking. But the time came when liquor became my enemy. I don't know just when liquor turned against me and became my enemy, but I know it happened, because I began to get into trouble. And since I realize that liquor is now my enemy, my main business now is keeping sober. Making a living or keeping house is no longer my main business. It's secondary to the business of keeping sober. *Do I realize that my main business is keeping sober?*

Meditation for the Day

I can depend on God to supply me with all the power I need to face any situation, provided that I will sincerely believe in that power and honestly ask for it, at the same time making all my life conform to what I believe God wants me to be. I can come to God as a business manager would come to the owner of the business, knowing that to lay the matter before Him means immediate cooperation, providing the matter has merit.

Prayer for the Day

I pray that I may believe that God is ready and willing to supply me with all that I need. I pray that I may ask only for faith and strength to meet any situation.

FEB. 21—A.A. Thought for the Day

I go to the A.A. meetings because it helps me in my business of keeping sober. And I try to help other alcoholics when I can, because that's part of my business of keeping sober. I also have a partner in this business and that's God. I pray to Him every day to help me to keep sober. As long as I keep in mind that liquor can never be my friend again, but is now my deadly enemy, and as long as I remember that my main business is keeping sober and that it's the most important thing in my life, I believe I'll be prepared for that crucial moment when the idea of having a drink pops into my mind. *When that idea comes, will I be able to resist it and not take that drink?*

Meditation for the Day

I will be more afraid of spirit-unrest, of soul-disturbance, of any ruffling of the mind, than of earthquake or fire. When I feel the calm of my spirit has been broken by emotional upset, then I must steal away alone with God, until my heart sings and all is strong and calm again. Uncalm times are the only times when evil can find an entrance. I will beware of ungarded spots of unrest. I will try to keep calm, no matter what turmoil surrounds me.

Prayer for the Day

I pray that no emotional upsets will hinder God's power in my life. I pray that I may keep a calm spirit and a steady heart.

FEB. 22—A.A. Thought for the Day

Now we can take an inventory of the good things that have come to us through A.A. To begin with, we're sober today. That's the biggest asset on any alcoholic's books. Sobriety to us is like good-will in business. Everything else depends on that. Most of us have jobs which we owe to our sobriety. We know we couldn't hold these jobs if we were drinking, so our jobs depend on our sobriety. Most of us have wives or husbands and children, which we either had lost or might have lost, if we hadn't stopped drinking. We have friends in A.A., real friends who are always ready to help us. *Do I realize that my job, my family and my real friends are dependent upon my sobriety?*

Meditation for the Day

I must trust God to the best of my ability. This lesson has to be learned. My doubts and fears continually drive me back into the wilderness. Doubts lead me astray, because I am not trusting God. I must trust God's love. It will never fail me, but I must learn not to fail it by my doubts and fears. We all have much to learn in turning out fear by faith. All our doubts arrest God's work through us. I must not doubt. I must believe in God and continually work at strengthening my faith.

Prayer for the Day

I pray that I may live the way God wants me to live. I pray that I may get into that stream of goodness in the world.

FEB. 23—A.A. Thought for the Day

Besides our jobs, our families, our friends, and our sobriety, we have something else which many of us found through A.A. That's faith in a Power greater than ourselves, to which we can turn for help: faith in that Divine Principle in the universe which we call God and which is on our side as long as we do the right thing. There have been many days in the past when, if we had taken an inventory, we'd have found ourselves very much in the red, without sobriety, and therefore without jobs, families, friends, or faith in God. We now have these things because we're sober. *Do I make one resolution every day of my life—to stay sober?*

Meditation for the Day

Love the busy life. It is a joy-filled life. Take your fill of joy in the Spring. Live outdoors whenever possible. Sun and air are nature's great healing forces. That inward joy changes poisoned blood into a pure, healthy, life-giving flow. But never forget that the real healing of the spirit comes from within, from the close, loving contact of your spirit with God's spirit. Keep in close communion with God's spirit day by day.

Prayer for the Day

I pray that I may learn to live the abundant life. I pray that I may enjoy a close contact with God this day and be glad in it.

FEB. 24—A.A. Thought for the Day

When we came to our first A.A. meeting, we looked up at the wall at the end of the room and saw the sign: "But for the Grace of God." We knew right then and there that we would have to call on the Grace of God in order to get sober and get over our soul-sickness. We heard speakers tell how they had come to depend on a Power greater than themselves. That made sense to us and we made up our minds to try it. *Am I depending on the Grace of God to help me stay sober?*

Meditation for the Day

Share your love, your joy, your happiness, your time, your food, your money gladly with all. Give out all the love you can with a glad, free heart and hand. Do all you can for others and back will come countless stores of blessings. Sharing draws others to you. Take all who come as sent by God and give them a royal welcome. You may never see the results of your sharing. Today they may not need you, but tomorrow may bring results from the sharing you did today.

Prayer for the Day

I pray that I may make each visitor desire to return. I pray that I may never make anyone feel repulsed or unwanted.

FEB. 25—A.A. Thought for the Day

Some people find it hard to believe in a Power greater than themselves. But not to believe in such a Power forces us to atheism. It has been said that atheism is blind faith in the strange proposition that this universe originated in a cipher and aimlessly rushes nowhere. That's practically impossible to believe. I think we all can agree that alcohol is a power greater than ourselves. It certainly was in my case. I was helpless before the power of alcohol. *Do I remember the things that happened to me because of the power of alcohol?*

Meditation for the Day

The spiritual and moral will eventually overcome the material and unmoral. That is the purpose and destiny of the human race. Gradually the spiritual is overcoming the material in our minds. Gradually the moral is overcoming the unmoral. Faith, fellowship, and service are cures for most of the ills of the world. There is nothing in the field of personal relationships that they cannot do.

Prayer for the Day

I pray that I may do my share in making a better world. I pray that I may be part of the cure for the ills of the world.

FEB. 26—A.A. Thought for the Day

When we came into A.A., we came to believe in a Power greater than ourselves. We came to believe in that Divine Principle in the universe which we call God, and to which we can turn for help. Each morning we have a quiet time. We ask God for the power to stay sober for the next twenty-four hours. And each night we thank Him for helping us to keep sober that day. *Do I believe that each man or woman I see in A.A. is a demonstration of the power of God to change a human being from a drunkard to a sober person?*

Meditation for the Day

I should pray for faith as a thirsty person prays for water in a desert. Do I know what it means to feel sure that God will never fail me? Am I sure of this as I am sure that I still breathe? I should pray daily and most diligently that my faith may increase. There is nothing lacking in my life because, really, all I need is mine, only I lack the faith to know it. I am like a rich man's child who sits in rags when all around me are stores of all I could desire.

Prayer for the Day

I pray for the realization that God has everything I need. I pray that I may know that His power is always available.

FEB. 27—A.A. Thought for the Day

When we came into A.A., the first thing we did was to admit that we couldn't do anything about our drinking. We admitted that alcohol had us licked and that we were helpless against it. We never could decide whether or not to take a drink. We always took the drink. And since we couldn't do anything about it ourselves, we put our whole drink problem into the hands of God. We turned the whole thing over to that Power greater than ourselves. And we have nothing more to do about it, except to trust God to take care of the problem for us. *Have I done this honestly and fully?*

Meditation for the Day

This is the time for my spirit to touch the spirit of God. I know that the feeling of the spirit-touch is more important than all the sensations of material things. I must seek a silence of spirit-touching with God. Just a moment's contact and all the fever of life leaves me. Then I am well, whole, calm, and able to rise and minister to others. God's touch is a potent healer. I must feel that touch and sense God's presence.

Prayer for the Day

I pray that the fever of resentment, worry, and fear may melt into nothingness. I pray that health, joy, peace, and serenity may take its place.

FEB. 28—A.A. Thought for the Day

We should be free from alcohol for good. It's out of our hands and in the hands of God, so we don't need to worry about it or even think about it any more. But if we haven't done this honestly and fully, the chances are that it will become our problem again. Since we don't trust God to take care of the problem for us, we reach out and take the problem back to ourselves. Then it's our problem again and we're in the same old mess we were in before. We're helpless again and we drink. *Do I trust God to take care of the problem for me?*

Meditation for the Day

No work is of value without preparation. Every spiritual work must have behind it much spiritual preparation. Cut short times of prayer and times of spiritual preparation and many hours of work may be profitless. From the point of view of God, one poor tool working all the time, but doing bad work because of lack of preparation, is of small value compared with the sharp, keen, perfect instrument working for only a short time, but which turns out perfect work because of long hours of spiritual preparation.

Prayer for the Day

I pray that I may spend more time alone with God. I pray that I may get more strength and joy from such times, so that they will add much to my work.

MARCH 1—A.A. Thought for the Day

When I find myself thinking about taking a drink, I say to myself: " Don't reach out and take that problem back. You've given it to God and there's nothing you can do about it." So I forget about the drink. One of the most important parts of the A.A. program is to give our drink problem to God honestly and fully and never to reach out and take the problem back to ourselves. If we let God have it and keep it for good and then co-operate with Him, we'll stay sober. *Have I determined not to take the drink problem back to myself?*

Meditation for the Day

Constant effort is necessary if I am to grow spiritually and develop my spiritual life. I must keep the spiritual rules persistently, perseveringly, lovingly, patiently, and hopefully. By keeping them, every mountain of difficulty shall be laid low, the rough places of poverty of spirit shall be made smooth, and all who know me shall know that God is the Lord of all my ways. To get close to the spirit of God is to find life and healing and strength.

Prayer for the Day

I pray that God's spirit may be everything to my soul. I pray that God's spirit may grow within me.

MARCH 2—A.A. Thought for the Day

Over a period of drinking years, we've proved to ourselves and to everybody else that we can't stop drinking by our own will power. We have been proved helpless before the power of alcohol. So the only way we could stop drinking was by turning to a Power greater than ourselves. We call that Power God. The time that you really get this program is when you get down on your knees and surrender yourself to God, as you understand Him. Surrender means putting your life into God's hands. *Have I made a promise to God that I will try to live the way He wants me to live?*

Meditation for the Day

Spirit-power comes from communication with God in prayer and times of quiet meditation. I must constantly seek spirit-communication with God. This is a matter directly between me and God. Those who seek it through the medium of the church do not always get the joy and the wonder of spirit-communication with God. From this communication comes life, joy, peace, and healing. Many people do not realize the power that can come to them from direct spirit-communication.

Prayer for the Day

I pray that I may feel that God's power is mine. I pray that I may be able to face anything through that power.

MARCH 3—A.A. Thought for the Day

After we've made a surrender, the drink problem is out of our hands and in the hands of God. The thing we have to do is to be sure that we never reach out and take the problem back into our own hands. Leave it in God's hands. Whenever I'm tempted to take a drink, I must say to myself: "I can't do that. I've made a bargain with God not to drink. I know God doesn't want me to drink and so I won't do it." At the same time I say a little prayer to God for the strength needed to keep the bargain with Him. *Am I going to keep my bargain with God?*

Meditation for the Day

I will try to grow in this new life. I will think of spiritual things often and unconsciously I will grow. The nearer I get to the new life, the more I will see my unfitness. My sense of failure is a sure sign that I am growing in the new life. It is only struggle that hurts. In sloth—physical, mental, or spiritual—there is no sense of failure or discomfort. With struggle and effort, I am conscious not of strength but of weakness until I am really living the new life. But in the struggle, I can always rely on the power of God to help me.

Prayer for the Day

I pray that I may see signs of my growth in the new life. I pray that I may always keep trying to grow.

MARCH 4—A.A. Thought for the Day

Having surrendered our lives to God and put our drink problem in His hands doesn't mean that we'll never be tempted to drink. So we must build up strength for the time when temptation will come. In this quiet time, we read and pray and get our minds in the right mood for the day. Starting the day right is a great help in keeping sober. As the days go by and we get used to the sober life, it gets easier and easier. We begin to develop a deep gratitude to God for saving us from that old life. And we begin to enjoy peace and serenity and quiet happiness. *Am I trying to live the way God wants me to live?*

Meditation for the Day

The elimination of selfishness is the key to happiness and can only be accomplished with God's help. We start out with a spark of the Divine Spirit but a large amount of selfishness. As we grow and come in contact with other people, we can take one of two paths. We can become more and more selfish and practically extinguish the Divine Spark within us, or we can become more unselfish and develop our spirituality until it becomes the most important thing in our lives.

Prayer for the Day

I pray that I may grow more and more unselfish, honest, pure, and loving. I pray that I may take the right path every day.

MARCH 5—A.A. Thought for the Day

Sometimes we try too hard to get this program. It is better to relax and accept it. It will be given to us, with no effort on our part, if we stop trying too hard to get it. Sobriety can be a free gift of God, which he gives us by His grace when He knows we are ready for it. But we have to be ready. Then we must relax, take it easy, and accept the gift with gratitude and humility. We must put ourselves in God's hands. We must say to God: "Here am I and here are all my troubles. I've made a mess of things and can't do anything about it. You take me and all my troubles and do anything you want with me." *Do I believe that the grace of God can do for me what I could never do for myself?*

Meditation for the Day

Fear is the curse of the world. Many are our fears. Fear is everywhere. I must fight fear as I would a plague. I must turn it out of my life. There is no room for fear in the heart in which God dwells. Fear cannot exist where true love is or where faith abides. So I must have no fear. Fear is evil, but "perfect love casteth out all fear." Fear destroys hope and hope is necessary for all of humanity.

Prayer for the Day

I pray that I may have no fear. I pray that I may cast all fear out of my life.

MARCH 6—A.A. Thought for the Day

In A.A., we must surrender, give up, admit that we're helpless. We surrender our lives to God and ask Him for help. When He knows that we're ready, He gives us by His grace the free gift of sobriety. And we can't take any credit for having stopped drinking, because we didn't do it by our own willpower. There's no place for pride or boasting. We can only be grateful to God for doing for us what we could never do for ourselves. *Do I believe that God has made me a free gift of the strength to stay sober?*

Meditation for the Day

I must work for God, with God, and through God's help. By helping to bring about a true fellowship of human beings, I am working for God. I am also working with God because this is the way God works, and He is with me when I am doing such work. I cannot do good work, however, without God's help. In the final analysis, it is through the grace of God that any real change in human personality takes place. I have to rely on God's power, and anything I accomplish is through His help.

Prayer for the Day

I pray that I may work for God and with God. I pray that I may be used to change human personalities through God's help.

MARCH 7—A.A. Thought for the Day

There are two important things we have to do if we want to get sober and stay sober. First, having admitted that we're helpless before alcohol, we have to turn our alcoholic problem over to God and trust Him to take care of it for us. This means asking Him every morning for the strength to stay sober that day and thanking Him every night. It means really leaving the problem in God's hands and not reaching out and taking the problem back to ourselves. Second, having given our drink problem to God, we must cooperate with Him by doing something about it ourselves. *Am I doing these two things?*

Meditation for the Day

I must prepare myself by doing each day what I can to develop spiritually and to help others to do so. God tests me and trains me and bends me to His will. If I am not properly trained, I cannot meet the test when it comes. I must want God's will for me above all else. I must not expect to have what I am not prepared for. This preparation consists of quiet communion with God every day and gradually gaining the strength I need.

Prayer for the Day

I pray that I may really try to do God's will in all my affairs. I pray that I may do all I can to help others find God's will for them.

MARCH 8—A.A. Thought for the Day

We must go to A.A. meetings regularly. We must learn to think differently. We must change from alcoholic thinking to sober thinking. We must reeducate our minds. We must try to help other alcoholics. We must cooperate with God by spending at least as much time and energy on the A.A. program as we did on drinking. We must follow the A.A. program to the best of our ability. *Have I turned my alcoholic problem over to God and am I cooperating with Him?*

Meditation for the Day

The joy of true fellowship shall be mine in full measure. I will revel in the joy of real fellowship. There will come back a wonderful joy, if I share in fellowship now. Fellowship among spiritually-minded people is the embodiment of God's purpose for this world. To realize this will bring me a new life-joy. If I share in humanity's joy and travail, a great blessing will be mine. I can truly live a life not of earth, but a heaven-life here and now.

Prayer for the Day

I pray that I may be helped and healed by true spiritual fellowship. I pray that I may sense His presence in spiritual fellowship with His children.

MARCH 9—A.A. Thought for the Day

If we had absolute faith in the power of God to keep us from drinking and if we turned our drink problem entirely over to God without reservations, we wouldn't have to do anything more about it. We'd be free from drink once and for all. But since our faith is apt to be weak, we have to strengthen and build up this faith. We do this in several ways. One way is by going to meetings and listening to others tell how they have found all the strength they need to overcome drink. *Is my faith being strengthened by this personal witness of other alcoholics?*

Meditation for the Day

It is the quality of my life that determines its value. In order to judge the value of a person's life, we must set up a standard. The most valuable life is one of honesty, purity, unselfishness, and love. All people's lives ought to be judged by this standard in determining their value to the world. By this standard, most of the so-called heroes of history were not great men. "What shall it profit a man if he gain the whole world, if he loseth his own soul?"

Prayer for the Day

I pray that I may be honest, pure, unselfish, and loving. I pray that I may make the quality of my life good by these standards.

MARCH 10—A.A. Thought for the Day

We also strengthen our faith by working with other alcoholics and finding that we can do nothing ourselves to help them, except to tell them our own story of how we found the way out. If the other person is helped, it's by the grace of God and not by what we do or say. Our own faith is strengthened when we see another alcoholic find sobriety by turning to God. And finally we strengthen our faith by having quiet times every morning. *Do I ask God in this quiet time for the strength to stay sober this day?*

Meditation for the Day

My five senses are my means of communication with the material world. They are the links between my physical life and the material manifestations around me. But I must sever all connections with the material world when I wish to hold communion with the Great Spirit of the universe. I have to hush my mind and bid all my senses be still, before I can become attuned to receive the music of the heavenly spheres.

Prayer for the Day

I pray that I may get my spirit in tune with the Spirit of the universe. I pray that through faith and communion with Him I may receive the strength I need.

MARCH 11—A.A. Thought for the Day

By having quiet times each morning, we come to depend on God's help during the day, especially if we should be tempted to take a drink. And we can honestly thank Him each night for the strength He has given us. So our faith is strengthened by these quiet times of prayer. By listening to other members, by working with other alcoholics, by times of quiet meditation, our faith in God gradually becomes strong. *Have I turned my drink problem entirely over to God, without reservations?*

Meditation for the Day

It seems as though, when God wants to express to men what He is like, He makes a very beautiful character. Think of a personality as God's expression of character attributes. Be as fit an expression of Godlike character as you can. When the beauty of a person's character is impressed upon us, it leaves an image which in turn reflects through our own actions. So look for beauty of character in those around you.

Prayer for the Day

I pray that I may look at great souls until their beauty of character becomes a part of my soul. I pray that I may reflect this character in my own life.

MARCH 12—A.A. Thought for the Day

The Prodigal Son "took his journey into a far country and wasted his substance with riotous living." That's what we alcoholics do. We waste our substance with riotous living. "When he came to himself, he said: 'I will arise and go to my father.'" That's what you do in A.A. You come to yourself. Your alcoholic self is not your real self. Your sane, sober, respectable self is your real self. That's why we alcoholics are so happy in A.A. *Have I come to myself?*

Meditation for the Day

Simplicity is the keynote of a good life. Choose the simple things always. Life can become complicated if you let it be so. You can be swamped by difficulties if you let them take up too much of your time. Every difficulty can be either solved or ignored and something better substituted for it. Love the humble things of life. Reverence the simple things. Your standard must never be the world's standard of wealth and power.

Prayer for the Day

I pray that I may love the simple things of life. I pray that I may keep my life uncomplicated and free.

MARCH 13—A.A. Thought for the Day

We've got rid of our false, drinking selves and found our real, sober selves. And we turn to God, our Father, for help, just as the Prodigal Son arose and went to his father. At the end of the story, the father of the Prodigal Son says: "He was dead and is alive again, he was lost and is found." We alcoholics who have found sobriety in A.A. were certainly dead and are alive again. We were lost and are found. *Am I alive again?*

Meditation for the Day

Gently breathe in God's spirit, that spirit which, if not barred out by selfishness, will enable you to do good works. This means rather that God will be enabled to do good works through you. You can become a channel for God's spirit to flow through you and into the lives of others. The works that you can do will only be limited by your spiritual development. Let your spirit be in harmony with God's spirit and there is no limit to what you can do in the realm of human relationships.

Prayer for the Day

I pray that I may become a channel for God's spirit. I pray that God's spirit may flow through me into the lives of others.

MARCH 14—A.A. Thought for the Day

Can I get well? If I mean: "Can I ever drink normally again," the answer is no. But if I mean, "Can I stay sober?" the answer is definitely yes. I can get well by turning my drink problem over to a Power greater than myself, that Divine Principle in the universe which we call God, and by asking that Power each morning to give me the strength to stay sober for the next twenty-four hours. I know from the experience of thousands of people that if I honestly want to get well, I can get well. *Am I faithfully following the A.A. program?*

Meditation for the Day

Persevere in all that God's guidance moves you to do. The persistent carrying out of what seems right and good will bring you to that place where you would be. If you look back over God's guidance, you will see that His leading has been very gradual and that only as you have carried out His wishes, as far as you can understand them, has God been able to give you more clear and definite leading. You are led by God's touch on a quickened, responsive mind.

Prayer for the Day

I pray that I may persevere in doing what seems right. I pray that I may carry out all of God's leading, as far as I can understand it.

MARCH 15—A.A. Thought for the Day

We alcoholics were on a merry-go-round, going round and round, and we couldn't get off. That merry-go-round is a kind of hell on earth. In A.A. I got off that merry-go-round by learning to stay sober. I pray to my Higher Power every morning to help me to keep sober. And I get the strength from that Power to do what I could never do with my own strength. I do not doubt the existence of that Power. We're not speaking into a vacuum when we pray. That Power is there, if we will use it. *Am I off the merry-go-round of drinking for good?*

Meditation for the Day

I must remember that in spiritual matters I am only an instrument. It is not mine to decide how or when I am to act. God plans all spiritual matters. It is up to me to make myself fit to do God's work. All that hinders my spiritual activity must be eliminated. I can depend on God for all the strength I need to overcome those faults which are blocks. I must keep myself fit, so that God can use me as a channel for His spirit.

Prayer for the Day

I pray that my selfishness may not hinder my progress in spiritual matters. I pray that I may be a good instrument for God to work with.

MARCH 16—A.A. Thought for the Day

Before we decide to quit drinking, most of us have to come up against a blank wall. We see that we're licked, that we have to quit. But we don't know which way to turn for help. There seems to be no door in that blank wall. A.A. opens the door that leads to sobriety. By encouraging us to honestly admit that we're alcoholics and to realize that we can't take even one drink, and by showing us which way to turn for help, A.A. opens the door in that blank wall. *Have I gone through that door to sobriety?*

Meditation for the Day

I must have a singleness of purpose to do my part in God's work. I must not let material distractions interfere with my job of improving personal relationships. It is easy to become distracted by material affairs, so that I lose my singleness of purpose. I do not have time to be concerned about the multifarious concerns of the world. I must concentrate and specialize on what I can do best.

Prayer for the Day

I pray that I may not become distracted by material affairs. I pray that I may concentrate on doing what I can do best.

MARCH 17—A.A. Thought for the Day

A.A. also helps us to hang onto sobriety. By having regular meetings so that we can associate with other alcoholics who have come through that same door in the wall, by encouraging us to tell the story of our own sad experiences with alcohol, and by showing us how to help other alcoholics, A.A. keeps us sober. Our attitude toward life changes from one of pride and selfishness to one of humility and gratitude. *Am I going to step back through that door in the wall to my old helpless, hopeless, drunken life?*

Meditation for the Day

Withdraw into the calm of communion with God. Rest in that calm and peace. When the soul finds its home of rest in God, then it is that real life begins. Only when you are calm and serene can you do good work. Emotional upsets make you useless. The eternal life is calmness and when you enter into that, then you live as an eternal being. Calmness is based on complete trust in God. Nothing in this world can separate you from the love of God.

Prayer for the Day

I pray that I may wear the world like a loose garment. I pray that I may keep serene at the center of my being.

MARCH 18—A.A. Thought for the Day

When we alcoholics first come into A.A. and we face the fact that we must spend the rest of our life without liquor, it often seems like an impossibility to us. So A.A. tells us to forget about the future and take it one day at a time. All we really have is now. We have no past time and no future time. As the saying goes: "Yesterday is gone, forget it; tomorrow never comes, don't worry; today is here, get busy." All we have is the present. The past is gone forever and the future never comes. When tomorrow gets here, it will be today. *Am I living one day at a time?*

Meditation for the Day

Persistence is necessary if you are to advance in spiritual things. By persistent prayer, persistent, firm, and simple trust, you achieve the treasures of the spirit. By persistent practice, you can eventually obtain joy, peace, assurance, security, health, happiness, and serenity. Nothing is too great, in the spiritual realm, for you to obtain, if you persistently prepare yourself for it.

Prayer for the Day

I pray that I may persistently carry out my spiritual exercises every day. I pray that I may strive for peace and serenity.

MARCH 19—A.A. Thought for the Day

When we were drinking, we used to be ashamed of the past. Remorse is terrible mental punishment: ashamed of ourselves for the things we've said and done, afraid to face people because of what they might think of us, afraid of the consequences of what we did when we were drunk. In A.A. we forget about the past. *Do I believe that God has forgiven me for everything I've done in the past, no matter how black it was, provided I'm honestly trying to do the right thing today?*

Meditation for the Day

God's spirit is all about you all day long. You have no thoughts, no plans, no impulses, no emotions, that He does not know about. You can hide nothing from Him. Do not make your conduct conform only to that of the world and do not depend on the approval or disapproval of others. God sees in secret, but He rewards openly. If you are in harmony with the Divine Spirit, doing your best to live the way you believe God wants you to live, you will be at peace.

Prayer for the Day

I pray that I may always feel God's presence. I pray that I may realize this Presence constantly all through the day.

MARCH 20—A.A. Thought for the Day

When we were drinking, we used to worry about the future. Worry is terrible mental punishment. What's going to become of me? Where will I end up? In the gutter or the sanitarium? We can see ourselves slipping, getting worse and worse, and we wonder what the finish will be. Sometimes we get so discouraged in thinking about the future that we toy with the idea of suicide. *In A.A. have I stopped worrying about the future?*

Meditation for the Day

Functioning on a material plane alone takes me away from God. I must also try to function on a spiritual plane. Functioning on a spiritual plane as well as on a material plane will make life what it should be. All material activities are valueless in themselves alone. But all activities, seemingly trivial or of seemingly great moment, are all alike if directed by God's guidance. I must try to obey God as I would expect a faithful, willing servant to carry out directions.

Prayer for the Day

I pray that the flow of God's spirit may come to me through many channels. I pray that I may function on a spiritual plane as well as on a material plane.

MARCH 21—A.A. Thought for the Day

In A.A. we forget about the future. We know from experience that as time goes on, the future takes care of itself. Everything works out well, as long as we stay sober. All we need to think about is today. When we get up in the morning and see the sun shining in the window, we thank God that He has given us another day to enjoy because we're sober, a day in which we may have a chance to help somebody. *Do I know that this day is all I have and that with God's help I can stay sober today?*

Meditation for the Day

All is fundamentally well. That does not mean that all is well on the surface of things. But it does mean that God's in His heaven and that He has a purpose for the world, which will eventually work out when enough human beings are willing to follow His way. "Wearing the world as a loose garment" means not being upset by the surface wrongness of things, but feeling deeply secure in the fundamental goodness and purpose in the universe.

Prayer for the Day

I pray that God may be with me in my journey through the world. I pray that I may know that God is planning that journey.

MARCH 22—A.A. Thought for the Day

We're all looking for the power to overcome drinking. When we alcoholics come into A.A., our first question is: "How do I get the strength to quit?" At first it seems to us that we will never get the necessary strength. We see older members who have found the power we are looking for, but we don't know the process by which they got it. This necessary strength comes in many ways. *Have I found all the strength I need?*

Meditation for the Day

You cannot have a spiritual need which God cannot supply. Your fundamental need is a spiritual need, the need of power to live the good life. The best spiritual supply is received by you when you want it to pass on to other people. You get it largely by giving it away. God gives you strength as you pass it on to another person. That strength means increased health; increased health means more good work, and more good work means more people helped. And so it goes on, a constant supply to meet all spiritual needs.

Prayer for the Day

I pray that my every spiritual need will be supplied by God. I pray that I may use the power I receive to help others.

MARCH 23—A.A. Thought for the Day

Strength comes from the fellowship you find when you come into A.A. Just being with men and women who have found the way out gives you a feeling of security. You listen to the speakers, you talk with other members, and you absorb the atmosphere of confidence and hope that you find in the place. *Am I receiving strength from the fellowship with other A.A. members?*

Meditation for the Day

God is with you, to bless and help you. His spirit is all around you. Waver not in your faith or in your prayers. All power is the Lord's. Say that to yourself often and steadily. Say it until your heart sings with joy for the safety and personal power that it means to you. Say it until the very force of the utterance drives back and puts to naught all the evils against you. Use it as a battle cry. All power is the Lord's. Then you will pass on to victory over all your sins and temptations, and you will begin to live a victorious life.

Prayer for the Day

I pray that with strength from God I may lead an abundant life. I pray that I may lead a life of victory.

MARCH 24—A.A. Thought for the Day

Strength comes from honestly telling your own experiences with drinking. In religion, they call it confession. We call it witnessing or sharing. You give a personal witness, you share your past experiences, the troubles you got into, the hospitals, the jails, the break-up of your home, the money wasted, the debts, and all the foolish things you did when you were drinking. This personal witness lets out the things you had kept hidden, brings them out into the open, and you find release and strength. *Am I receiving strength from my personal witnessing?*

Meditation for the Day

We cannot fully understand the universe. The simple fact is that we cannot even define space or time. They are both boundless, in spite of all we can do to limit them. We live in a box of space and time, which we have manufactured by our own minds and on that depends all our so-called knowledge of the universe. The simple fact is that we can never know all things, nor are we made to know them. Much of our lives must be taken on faith.

Prayer for the Day

I pray that my faith may be based on my own experience of the power of God in my life. I pray that I may know this one thing above all else in the universe.

MARCH 25—A.A. Thought for the Day

Strength comes from coming to believe in a Higher Power that can help you. You can't define this Higher Power, but you can see how it helps other alcoholics. You hear them talk about it and you begin to get the idea yourself. You try praying in a quiet time each morning and you begin to feel stronger, as though your prayers were heard. So you gradually come to believe there must be a Power in the world outside yourself, which is stronger than you and to which you can turn for help. *Am I receiving strength from my faith in a Higher Power?*

Meditation for the Day

Spiritual development is achieved by daily persistence in living the way you believe God wants you to live. Like the wearing away of a stone by steady drops of water, so will your daily persistence wear away all the difficulties and gain spiritual success for you. Never falter in this daily, steady persistence. Go forward boldly and unafraid. God will help and strengthen you, as long as you are trying to do His will.

Prayer for the Day

I pray that I may persist day by day in gaining spiritual experience. I pray that I may make this a lifetime work.

MARCH 26—A.A. Thought for the Day

Strength comes also from working with other alcoholics. When you are trying to help a new prospect with the program, you are building up your own strength at the same time. You see the other person in the condition you might be in yourself and it makes your resolve to stay sober stronger than ever. Often, you help yourself more than the other person, but if you do succeed in helping the prospect to get sober, you are stronger from the experience of having helped another person. *Am I receiving strength from working with others?*

Meditation for the Day

Faith is the bridge between you and God. It is the bridge which God has ordained. If all were seen and known, there would be no merit in doing right. Therefore God has ordained that we do not see or know directly. But we can experience the power of His spirit through our faith. It is the bridge between us and Him, which we can take or not, as we will. There could be no morality without free will. We must make the choice ourselves. We must make the venture of belief.

Prayer for the Day

I pray that I may choose and decide to cross the bridge of faith. I pray that by crossing this bridge I may receive the spiritual power I need.

MARCH 27—A.A. Thought for the Day

You get the power to overcome drinking through the fellowship of other
alcoholics who have found the way out.
You get power by honestly sharing
your past experience by a personal witness. You get power by coming to believe in a Higher Power, the Divine
Principle in the universe which can
help you. You get power by working
with other alcoholics. In these four
ways, thousands of alcoholics have
found all the power they needed to
overcome drinking. *Am I ready and
willing to accept this power and work
for it?*

Meditation for the Day

The power of God's spirit is the greatest power
in the universe. Our conquest of each other,
the great kings and conquerors, the conquest
of wealth, the leaders of the money society,
all amount to very little in the end. But he
that conquers himself is greater than he who
conquers a city. Material things have no per-
manence. But God's spirit is eternal. Everything really worthwhile in the world is the
result of the power of God's spirit.

Prayer for the Day

I pray that I may open myself to the power
of God's spirit. I pray that my relationships
with others may be improved by this spirit.

MARCH 28—A.A. Thought for the Day

When you come into an A.A. meeting, you're not just coming into a meeting, you're coming into a new life. I'm always impressed by the change I see in people after they've been in A.A. for a while. I sometimes take an inventory of myself, to see whether I have changed, and if so, in what way. Before I met A.A., I was very selfish. I wanted my own way in everything. I don't believe I ever grew up. When things went wrong, I sulked like a spoiled child and often went out and got drunk. *Am I still all get and no give?*

Meditation for the Day

There are two things that we must have if we are going to change our way of life. One is faith, the confidence in things unseen, the fundamental goodness and purpose in the universe. The other is obedience: that is, living according to our faith, living each day as we believe that God wants us to live, with gratitude, humility, honesty, purity, unselfishness, and love. Faith and obedience, these two, will give us all the strength we need to overcome sin and temptation and to live a new and more abundant life.

Prayer for the Day

I pray that I may have more faith and obedience. I pray that I may live a more abundant life as a result of these things.

MARCH 29—A.A. Thought for the Day

Before I met A.A., I was very dishonest. I lied to my spouse constantly about where I had been and what I'd been doing. I took time off from my work and pretended I'd been sick or gave some other dishonest excuse. I was dishonest with myself, as well as with other people. I would never face myself as I really was or admit when I was wrong. I pretended to myself that I was as good as the next person, although I suspected I wasn't. *Am I now really honest?*

Meditation for the Day

I must live in the world and yet live apart with God. I can go forth from my secret times of communion with God to the work of the world. To get the spiritual strength I need, my inner life must be lived apart from the world. I must wear the world as a loose garment. Nothing in the world should seriously upset me, as long as my inner life is lived with God. All successful living arises from this inner life.

Prayer for the Day

I pray that I may live my inner life with God. I pray that nothing shall invade or destroy that secret place of peace.

MARCH 30—A.A. Thought for the Day

Before I met A.A., I was very unloving. From the time I went away to school, I paid very little attention to my mother and father. I was on my own and didn't even bother to keep in touch with them. After I got married, I was very unappreciative of my spouse. Many a time I would go out all by myself to have a good time. I paid too little attention to our children and didn't try to understand them or show them affection. My few friends were only drinking companions, not real friends. *Have I gotten over loving nobody but myself?*

Meditation for the Day

Be calm, be true, be quiet. Do not get emotionally upset by anything that happens around you. Feel a deep, inner security in the goodness and purpose in the universe. Be true to your highest ideals. Do not let yourself slip back into the old ways of reacting. Stick to your spiritual guns. Be calm always. Do not talk back or defend yourself too much against accusation, whether false or true. Accept abuse as well as you accept praise. Only God can judge the real you.

Prayer for the Day

I pray that I may not be upset by the judgment of others. I pray that I may let God be the judge of the real me.

MARCH 31—A.A. Thought for the Day

Since I've been in A.A., have I made a start towards being more unselfish? Do I no longer want my own way in everything? When things go wrong and I can't have what I want, do I no longer sulk? Am I trying not to waste money on myself? And does it make me happy to see my family and my home have enough attention from me? *Am I trying not to be all get and no give?*

Meditation for the Day

Each day is a day of progress, steady progress forward, if you make it so. You may not see it, but God does. God does not judge by outward appearance. He judges by the heart. Let Him see in your heart a simple desire always to do His will. Though you may feel that your work has been spoiled or tarnished, God sees it as an offering for Him. When climbing a steep hill, a person is often more conscious of the weakness of his stumbling feet than of the view, the grandeur, or even of the upward progress.

Prayer for the Day

I pray that I may persevere in all good things. I pray that I may advance each day in spite of my stumbling feet.

APRIL 1—A.A. Thought for the Day

Since I've been in A.A., have I made a start towards becoming more honest? Do I no longer have to lie to my husband or wife? Do I try to have meals on time, and do I try to earn what I make at work? Am I trying to be honest? Have I faced myself as I really am and have I admitted to myself that I'm no good by myself, but have to rely on God to help me do the right thing? *Am I beginning to find out what it means to be alive and to face the world honestly and without fear?*

Meditation for the Day

God is all around us. His spirit pervades the universe. And yet we often do not let His spirit in. We try to get along without His help and we make a mess of our lives. We can do nothing of any value without God's help. All our human relationships depend on this. When we let God's spirit rule our lives, we learn how to get along with others and how to help them.

Prayer for the Day

I pray that I may let God run my life. I pray that I will never again make a mess of my life through trying to run it myself.

APRIL 2—A.A. Thought for the Day

Since I've been in A.A., have I made a start towards becoming more loving to my family and friends? Do I visit my parents? Am I more appreciative of my spouse than I was before? Am I grateful to my family for having put up with me? Have I found real understanding with my children? Do I feel that the friends I've found in A.A. are real friends? Do I believe that they are always ready to help me and do I want to help them if I can? *Do I really care now about other people?*

Meditation for the Day

Not what you do so much as what you are, that is the miracle-working power. You can be a force for good, with the help of God. God is here to help you and to bless you, here to company with you. You can be a worker with God. Changed by God's grace, you shed one garment of the spirit for a better one. In time, you throw that one aside for a yet finer one. And so from character to character, you are gradually transformed.

Prayer for the Day

I pray that I may accept ever challenge. I pray that each acceptance of a challenge may make me grow into a better person.

APRIL 3—A.A. Thought for the Day

When I was drinking, I was absolutely selfish, I thought of myself first, last, and always. The universe revolved around me at the center. When I woke up in the morning with a hangover, my only thought was how terrible I felt and about what I could do to make myself feel better. And the only thing I could think of was more liquor. To quit was impossible. I couldn't see beyond myself and my own need for another drink. *Can I now look out and beyond my own selfishness?*

Meditation for the Day

Remember that the first quality of greatness is service. In a way, God is the greatest servant of all, because He is always waiting for us to call on Him to help us in all good endeavor. His strength is always available to us, but we must ask it of Him through our own free will. It is a free gift, but we must sincerely seek for it. A life of service is the finest life we can live. We are here on earth to serve others. That is the beginning and the end of our real worth.

Prayer for the Day

I pray that I may cooperate with God in all good things. I pray that I may serve God and others and so lead a useful and happy life.

APRIL 4—A.A. Thought for the Day

When I came into A.A., I found men and women who had been through the same things I had been through. But now they were thinking more about how they could help others than they were about themselves. They were a lot more unselfish than I ever was. By coming to meetings and associating with them, I began to think a little less about myself and a little more about other people. I also learned that I didn't have to depend on myself alone to get out of the mess I was in. I could get a greater strength than my own. *Am I now depending less on myself and more on God?*

Meditation for the Day

You cannot help others unless you understand the person you are trying to help. To understand the problems and temptations of others, you must have been through them yourself. You must do all you can to understand others. You must study their backgrounds, their likes and dislikes, their reactions and their prejudices. When you see their weaknesses, do not confront the person with them. Share your own weaknesses, sins, and temptations and let other people find their own convictions.

Prayer for the Day

I pray that I may serve as a channel for God's power to come into the lives of others. I pray that I may try to understand them.

APRIL 5—A.A. Thought for the Day

People often ask what makes the A.A. program work. One of the answers is that A.A. works because it gets a person away from himself as the center of the universe. And it teaches him to rely more on the fellowship of others and on strength from God. Forgetting ourselves in fellowship, prayer, and working with others, is what makes the A.A. program work. *Are these things keeping me sober?*

Meditation for the Day

God is the great interpreter of one human personality to another. Even personalities who are the nearest together have much in their natures that remains a sealed book to each other. And only as God enters and controls their lives are the mysteries of each revealed to the other. Each personality is so different. God alone understands perfectly the language of each and can interpret between the two. Here we find the miracles of change and the true interpretation of life.

Prayer for the Day

I pray that I may be in the right relationship to God. I pray that God will interpret to me the personalities of other people, so that I can understand them and help them.

APRIL 6—A.A. Thought for the Day

All alcoholics have personality problems. They drink to escape from life, to counteract feelings of loneliness or inferiority, or because of some emotional conflict within them, so that they cannot adjust themselves to life. Alcoholics cannot stop drinking unless they find a way to solve their personality problems. That's why going on the wagon doesn't solve anything. That's why taking the pledge usually doesn't work. *Was my personality problem ever solved by going on the wagon or taking the pledge?*

Meditation for the Day

God irradiates your life with the warmth of His spirit. You must open up like a flower to this divine irradiation. Loosen your hold on earth, its cares, and its worries. Unclasp your hold on material things, relax your grip, and the tide of peace and serenity will flow in. Relinquish every material thing and receive it back again from God. Do not hold on to earth's treasures so firmly that your hands are too occupied to clasp God's hands as He holds them out to you in love.

Prayer for the Day

I pray that I may be open to receive God's blessing. I pray that I may be willing to relinquish my hold on material things and receive them back from God.

APRIL 7—A.A. Thought for the Day

In A.A. alcoholics find a way to solve their personality problems. They do this by recovering three things. First, they recover their personal integrity. They pull themselves together. They get honest with themselves and with other people. They face themselves and their problems honestly, instead of running away. They take a personal inventory of themselves to see where they really stand. Then they face the facts instead of making excuses for themselves. *Have I recovered my integrity?*

Meditation for the Day

When trouble comes, do not say: "Why should this happen to me?" Leave yourself out of the picture. Think of other people and their troubles and you will forget about your own. Gradually get away from yourself and you will know the consolation of unselfish service to others. After a while, it will not matter so much what happens to you. It is not so important any more, except as your experience can be used to help others who are in the same kind of trouble.

Prayer for the Day

I pray that I may become more unselfish. I pray that I may not be thrown off the track by letting the old selfishness creep back into my life.

APRIL 8—A.A. Thought for the Day

Second, alcoholics recover their faith in a Power greater than themselves. They admit that they're helpless by themselves and they call on that Higher Power for help. They surrender their lives to God, as they understand Him. They put their drink problem in God's hands and leave it there. They recover their faith in a Higher Power that can help them. *Have I recovered my faith?*

Meditation for the Day

You must make a stand for God. Believers in God are considered by some as peculiar people. You must even be willing to be deemed a fool for the sake of your faith. You must be ready to stand aside and let the fashions and customs of the world go by, when God's purposes are thereby forwarded. Be known by the marks that distinguish a believer in God. These are honesty, purity, unselfishness, love, gratitude, and humility.

Prayer for the Day

I pray that I may be ready to profess my belief in God before others. I pray that I may not be turned aside by the skepticism and cynicism of unbelievers.

APRIL 9—A.A. Thought for the Day

Third, alcoholics recover their proper relationship with other people. They think less about themselves and more about others. They try to help other alcoholics. They make new friends so that they're no longer lonely. They try to live a life of service instead of self-ishness. All their relationships with other people are improved. They solve their personality problems by recovering their personal integrity, their faith in a Higher Power, and their way of fellowship and service to others. *Is my drink problem solved as along as my personality problem is solved?*

Meditation for the Day

All that depresses you, all that you fear, is really powerless to harm you. These things are but phantoms. So arise from earth's bonds, from depression, distrust, fear, and all that hinders your new life. Arise to beauty, joy, peace, and work inspired by love. Rise from death to life. You do not even need to fear death. All past sins are forgiven if you live and love and work with God. Let nothing hinder your new life. Seek to know more and more of that new way of living.

Prayer for the Day

I pray that I may let God live in me as I work for Him. I pray that I may go out into the sunlight and work with God.

APRIL 10—A.A. Thought for the Day

When I came into A.A., I came into a new world. A sober world. A world of sobriety, peace, serenity, and happiness. But I know that if I take just one drink, I'll go right back into that old world. That alcoholic world. That world of drunkenness, conflict, and misery. That alcoholic world is not a pleasant place for an alcoholic to live in. Looking at the world through the bottom of a whiskey glass is no fun after you've become an alcoholic. *Do I want to go back to that alcoholic world?*

Meditation for the Day

Pride stands sentinel at the door of the heart and shuts out the love of God. God can only dwell with the humble and the obedient. Obedience to God's will is the key unlocking the door to God's kingdom. You cannot obey God to the best of your ability without in time realizing God's love and responding to that love. The rough stone steps of obedience lead up to where the mosaic floor of love and joy is laid. Where God's spirit is, there is your home. There is heaven for you.

Prayer for the Day

I pray that God may make His home in my humble and obedient heart. I pray that I obey his guidance to the best of my y.

APRIL 11—A.A. Thought for the Day

In that alcoholic world, one drink always leads to another and you can't stop till you're paralyzed. And the next morning it begins all over again. You eventually land in a hospital or jail. You lose your job. Your home is broken up. You're always in a mess. You're on the merry-go-round and you can't get off. You're in a squirrel cage and you can't get out. *Am I convinced that the alcoholic world is not a pleasant place for me to live in?*

Meditation for the Day

I must learn to accept self-discipline. I must try never to yield one point that I have already won. I must not let myself go in resentments, hates, fears, pride, lust, or gossip. Even if the discipline keeps me separated from some people who are without discipline, nevertheless I will carry on. I may have different ways and a different standard of living than some others. I may be actuated by different motives than some people. But I will try to live the way I believe God wants me to live, no matter what others say.

Prayer for the Day

I pray that I may be an example to others of a better way of living. I pray that I may carry on in spite of hindrances.

APRIL 12—A.A. Thought for the Day

This sober world is a pleasant place for an alcoholic to live in. Once you've got out of your alcoholic fog, you find that the world looks good. You find real friends in A.A. You get a job. You feel good in the morning. You eat a good breakfast and you do a good day's work at home or outside. And your family loves you and welcomes you because you're sober. *Am I convinced that this sober world is a pleasant place for an alcoholic to live in?*

Meditation for the Day

Our need is God's opportunity. First we must recognize our need. Often this means helplessness before some weakness or sickness and an admission of our need for help. Next comes faith in the power of God's spirit, available to us to meet that need. Before any need can be met, our faith must find expression. That expression of faith is all God needs to manifest His power in our lives. Faith is the key that unlocks the storehouse of God's resources.

Prayer for the Day

I pray that I may first admit my needs. I pray that then I may have faith that God will meet those needs, in the way which is best for me.

APRIL 13—A.A. Thought for the Day

Having found my way into this new world by the grace of God and the help of A.A., am I going to take that first drink, when I know that just one drink will change my whole world? Am I deliberately going back to the suffering of that alcoholic world? Or am I going to hang onto the happiness of this sober world? Is there any doubt about the answer? *With God's help, am I going to hang onto A.A. with both hands?*

Meditation for the Day

I will try to make the world better and happier by my presence in it. I will try to help other people find the way God wants them to live. I will try to be on the side of good, in the stream of righteousness, where all things work for good. I will do my duty persistently and faithfully, not sparing myself. I will be gentle with all people. I will try to see other people's difficulty and help them to correct it. I will always pray to God to act as interpreter between me and the other person.

Prayer for the Day

I pray that I may live in the spirit of prayer. I pray that I may depend on God for the strength I need to help me to do my part in making the world a better place.

RIL 14—A.A. Thought for the Day

A police captain once told about certain cases he had come across in his police work. The cause of the tragedy in each case was drunkenness. He told his audience about a man who got into an argument with his wife while he was drunk and beat her to death. Then he went out and drank some more. The police captain also told about a man who got too near the edge of an old quarry hole when he was drunk and fell one hundred and fifty feet to his death. *When I read or hear these stories, do I think about our motto: "But for the grace of God"?*

Meditation for the Day

I must keep balance by keeping spiritual things at the center of my life. God will give me this poise and balance if I pray for it. This poise will give me power in dealing with the lives of others. This balance will manifest itself more and more in my own life. I should keep material things in their proper place and keep spiritual things at the center of my life. Then I will be at peace amid the distractions of everyday living.

Prayer for the Day

I pray that I may dwell with God at the center of my life. I pray that I may keep inner peace at the center of my being.

APRIL 15—A.A. Thought for the Day

Terrible things could have happened to any one of us. We never will know what might have happened to us when we were drunk. We usually thought: "That couldn't happen to me." But any one of us could have killed somebody or have been killed ourselves, if we were drunk enough. But fear of these things never kept us from drinking. *Do I believe that in A.A. we have something more effective than fear?*

Meditation for the Day

I must keep calm and unmoved in the vicissitudes of life. I must go back into the silence of communion with God to recover this calm when it is lost even for one moment. I will accomplish more by this calmness than by all the activities of a long day. At all cost I will keep calm. I can solve nothing when I am agitated. I should keep away from things that are upsetting emotionally. I should run on an even keel and not get tipped over by emotional upsets. I should seek for things that are calm and good and true and stick to those things.

Prayer for the Day

I pray that I may not argue nor contend, but merely state calmly what I believe to be true. I pray that I may keep myself in that state of calmness that comes from faith in God's purpose for the world.

APRIL 16—A.A. Thought for the Day

In A.A. we have insurance. Our faith in God is a kind of insurance against the terrible things that might happen to us if we ever drink again. By putting our drink problem in the hands of God, we've taken out a sort of insurance policy, which insures us against the ravages of drink, as our homes are insured against destruction by fire. *Am I paying my A.A. insurance premiums regularly?*

Meditation for the Day

I must try to love all humanity. Love comes from thinking of every man or woman as your brother or sister, because they are children of God. This way of thinking makes me care enough about them to really want to help them. I must put this kind of love into action by serving others. Love means no severe judging, no resentments, no malicious gossip, and no destructive criticism. It means patience, understanding, compassion, and helpfulness.

Prayer for the Day

I pray that I may realize that God loves me, since He is the Father of us all. I pray that I in turn may have love for all of His children.

APRIL 17—A.A. Thought for the Day

Every time we go to an A.A. meeting, every time we say the Lord's prayer, every time we have a quiet time before breakfast, we're paying a premium on our insurance against taking that first drink. And every time we help another alcoholic, we're making a large payment on our drink insurance. We're making sure that our policy doesn't lapse. *Am I building up an endowment in serenity, peace, and happiness that will put me on easy street for the rest of my life?*

Meditation for the Day

I gain faith by my own experience of God's power in my life. The constant, persistent recognition of God's spirit in all my personal relationships, the ever-accumulating weight of evidence in support of God's guidance, the numberless instances in which seeming chance or wonderful coincidence can be traced to God's purpose in my life. All these things gradually engender a feeling of wonder, humility, and gratitude to God. These in turn are followed by a more sure and abiding faith in God and His purposes.

Prayer for the Day

I pray that my faith may be strengthened every day. I pray that I may find confirmation of my life in the good things that have come into my life.

APRIL 18—A.A. Thought for the Day

As I look back over my drinking career, have I learned that you take out of life what you put into it? When I put drinking into my life, did I take out a lot of bad things? Hospitals with the D.T.'s? Jails for drunken driving? Loss of job? Loss of home and family? *When I put drinking into my life, was almost everything I took out bad?*

Meditation for the Day

I should strive for a friendliness and helpfulness that will affect all who come near to me. I should try to see something to love in them. I should welcome them, bestow little courtesies and understandings on them, and help them if they ask for help. I must send no one away without a word of cheer, a feeling that I really care about them. God may have put the impulse in some despairing one's mind to come to me. I must not fail God by repulsing that person. They may not want to communicate with me unless they are sure of a warm welcome.

Prayer for the Day

I pray that I may warmly welcome all who come to me for help. I pray that I may make them feel that I really care.

APRIL 19—A.A. Thought for the Day

Since I've been putting sobriety into my life, I've been taking out a lot of good things. I can describe it best as a kind of quiet satisfaction. I feel good. I feel right with the world, on the right side of the fence. As long as I put sobriety into my life, almost everything I take out is good. The satisfaction you get out of living a sober life is made up of a lot of little things. You have the ambition to do things you didn't feel like doing when you were drinking. *Am I getting satisfaction out of living a sober life?*

Meditation for the Day

It is a glorious way—the upward way. There are wonderful discoveries in the realm of the spirit. There are tender intimacies in the quiet times of communion with God. There is an amazing, almost incomprehensible understanding of the other person. On the upward way, you can have all the strength you need from that Higher Power. You cannot make too many demands on Him for strength. He gives you all the power you need, as long as you are moving along the upward way.

Prayer for the Day

I pray that I may see the beautiful horizons ahead on the upward way. I pray that I may keep going forward to the more abundant life.

APRIL 20—A.A. Thought for the Day

The satisfaction you get out of living a sober life is made up of a lot of little things, but they add up to a satisfactory and happy life. You take out of life what you put into it. So I'd say to people coming into A.A.: "Don't worry about what life will be like without liquor. Just hang in there and a lot of good things will happen to you. And you'll have that feeling of quiet satisfaction and peace and serenity and gratitude for the grace of God." *Is my life becoming really worth living?*

Meditation for the Day

There are two paths, one up and one down. We have been given free will to choose either path. We are captains of our souls to this extent only. We can choose the good or the bad. Once we have chosen the wrong path, we go down and down, eventually to death. But if we choose the right path, we go up and up, until we come to the resurrection day. On the wrong path, we have no power for good because we do not choose to ask for it. But on the right path, we are on the side of good and we have all the power of God's spirit behind us.

Prayer for the Day

I pray that I may be in the stream of goodness. I pray that I may be on the right side, on the side of all good in the universe.

APRIL 21—A.A. Thought for the Day

After we've been in A.A. for a while, we find out that if we're going to stay sober, we have to be humble people. The men and women in A.A. who have achieved sobriety are all humble people. When I stop to think that but for the grace of God I might be drunk right now, I can't help feeling humble. Gratitude to God for His grace makes me humble. When I think of the kind of person I was not so long ago, when I think of the person I left behind me, I have nothing to be proud of. *Am I grateful and humble?*

Meditation for the Day

I must arise from the death of sin and self-ishness and put on a new life of integrity. All the old sins and temptations must be laid in the grave and a new existence rise from the ashes. Yesterday is gone. All my sins are forgiven if I am honestly trying to do God's will today. Today is here, the time of resurrection and renewal. I must start now, today, to build a new life of complete faith and trust in God and a determination to do His will in all things.

Prayer for the Day

I pray that I may share in making the world a better place to live in. I pray that I may do what I can to bring goodness a little nearer to the earth.

APRIL 22—A.A. Thought for the Day

People believe in A.A. when they see it work. An actual demonstration is what convinces them. What they read in books, what they hear people say doesn't always convince them. But when they see a real honest-to-goodness change take place in a person, a change from a drunkard to a sober, useful citizen, that's something they can believe because they can see it. There's really only one thing that proves to me that A.A. works. *Have I seen the change in people who come into A.A.?*

Meditation for the Day

Divine control and unquestioning obedience to God are the only conditions necessary for a spiritual life. Divine control means absolute faith and trust in God, a belief that God is the Divine Principle in the universe and that He is the Intelligence and the Love that controls the universe. Unquestioning obedience to God means living each day the way you believe God wants you to live, constantly seeking the guidance of God in every situation and being willing to do the right thing at all times.

Prayer for the Day

I pray that I may always be under Divine Control and always practice unquestioning obedience to God. I pray that I may be always ready to serve Him.

APRIL 23—A.A. Thought for the Day

Men and women keep coming into A.A., licked by alcohol, often given up by doctors as hopeless cases, they themselves admitting they're helpless to stop drinking. When I see these men and women get sober and stay sober over a period of months and years, I know that A.A. works. The change I see in people who come into A.A. not only convinces me that A.A. works, but it also convinces me that there must be a Power greater than ourselves which helps us to make that change. *Am I convinced that a Higher Power can help me to change?*

Meditation for the Day

Cooperation with God is the great necessity for our lives. All else follows naturally. Cooperation with God is the result of our consciousness of His presence. Guidance is bound to come to us as we live more and more with God, as our consciousness becomes more and more attuned to the great Consciousness of the universe. We must have many quiet times when we not so much ask to be shown and led by God, as to feel and realize His presence. New spiritual growth comes naturally from cooperation with God.

Prayer for the Day

I pray that God may supply me with strength and show me the direction in which He wants me to grow. I pray that these things may come naturally from my cooperation with Him.

APRIL 24—A.A. Thought for the Day

It's been proved that we alcoholics can't get sober by our will power. We've failed again and again. Therefore I believe there must be a Higher Power which helps me. I think of that power as the grace of God. And I pray to God every morning for the strength to stay sober today. I know that Power is there because it never fails to help me. *Do I believe that A.A. works through the grace of God?*

Meditation for the Day

Once I am "born of the spirit," that is my life's breath. Within me is the life of life, so that I can never perish. The life that down the ages has kept God's children through peril, adversity, and sorrow. I must try never to doubt or worry, but follow where the life of the spirit leads. How often, when little I know it, God goes before me to prepare the way, to soften a heart, or to overrule a resentment. As the life of the spirit grows, natural wants become less important.

Prayer for the Day

I pray that my life may become centered in God more than in self. I pray that my will may be directed towards doing His will.

APRIL 25—A.A. Thought for the Day

I don't believe that A.A. works because I read it in a book or because I hear people say so. I believe it because I see people getting sober and staying sober. An actual demonstration is what convinces me. When I see the change in people, I can't help believing that A.A. works. We could listen to talk about A.A. all day and still not believe it, but when we see it work, we have to believe it. Seeing is believing. *Do I see A.A. work every day?*

Meditation for the Day

Try saying: "God bless her (or him)" of anyone who is in disharmony with you. Also say it of those who are in trouble through their own fault. Say it, willing that showers of blessings may fall upon them. Let God do the blessing. Leave to God the necessary correcting or disciplining. You should only desire blessing for them. Leave God's work to God. Occupy yourself with the task that He gives you to do. God's blessing will also break down all your own difficulties and build up all your successes.

Prayer for the Day

I pray that I may use God's goodness so that it will be a blessing to others. I pray that I may accept God's blessing so that I will have harmony, beauty, joy, and happiness.

APRIL 26—A.A. Thought for the Day

The A.A. program is one of submission, release, and action. When we're drinking, we're submitting to a power greater than ourselves, liquor. Our own wills are no use against the power of liquor. One drink and we're sunk. In A.A. we stop submitting to the power of liquor. Instead, we submit to a Power, also greater than ourselves, which we call God. *Have I submitted myself to that Higher Power?*

Meditation for the Day

Ceaseless activity is not God's plan for your life. Times of withdrawal for renewed strength are always necessary. Wait for the faintest tremor of fear and stop all work, everything, and rest before God until you are strong again. Deal in the same way with all tired feelings. Then you need rest of body and renewal of spirit-force. Saint Paul said: "I can do all things through Him who strengthens me." This does not mean that you are to do all things and then rely on God to find strength. It means that you are to do the things you believe God wants you to do and only then can you rely on His supply of power.

Prayer for the Day

I pray that God's spirit may be my master always. I pray that I may learn how to rest and listen, as well as how to work.

APRIL 27—A.A. Thought for the Day

By submitting to God, we're released from the power of liquor. It has no more hold on us. We're also released from the things that were holding us down: pride, selfishness, and fear. And we're free to grow into a new life, which is so much better than the old life that there's no comparison. This release gives us serenity and peace with the world. *Have I been released from the power of alcohol?*

Meditation for the Day

We know God by spiritual vision. We feel that He is beside us. We feel His presence. Contact with God is not made by the senses. Spirit-consciousness replaces sight. Since we cannot see God, we have to perceive Him by spiritual perception. God has to span the physical and the spiritual with the gift to us of spiritual vision. Many persons, though they cannot see God, have had a clear spiritual consciousness of Him. We are inside a box of space and time, but we know there must be something outside of that box, limitless space, eternity of time, and God.

Prayer for the Day

I pray that I may have a consciousness of God's presence. I pray that God will give me spiritual vision.

APRIL 28—A.A. Thought for the Day

We're so glad to be free from liquor that we do something about it. We get into action. We come to meetings regularly. We go out and try to help other alcoholics. We pass on the good news whenever we get a chance. In a spirit of thankfulness to God, we get into action. The A.A. program is simple. Submit yourself to God, find release from liquor and get into action. Do these things and keep doing them and you're all set for the rest of your life. *Have I got into action?*

Meditation for the Day

God's eternal quest must be the tracking down of souls. You should join Him in His quest. Through briars, through waste places, through glades, up mountain heights, down into valleys. God leads you. But ever with His leadership goes your helping hand. Glorious to follow where the Leader goes. You are seeking lost sheep. You are bringing the good news into places where it has not been known before. You may not know which soul you will help, but you can leave all results to God. Just go with Him in His eternal quest for souls.

Prayer for the Day

I pray that I may follow God in His eternal quest for souls. I pray that I may offer God my helping hand.

APRIL 29—A.A. Thought for the Day

The A.A. program is one of faith, hope, and charity. It's a program of hope because when new members come into A.A., the first thing they get is hope. They hear older members tell how they had been through the same kind of hell that they have and how they found the way out through A.A. And this gives them hope that if others can do it, they can do it. *Is hope still strong in me?*

Meditation for the Day

The rule of God's kingdom is perfect order, perfect harmony, perfect supply, perfect love, perfect honesty, perfect obedience. There is no discord in God's kingdom, only some things still unconquered in God's children. The difficulties of life are caused by disharmony in the individual man or woman. People lack power because they lack harmony with God and with each other. They think that God fails because power is not manifested in their lives. God does not fail. People fail because they are out of harmony with Him.

Prayer for the Day

I pray that I may be in harmony with God and with other people. I pray that this harmony will result in strength and success.

APRIL 30—A.A. Thought for the Day

The A.A. program is one of faith because we find that we must have faith in a Power greater than ourselves if we are going to get sober. We're helpless before alcohol, but when we turn our drink problem over to God and have faith that He can give us all the strength we need, then we have the drink problem licked. Faith in that Divine Principle in the universe which we call God is the essential part of the A.A. program. *Is faith still strong in me?*

Meditation for the Day

Each one of us is a child of God, and as such, we are full of the promise of spiritual growth. A young person is like the springtime of the year. The full time of the fruit is not yet, but there is promise of the blossom. There is a spark of the Divine in every one of us. Each has some of God's spirit which can be developed by spiritual exercise. Know that your life is full of glad promise. Such blessings can be yours, such joys, such wonders, as long as you develop in the sunshine of God's love.

Prayer for the Day

I pray that I may develop the divine spark within me. I pray that by so doing I may fulfill the promise of a more abundant life.

MAY 1—A.A. Thought for the Day

The A.A. program is one of charity because the real meaning of the word *charity* is to care enough about other people to really want to help them. To get the full benefit of the program, we must try to help other alcoholics. We may try to help somebody and think we have failed, but the seed we have planted may bear fruit some time. We never know the results even a word of ours might have. But the main thing is to have charity for others, a real desire to help them, whether we succeed or not. *Do I have real charity?*

Meditation for the Day

All material things, the universe, the world, even our bodies, may be Eternal Thought expressed in time and space. The more the physicists and astronomers reduce matter, the more it becomes a mathematical formula, which is thought. In the final analysis, matter is thought. When Eternal thought expresses itself within the framework of space and time, it becomes matter. Our thoughts, within the box of space and time, cannot know anything first hand, except material things. But we can deduce that outside the box of space and time is Eternal Thought, which we can call God.

Prayer for the Day

I pray that I may be a true expression of Eternal Thought. I pray that God's thoughts may work through my thoughts.

MAY 2—A.A. Thought for the Day

In A.A. we often hear the slogan "Easy Does It." Alcoholics always do everything to excess. They drink too much. They worry too much. They have too many resentments. They hurt themselves physically and mentally by too much of everything. So when they come into A.A., they have to learn to take it easy. None of us knows how much longer we have to live. It's probable that we wouldn't have lived very long if we had continued to drink the way we used to. By stopping drinking, we have increased our chances of living for a while longer. *Have I learned to take it easy?*

Meditation for the Day

You must be, before you can do. To accomplish much, be much. In all cases, the doing must be the expression of the being. It is foolish to think that we can accomplish much in personal relationships, without first preparing ourselves by being honest, pure, unselfish, and loving. We must choose the good and keep choosing it, before we are ready to be used by God to accomplish any thing worth while. We will not be given the opportunities until we are ready for them. Quiet times of communion with the Higher Power are good preparation for creative action.

Prayer for the Day

I pray that I may constantly prepare myself for better things to come. I pray that I may only have opportunities when I am ready for them.

MAY 3—A.A. Thought for the Day

A.A. teaches us to take it easy. We learn how to relax and to stop worrying about the past or the future, to give up our resentments and hates and tempers, to stop being critical of people, and to try to help them instead. That's what "Easy Does It" means. So in the time that's left to me to live, I'm going to try to take it easy, to relax and not to worry, to try to be helpful to others and to trust God. *For what's left of my life, is my motto going to be "Easy Does It"?*

Meditation for the Day

I must overcome myself before I can truly forgive other people for injuries done to me. The self in me cannot forgive injuries. The very thought of wrongs means that my self is in the foreground. Since the self cannot forgive, I must overcome my selfishness. I must cease trying to forgive those who fretted and wronged me. It is a mistake for me even to think about these injuries. I must aim at overcoming myself in my daily life and then I will find there is nothing in me that remembers injury, because the only thing injured, my selfishness, is gone.

Prayer for the Day

I pray that I may hold no resentments. I pray that my mind may be washed clean of all past hates and fears.

MAY 4—A.A. Thought for the Day

When I was drinking, I always tried to build myself up. I used to tell tall stories about myself. I told them so often that I half believe some of them now, even though I know they aren't true. I used to hang around the low-brow barrooms so I could feel superior to the other customers. The reason I always tried to build myself up was that I knew deep down in my heart that I really didn't amount to anything. It was a kind of defense against my feeling of inferiority. *Do I still build myself up?*

Meditation for the Day

God thought about the universe and brought it into being. His thought brought me into being. I must think God's thought after Him. I must often keep my mind occupied with thoughts about God and meditate on the way He wants me to live. I must train my mind constantly in quiet times of communion with God. It is the work of a lifetime to develop to full stature spiritually. This is what I am on earth for. It gives meaning to my life.

Prayer for the Day

I pray that I may think God's thoughts after Him. I pray that I may live as He wants me to live.

MAY 5—A.A. Thought for the Day

I had to show off and boast so that people would think I amounted to something, when, of course, both they and I knew that I really didn't amount to anything. I didn't fool anybody. Although I've been sober for quite a while, the old habit of building myself up is still with me. I still have a tendency to think too well of myself and to pretend to be more than I really am. *Am I always in danger of becoming conceited just because I'm sober?*

Meditation for the Day

I cannot ascertain the spiritual with my intellect. I can only do it by my own faith and spiritual faculties. I must think of God more with my heart than with my head. I can breathe in God's very spirit in the life around me. I can keep my eyes turned towards the good things in the world. I am shut up in a box of space and time, but I can open a window in that box by faith. I can empty my mind of all the limitations of material things. I can sense the Eternal.

Prayer for the Day

I pray that whatever is good I may have. I pray that I may leave to God the choice of what good will come to me.

MAY 6—A.A. Thought for the Day

I've noticed that the ones who do the most for A.A. are not in the habit of boasting about it. The danger of building myself up too much is that, if I do, I'm in danger of having a fall. That pattern of thought goes with drinking. If one side of a boat gets too far up out of the water, it's liable to tip over. Building myself up and drinking go together. One leads to the other. So if I'm going to stay sober, I've got to keep small. *Have I got the right perspective on myself?*

Meditation for the Day

The way sometimes seems long and weary. So many people today are weary. The weariness of others must often be shared by me. The weary and the heavy-laden, when they come to me, should be helped to find the rest that I have found. There is only one sure cure for world-weariness and that is turning to spiritual things. In order to help bring about the turning of the weary world to God, I must dare to suffer, dare to conquer selfishness in myself, and dare to be filled with spiritual peace in the face of all the weariness of the world.

Prayer for the Day

I pray that I may be a help to discouraged people. I pray that I may have the courage to help bring about what the weary world needs but does not know how to get.

MAY 7—A.A. Thought for the Day

It's very important to keep in a grateful frame of mind, if we want to stay sober. We should be grateful that we're living in a day and age when an alcoholic isn't treated as he often used to be treated before Alcoholics Anonymous was started. In the old days, every town had its town drunk who was regarded with scorn and ridiculed by the rest of the townspeople. We have come into A.A. and found all the sympathy, understanding, and fellowship that we could ask for. There's no other group like A.A. in the world. *Am I grateful?*

Meditation for the Day

God takes our efforts for good and blesses them. God needs our efforts. We need God's blessing. Together, they mean spiritual success. Our efforts are necessary. We cannot merely relax and drift with the tide. We must often direct our efforts against the tide of materialism around us. When difficulties come, our efforts are needed to surmount them. But God directs our efforts into the right channels and God's power is necessary to help us choose the right.

Prayer for the Day

I pray that I may choose the right. I pray that I may have God's blessing and direction in all my efforts for good.

MAY 8—A.A. Thought for the Day

I'm grateful that I found a program in A.A. that could keep me sober. I'm grateful that A.A. has shown me the way to faith in a Higher Power, because the renewing of that faith has changed my way of life. And I've found a happiness and contentment that I had forgotten existed, by simply believing in God and trying to live the kind of a life that I know He wants me to live. As long as I stay grateful, I'll stay sober. *Am I in a grateful frame of mind?*

Meditation for the Day

God can work through you better when you are not hurrying. Go very slowly, very quietly, from one duty to the next, taking time to rest and pray between. Do not be too busy. Take everything in order. Venture often into the rest of God and you will find peace. All work that results from resting with God is good work. Claim the power to work miracles in human lives. Know that you can do many things through the Higher Power. Know that you can do good things through God who rests you and gives you strength. Partake regularly of rest and prayer.

Prayer for the Day

I pray that I may not be in too much of a hurry. I pray that I may take time out often to rest with God.

MAY 9—A.A. Thought for the Day

We alcoholics used so little self-control when we were drinking, we were so absolutely selfish, that it does us good to give up something once in a while. Using self-discipline and denying ourselves a few things is good for us. At first, giving up liquor is a big enough job for all of us, even with God's help. But later on, we can practice self-discipline in other ways to keep a firm grip on our minds so that we don't start any wishful thinking. If we day-dream too much, we'll be in danger of slipping. *Am I practicing enough self-discipline?*

Meditation for the Day

In material things, you must rely on your own wisdom and that of others. In spiritual things, you cannot rely so much on your own wisdom as on God's guidance. In dealing with personalities, it is a mistake to step out too much on your own. You must try to be guided by God in all human relationships. You cannot accomplish much of value in dealing with people until God knows you are ready. You alone do not have the power or wisdom to put things right between people. You must rely on God to help you in these vital matters.

Prayer for the Day

I pray that I may rely on God in dealing with people's problems. I pray that I may try to follow His guidance in all personal relationships.

One thing that keeps me sober is a feeling of loyalty to the other members of the group. I know I'd be letting them down if I ever took a drink. When I was drinking, I wasn't loyal to anybody. I should have been loyal to my family, but I wasn't. I let them down by my drinking. When I came into A.A., I found a group of people who were not only helping each other to stay sober, but who were loyal to each other by staying sober themselves. *Am I loyal to my group?*

Meditation for the Day

Calmness is constructive of good. Agitation is destructive of good. I should not rush into action. I should first "be still and know that He is God." Then I should act only as God directs me through my conscience. Only trust, perfect trust in God, can keep me calm when all around me are agitated. Calmness is trust in action. I should seek all things which can help me to cultivate calmness. To attain material things, the world learns to attain speed. To attain spiritual things, I have to learn to attain a state of calm.

Prayer for the Day

I pray that I may learn how to have inner peace. I pray that I may be calm, so that God can work through me.

MAY 11—A.A. Thought for the Day

We can depend on those members of any group who have gone all out for the program. They come to meetings. They work with other alcoholics. We don't have to worry about their slipping. They're loyal members of the group. I'm trying to be a loyal member of the group. When I'm tempted to take a drink, I tell myself that if I did I'd be letting down the other members who are the best friends I have. *Am I going to let them down, if I can help it?*

Meditation for the Day

Wherever there is true fellowship and love between people, God's spirit is always there as the Divine Third. In all human relationships, the Divine Spirit is what brings them together. When a life is changed through the channel of another person, it is God, the Divine Third, who always makes the change, using the person as a means. The moving power behind all spiritual things, all personal relationships between people is God, the Divine Third, who is always there. No personal relationships can be entirely right without the presence of God's Spirit.

Prayer for the Day

I pray that I may be used as a channel by God's spirit. I pray that I may feel that the Divine Third is always there to help me.

MAY 12—A.A. Thought for the Day

When we come into A.A., looking for a way out of drinking, we really need a lot more than that. We need fellowship. We need to get the things that are troubling us out into the open. We need a new outlet for our energies and we need a new strength beyond ourselves that will help us face life instead of running away from it. In A.A. we find these things that we need. *Have I found the things that I need?*

Meditation for the Day

Turn out all thoughts of doubt and fear and resentment. Never tolerate them if you can help it. Bar the windows and doors of your mind against them, as you would bar your home against a thief who would steal in to take away your treasures. What greater treasures can you have than faith and courage and love? All these are stolen from you by doubt and fear and resentment. Face each day with peace and hope. They are results of true faith in God. Faith gives you a feeling of protection and safety that you can get in no other way.

Prayer for the Day

I pray that I may feel protected and safe, but not only when I am in the harbor. I pray that I may have protection and safety even in the midst of the storms of life.

MAY 13—A.A. Thought for the Day

In A.A. we find fellowship and release and strength. And having found these things, the real reasons for our drinking are taken away. Then drinking has no more justification in our minds. We no longer need to fight against drink. Drink just naturally leaves us. At first, we are sorry that we can't drink, but we get so that we are glad that we don't have to drink. *Am I glad that I don't have to drink?*

Meditation for the Day

Try never to judge. The human mind is so delicate and so complex that only its Maker can know it wholly. Each mind is so different, actuated by such different motives, controlled by such different circumstances, influenced by such different sufferings, you cannot know all the influences that have gone to make up a personality. Therefore, it is impossible for you to judge wholly that personality. But God knows that person wholly and He can change it. Leave to God the unravelling of the puzzles of personality. And leave it to God to teach you the proper understanding.

Prayer for the Day

I pray that I may not judge other people. I pray that I may be certain that God can set right what is wrong in every personality.

MAY 14—A.A. Thought for the Day

Having gotten over drinking, we have only just begun to enjoy the benefits of A.A. We find new friends, so that we are no longer lonely. We find new relationships with our families, so that we are happy at home. We find release from our troubles and worries through a new way of looking at things. We find an outlet for our energies in helping other people. *Am I enjoying these benefits of A.A.?*

Meditation for the Day

The kingdom of heaven is within you. God sees, as no one can see, what is within you. He sees you growing more and more like Himself. That is your reason for existence, to grow more and more like God, to develop more and more the spirit of God within you. You can often see in others those qualities and aspirations which you yourself possess. So also can God recognize His own spirit in you. Your motives and aspirations can only be understood by those who have attained the same spiritual level as you have.

Prayer for the Day

I pray that I may not expect complete understanding from others. I pray that I may only expect this from God, as I try to grow more like Him.

MAY 15—A.A. Thought for the Day

In A.A. we find a new strength and peace from the realization that there must be a Power greater than ourselves which is running the universe and which is on our side when we live a good life. So the A.A. program really never ends. You begin by overcoming drink and you go on from there to many new opportunities for happiness and usefulness. *Am I really enjoying the full benefits of A.A.?*

Meditation for the Day

"Seek ye first the Kingdom of God and His righteousness and all these things shall be added unto you." We should not seek material things first, but seek spiritual things first and material things will come to us, as we honestly work for them. Many people seek material things first and think they can then grow into knowledge of spiritual things. You cannot serve God and Mammon at the same time. The first requisites of an abundant life are the spiritual things: honesty, purity, unselfishness, and love. Until you have these qualities, quantities of material things are of little real use to you.

Prayer for the Day

I pray that I may put much effort into acquiring spiritual things. I pray that I may not expect good things until I am right spiritually.

MAY 16—A.A. Thought for the Day

In the story of the Good Samaritan, the wayfarer fell among robbers and was left lying in the gutter, half dead. And a priest and a Levite both passed by on the other side of the road. But the Good Samaritan was moved with compassion and came to him and bound up his wounds and brought him to an inn and took care of him. *Do I treat another alcoholic like the priest and the Levite or like the Good Samaritan?*

Meditation for the Day

Never weary in prayer. When one day you see how unexpectedly your prayer has been answered, then you will deeply regret that you have prayed so little. Prayer changes things for you. Practice praying until your trust in God has become strong. And then pray on, because it has become so much a habit that you need it daily. Keep praying until prayer seems to become communion with God. That is the note on which true times of prayer should end.

Prayer for the Day

I pray that I may form the habit of daily prayer. I pray that I may find the strength I need, as a result of this communion.

MAY 17—A.A. Thought for the Day

A lot of well-meaning people treat an alcoholic like the priest and the Levite. They pass by on the other side by scorning him and telling him what a low person he is, with no will-power. Whereas, he really has fallen for alcohol, in the same way as the man in the story fell among robbers. And the member of A.A. who is working with others is like the Good Samaritan. Am I moved with compassion? *Do I take care of another alcoholic whenever I can?*

Meditation for the Day

I must constantly live in preparation for something better to come. All of life is a preparation for something better. I must anticipate the morning to come. I must feel, in the night of sorrow, that understanding joy that tells of confident expectation of better things to come. "Sorrow may endure for a night, but joy cometh in the morning." Know that God has something better in store for you, as long as you are making yourself ready for it. All your existence in this world is a training for a better life to come.

Prayer for the Day

I pray that when life is over, I will return to an eternal, spaceless life with God. I pray that I may make this life a preparation for a better life to come.

MAY 18—A.A. Thought for the Day

We're in A.A. for two main reasons: to keep sober ourselves and to help others to keep sober. It's a well-known fact that helping others is a big part of keeping sober yourself. It's also been proved that it's very hard to keep sober all by yourself. A lot of people have tried it and failed. They come to a few A.A. meetings and then stay sober alone for a few months, but usually they eventually get drunk. *Do I know that I can't stay sober successfully alone?*

Meditation for the Day

Look by faith into that place beyond space or time where God dwells and whence you came and to which you shall eventually return. "Look unto Him and be saved." To look beyond material things is within the power of everyone's imagination. Faith's look saves you from despair. Faith's look saves you from worry and care. Faith's look brings a peace beyond all understanding. Faith's look brings you all the strength you need. Faith's look gives you a new and vital power and a wonderful peace and serenity.

Prayer for the Day

I pray that I may have faith's look. I pray that by faith I may look beyond the now to eternal life.

MAY 19—A.A. Thought for the Day

Fellowship is a big part of staying sober. The doctors call it group therapy. We never go to an A.A. meeting without taking something out of it. Sometimes we don't feel like going to a meeting and we think of excuses for not going. But we usually end up by going anyway. And we always get some lift out of every meeting. Meetings are part of keeping sober. And we get more out of a meeting if we try to contribute something to it. *Am I contributing my share at meetings?*

Meditation for the Day

"He brought me up out of a horrible pit, out of the miry clay, and set my feet upon a rock and established my goings." The first part, "He brought me up out of a horrible pit," means that by turning to God and putting my problems in His hands, I am able to overcome my sins and temptations. "He set my feet upon a rock" means that when I trust God in all things, I have true security. "He established my goings" means that if I honestly try to live the way God wants me to live, I will have God's guidance in my daily living.

Prayer for the Day

I pray that my feet may be set upon a rock. I pray that I may rely on God to guide my comings and goings.

MAY 20—A.A. Thought for the Day

If we get up in a meeting and tell something about ourselves in order to help the other person, we feel a whole lot better. It's the old law of the more you give the more you get. Witnessing and confession are part of keeping sober. You never know when you may help somebody. Helping others is one of the best ways to stay sober yourself. And the satisfaction you get out of helping a fellow human being is one of the finest experiences you can have. *Am I helping others?*

Meditation for the Day

Without God, no real victory is ever won. All the military victories of great conquerors have passed into history. The world might be better off without military conquerors. The real victories are won in the spiritual realm. "He that conquers himself is greater than he who conquers a city." The real victories are victories over sin and temptation, leading to a victorious and abundant life. Therefore, keep a brave and trusting heart. Face all your difficulties in the spirit of conquest. Remember that where God is, there is the true victory.

Prayer for the Day

I pray that the forces of evil in my life will flee before God's presence. I pray that with God I will win the real victory over myself

MAY 21—A.A. Thought for the Day

One of the finest things about A.A. is the sharing. Sharing is a wonderful thing because the more you share the more you have. In our old drinking days, we didn't do much sharing. We used to keep things to ourselves, partly because we were ashamed, but mostly because we were selfish. And we were very lonely because we didn't share. When we came into A.A., the first thing we found was sharing. We heard other alcoholics frankly sharing their experiences with hospitals, jails, and all the usual mess that goes with drinking. *Am I sharing?*

Meditation for the Day

Character is developed by the daily discipline of duties done. Be obedient to the heavenly vision and take the straight way. Do not fall into the error of calling "Lord, Lord," and doing not the things that should be done. You need a life of prayer and meditation, but you must still do your work in the busy ways of life. The busy person is wise to rest and wait patiently for God's guidance. If you are obedient to the heavenly vision, you can be at peace.

Prayer for the Day

I pray that I may be obedient to the heavenly vision. I pray if I fall, I will pick myself up and go on.

MAY 22—A.A. Thought for the Day

What impresses us most at an A.A. meeting is the willingness to share, without holding anything back. And pretty soon we find ourselves sharing also. We start telling our own experiences and by so doing we help the other person. And when we've got these things off our chest, we feel a lot better. It does us a lot of good to share with some other poor unfortunate person who's in the same box that we were in. And the more we share, the more we have left for ourselves. *Do I know that the more I share, the better chance I'll have to stay sober?*

Meditation for the Day

Constantly claim God's strength. Once convinced of the right of a course of action, once reasonably sure of God's guidance, claim that strength now. You can claim all the strength you need to meet any situation. You can claim a new supply when your own supply is exhausted. You have a right to claim it and you should use your right. A beggar supplicates, a son appropriates. When you supplicate, you are often kept waiting, but when you appropriate God's strength in a good cause, you have it at once.

Prayer for the Day

I pray that I may claim God's strength whenever I need it. I pray that I may try to live as a child of God.

MAY 23—A.A. Thought for the Day

The twelfth step of A.A., working with others, can be subdivided into five parts, five words beginning with the letter C—confidence, confession, conviction, conversion, and continuance. The first thing in trying to help other alcoholics is to get their confidence. We do this by telling them our own experiences with drinking, so that they see that we know what we're talking about. If we share our experiences frankly, they will know that we are sincerely trying to help them. They will realize that they're not alone and that others have had experiences as bad or worse than theirs. This gives them confidence that they can be helped. *Do I care enough about other alcoholics to get their confidence?*

Meditation for the Day

I fail not so much when tragedy happens as I did before the happening, by all the little things I might have done, but did not do. I must prepare for the future by doing the right thing at the right time now. If a thing should be done, I should deal with that thing today and get it righted with God before I allow myself to undertake any new duty. I should look upon myself as performing God's errands and then coming back to Him to tell Him in quiet communion that the message has been delivered or the task done.

Prayer for the Day

I pray that I may seek no credit for the results of what I do. I pray that I may leave the outcome of my actions to God.

MAY 24—A.A. Thought for the Day

In twelfth-step work, the second thing is confession. By frankly sharing with prospects, we get them talking about their own experiences. They will open up and confess things to us that they haven't been able to tell other people. And they feel better when this confession has been made. It's a great load off their minds to get these things out into the open. It's the things that are kept hidden that weigh on the mind. They feel a sense of release and freedom when they have opened up their hearts to us. *Do I care enough about other alcoholics to help them to make a confession?*

Meditation for the Day

I should help others all I can. Every troubled soul that God puts in my path is the one for me to help. As I sincerely try to help, a supply of strength will flow into me from God. My circle of helpfulness will widen more and more. God hands out the spiritual food to me and I pass it on to others. I must never say that I have only enough strength for my own need. The more I give away, the more I will keep. That which I keep to myself, I will lose in the end.

Prayer for the Day

I pray that I may have a sincere willingness to give. I pray that I may not hold back the strength I have received for myself alone.

MAY 25—A.A. Thought for the Day

In twelfth-step work, the third thing is conviction. Prospects must be convinced that they honestly want to stop drinking. They must see and admit that their life is unmanageable. They must face the fact that they must do something about their drinking. They must be absolutely honest with themselves and face themselves as they really are. They must be convinced that they must give up drinking and they must see that their whole life depends on this conviction. *Do I care enough about other alcoholics to help them reach this conviction?*

Meditation for the Day

There is no limit to what you can accomplish in helping others. Keep that thought always. Never relinquish any work or give up the thought of any accomplishment because it seems beyond your power. God will help you in all good work. Only give it up if you feel that it's not God's will for you. In helping others, think of the tiny seed under the dark, hard ground. There is no certainty that, when it has forced its way up to the surface, sunlight and warmth will greet it. Often a task seems beyond your power, but there is no limit to what you can accomplish with God's help.

Prayer for the Day

I pray that I may never become discouraged in helping others. I pray that I may always rely on the power of God to help me.

MAY 26—A.A. Thought for the Day

In twelfth-step work, the fourth thing is conversion. Conversion means change. Prospects must learn to change their way of thinking. Until now, everything they've done has been connected with drinking. Now they must face a new kind of life, without liquor. They must see and admit that they cannot overcome drinking by their own willpower, so they must turn to a Higher Power for help. They must start each day by asking this Higher Power for the strength to stay sober. This conversion to belief in a Higher Power comes gradually, as they try it and find that it works. *Do I care enough about other alcoholics to help them to make this conversion?*

Meditation for the Day

Discipline of yourself is absolutely necessary before the power of God is given to you. When you see others manifesting the power of God, you probably have not seen the discipline that went before. They made themselves ready. All your life is a preparation for more good to be accomplished when God knows that you are ready for it. So keep disciplining yourself in the spiritual life every day. Learn so much of the spiritual laws that your life cannot again be a failure. Others will see the outward manifestation of the inward discipline in your daily living.

Prayer for the Day

I pray that I may manifest God's power in my daily living. I pray that I may discipline myself so as to be ready to meet every opportunity.

MAY 27—A.A. Thought for the Day

In twelfth-step work, the fifth thing is continuance. Continuance means our staying with prospects after they have started on the new way of living. We must stick with them and not let them down. We must encourage them to go to meetings regularly for fellowship and help. They will learn that keeping sober is a lot easier in the fellowship of others who are trying to do the same thing. We must continue to help prospects by going to see them regularly or telephoning them or writing them so that they don't get out of touch with A.A. Continuance means good sponsorship. *Do I care enough about other alcoholics to continue with them as long as necessary?*

Meditation for the Day

Every strong and beautiful flower must have a strong root in the ground. It must send a root down so that it may be rooted and grounded while at the same time it sends a shoot up to be the flower that shall gladden the world. Both growths are necessary. Without a strong root, it would soon wither. The higher the growth upward, the deeper must be the rooting. My life cannot flower into success and helpfulness unless it is rooted in a strong faith, or unless it feels deeply secure in the goodness and purpose of the universe.

Prayer for the Day

I pray that my life may be deeply rooted in faith. I pray that I may feel deeply secure.

MAY 28—A.A. Thought for the Day

In A.A. we learn that since we are alcoholics we can be uniquely useful people. That is, we can help other alcoholics when perhaps somebody who has not had our experience with drinking could not help them. That makes us uniquely useful. The A.A.s are a unique group of people because they have taken their own greatest defeat and failure and sickness and used it as a means of helping others. We who have been through the same thing are the ones who can best help other alcoholics. *Do I believe that I can be uniquely useful?*

Meditation for the Day

I should try to practice the presence of God. I can feel that He is with me and near me, protecting and strengthening me always. In spite of every difficulty, every trial, every failure, the presence of God suffices. Just to believe that He is near me brings strength and peace. I should try to live as though God were beside me. I cannot see Him because I was not made with the ability to see Him else there were no room for faith. But I can feel His spirit with me.

Prayer for the Day

I pray that I may try to practice the presence of God. I pray that by doing so I may never feel alone or helpless again.

MAY 29—A.A. Thought for the Day

We who have learned to put our drink problem in God's hands can help others to do so. We can be used as a connection between an alcoholic's need and God's supply of strength. We in Alcoholics Anonymous can be uniquely useful, just because we have the misfortune or fortune to be alcoholics ourselves. Do I want to be a uniquely useful person? *Will I use my own greatest defeat and failure and sickness as a weapon to help others?*

Meditation for the Day

I will try to help others. I will try not to let a day pass without reaching out an arm of love to someone. Each day I will try to do something to lift another human being out of the sea of discouragements into which he or she has fallen. My helping hand is needed to raise the helpless to courage, to strength, to faith, to health. In my own gratitude, I will turn and help other alcoholics with the burden that is pressing too heavily upon them.

Prayer for the Day

I pray that I may be used by God to lighten many burdens. I pray that many souls may be helped through my efforts.

MAY 30—A.A. Thought for the Day

I am part of A.A., one among many, but I am one. I need the A.A. principles for the development of the buried life within me. A.A. may be human in its organization, but it is Divine in its purpose. The purpose is to point me toward God and a better life. Participating in the privilege of the movement, I shall share in the responsibilities, taking it upon myself to carry my fair share of the load, not grudgingly but joyfully. To the extent that I fail in my responsibilities, A.A. fails. To the extent that I succeed, A.A. succeeds. *Do I accept this as my A.A. credo?*

Meditation for the Day

"Praise the Lord." What does praising God mean? It means being grateful for all the wonderful things in the universe and for all the blessings in your life. So praise God by being grateful and humble. Praise of this kind has more power to vanquish evil than has mere resignation. The truly grateful and humble person who is always praising God, is not tempted to do wrong. You will have a feeling of security because you know that fundamentally all is well. So look up to God and praise Him.

Prayer for the Day

I pray that I may be grateful for all my blessings. I pray that I may be humble because I know that I do not deserve them.

MAY 31—A.A. Thought for the Day

I shall not wait to be drafted for service to A.A. I shall volunteer. I shall be loyal in my attendance, generous in my giving, kind in my criticism, creative in my suggestions, loving in my attitudes. I shall give to A.A. my interest, my enthusiasm, my devotion, and most of all, myself. *Do I also accept this as my A.A. credo?*

Meditation for the Day

Prayer is of many kinds, but of whatever kind, prayer is the linking up of the soul and mind to God. So, if prayer is only a glance of faith, a look or a word of love, or just a feeling of confidence in the goodness and purpose in the universe, still the result of that prayer is added strength to meet all temptations and to overcome them. Even if no supplication is expressed, all the supply of strength that is necessary is secured, because the soul, being linked and united to God, receives from Him all spiritual help needed. The soul, when in its human body, still needs the things belonging to its heavenly habitation.

Prayer for the Day

I pray that I may be taught how to pray. I pray that I may be linked through prayer to the mind and will of God.

JUNE 1—A.A. Thought for the Day

Some things I do not miss since becoming dry: that over-all awful feeling physically, including the shakes, a spliting headache, pains in my arms and legs, bleary eyes, fluttering stomach, droopy shoulders, weak knees, a three-day beard, and a flushed complexion. Also, facing my wife or my husband at breakfast. Also, composing the alibi and sticking to it. Also, trying to shave or put on make-up with a shaky hand. Also, opening up my wallet to find it empty. *I don't miss these things, do I?*

Meditation for the Day

You were born with a spark of the Divine within you. It had been all but smothered by the life you were living. That celestial fire has to be tended and fed so that it will grow eventually into a real desire to live the right way. By trying to do the will of God, you grow more and more in the new way of life. By thinking of God, praying to Him, and having communion with Him, you gradually grow more like Him. The way of your transformation from the material to the spiritual is the way of Divine Companionship.

Prayer for the Day

I pray that I may tend the spark of the Divine within me so that it will grow. I pray that I may be gradually transformed from the old life to the new life.

JUNE 2—A.A. Thought for the Day

Some more things I do not miss since becoming dry: wondering if the car is in the garage and how I got home; struggling to remember where I was and what I did since my last conscious moment; trying to delay getting off to work, and wondering how I will look when I get there; dreading the day ahead of me. *I'm quite sure that I don't miss these things, am I not?*

Meditation for the Day

You cannot believe in God and keep your selfish ways. The old self shrivels up and dies, and upon the re-born soul God's image becomes stamped. The gradual elimination of selfishness in the growth of love for God and your fellow human beings is the goal of life. At first, you have only a faint likeness to the Divine, but the picture grows and takes on more and more of the likeness of God until those who see you can see in you some of the power of God's grace at work in a human life.

Prayer for the Day

I pray that I may develop that faint likeness I have to the Divine. I pray that others may see in me some of the power of God's grace at work.

JUNE 3—A.A. Thought for the Day

Some more things I do not miss since becoming dry: running all over town to find a bar open to get that "pick-me--up"; meeting my friends and trying to cover up that I feel awful; looking at myself in a mirror and calling myself a damn fool; struggling with myself to snap out of it for two or three days; wondering what it is all about. *I'm positive I don't miss these things, am I not?*

Meditation for the Day

Love is the power that transforms your life. Try to love your family and your friends and then try to love everybody that you possibly can, even the "sinners and publicans" —everybody. Love for God is an even greater thing. It is the result of gratitude to God and it is the acknowledgement of the blessing that God has sent you. Love for God acknowledges His gifts and leaves the way open for God to shower yet more blessings on your thankful heart. Say: "Thank you, God," until it becomes a habit.

Prayer for the Day

I pray that I may try to love God and all people. I pray that I may continually thank God for all His blessings.

JUNE 4—A.A. Thought for the Day

Some things I like since becoming dry: feeling good in the morning; full use of my intelligence; joy in my work; the love and trust of my children; lack of remorse; the confidence of my friends; the prospect of a happy future; the appreciation of the beauties of nature; knowing what it is all about. *I'm sure that I like these things, am I not?*

Meditation for the Day

Molding your life means cutting and shaping your material into something good, something which can express the spiritual. All material things are the clay out of which we mold something spiritual. You must first recognize the selfishness in your desires and motives, actions and words, and then mold that selfishness until it is sublimated into a spiritual weapon for good. As the work of molding proceeds, you see more and more clearly what must be done to mold your life into something better.

Prayer for the Day

I pray that I may mold my life into something useful and good. I pray that I may not be discouraged by the slow progress that I make.

JUNE 5—A.A. Thought for the Day

We alcoholics are fortunate to be living in a day and age when there is such a thing as Alcoholics Anonymous. Before A.A. came into being, there was very little hope for the alcoholic. A.A. is a great rebuilder of human wreckage. It takes men and women whose personality problem expresses itself in alcoholism and offers them a program which, if they are willing to accept it, allows them not only to get sober, but also to find a much better way of living. *Have I found a better way of living?*

Meditation for the Day

Very quietly God speaks through your thoughts and feelings. Heed the Divine voice of your conscience. Listen for this and you will never be disappointed in the results in your life. Listen for this small, still voice and your tired nerves will become rested. The Divine voice comes to you as strength as well as tenderness, as power as well as restfulness. Your moral strength derives its effectiveness from the power that comes when you listen patiently for the still, small voice.

Prayer for the Day

I pray that I may listen for the still, small voice of God. I pray that I may obey the leading of my conscience.

JUNE 6—A.A. Thought for the Day

Drinking is the way we alcoholics express our maladjustments to life. I believe that I was a potential alcoholic from the start. I had an inferiority complex. I didn't make friends easily. There was a wall between me and other people. And I was lonely. I was not well adjusted to life. *Did I drink to escape from myself?*

Meditation for the Day

According to the varying needs of each person, so does each person think of God. It is not necessary that you think of God as others think of Him, but it is necessary that you think of Him as supplying what you personally need. The weak need God's strength. The strong need God's tenderness. The tempted and fallen need God's saving grace. The righteous need God's pity for sinners. The lonely need God as a friend. The fighters for righteousness need a leader in God. You may think of God in any way you wish. We usually do not turn to God until we need Him.

Prayer for the Day

I pray that I may think of God as supplying my needs. I pray that I will bring all my problems to Him for help in meeting them.

JUNE 7—A.A. Thought for the Day

Alcoholism is a progressive illness. We go through the three stages of social drinking, trouble drinking, and merry-go-round drinking. We land in hospitals and jails. We eventually lose our homes, our families, and our self-respect. Yes, alcoholism is a progressive illness and there are only three ends to it—the insane asylum, the morgue, or total abstinence. *Will I choose not to take the first drink?*

Meditation for the Day

You not only can live a new life but you also can grow in grace and power and beauty. Reach ever forward and upward after the things of the spirit. In the animal world, the very form of an animal changes to enable it to reach that upon which it delights to feed. Your whole character changes as you reach upward for the things of the spirit— for beauty, for love, for honesty, for purity, and for unselfishness. Reaching after these things of the spirit, your whole nature becomes changed so that you can best receive and delight in the wonders of the abundant life.

Prayer for the Day

I pray that I may reach forward and upward. I pray that my character may be changed by this reaching upward for the things of the spirit.

JUNE 8—A.A. Thought for the Day

Once an alcoholic, always an alcoholic. We always get worse, never better. We are never cured. Our alcoholism can only be arrested. No matter how long we have been sober, if we try liquor again, we're as bad or worse than we ever were. There is no exception to this rule in the whole history of A.A. We can never recapture the good times of the past. They are gone forever. *Will I try to recapture them?*

Meditation for the Day

Your life has been given to you mainly for the purpose of training your soul. This life we live is not so much for the body as for the soul. We often choose the way of life that best suits the body, not the way that best suits the soul. God wants you to choose what suits the soul as well as the body. Accept this belief and a wonderful molding of character is the result. Reject it and God's purpose for your life is frustrated, and your spiritual progress is delayed. Your soul is being trained by the good you choose. Thus the purpose of your life is being accomplished.

Prayer for the Day

I pray that I may choose what is good for my soul. I pray that I may realize God's purpose for my life.

JUNE 9—A.A. Thought for the Day

We finally came to the bottom. We did not have to be financially broke, although many of us were. But we were spiritually bankrupt. We had a soul-sickness, a revulsion against ourselves and against our way of living. Life had become impossible for us. We had to end it all or do something about it. *Am I glad I did something about it?*

Meditation for the Day

Faith is not seeing, but believing. I am in a box of space and time and cannot see spacelessness or eternity. But God is not within the shell of time and space. He is timeless and spaceless. He cannot be fully comprehended by our finite minds. But we must try to make a union between our purposes and the purposes of God. By trying to merge our minds with the mind of God, a oneness of purpose results. This oneness of purpose puts us in harmony with God and others. Evil comes from being in disharmony with God and good comes from being in harmony with Him.

Prayer for the Day

I pray that I may be in harmony with God. I pray that I may get into the stream of goodness in the universe.

JUNE 10—A.A. Thought for the Day

If we have had some moral, religious, or spiritual training, we're better prospects for A.A. When we reach the bottom, at this crucial moment when we're thoroughly licked, we turn instinctively to whatever decency is left in us. We call upon whatever reserves of morality and faith are left down deep in our heart. *Have I had this spiritual experience?*

Meditation for the Day

The world wonders when it sees a person who can unexpectedly draw large and unsuspected sums from the bank for some emergency. But what the world has not seen are the countless small sums paid into that bank, earned by faithful work over a long time. And so is the bank of the spirit. The world sees the person of faith make a demand on God's stores of power and the demand is met. The world does not see what that person has been putting in, in thanks and praise, in prayer and communion, in small good deeds done faithfully, steadily over the years. .

Prayer for the Day

I pray that I may keep making deposits in God's bank. I pray that in my hour of need, I may call upon these.

JUNE 11—A.A. Thought for the Day

We alcoholics have to believe in some Power greater than ourselves. Yes, we have to believe in God. Not to believe in a Higher Power drives us to atheism. Atheism, it has been said before, is blind faith in the strange proposition that this universe originated in a cipher and aimlessly rushes nowhere. That's practically impossible to believe. So we turn to that Divine Principle in the universe which we call God. *Have I stopped trying to run my own life?*

Meditation for the Day

"Lord, we thank Thee for the great gift of peace, that peace which passeth all understanding, that peace which the world can neither give nor take away." That is the peace which only God can give in the midst of a restless world and surrounded by trouble and difficulty. To know that peace is to have received the stamp of the kingdom of God. When you have earned that peace, you are fit to judge between true and false values, between the values of the kingdom of God and the values of all that the world has to offer.

Prayer for the Day

I pray that today I may have inner peace. I pray that today I may be at peace with myself.

JUNE 12—A.A. Thought for the Day

When we came into A.A., we made a tremendous discovery. We found that we were sick persons rather than moral lepers. We were not such queer birds as we thought we were. We found other people who had the same illness that we had, who had been through the same experiences that we had been through. They had recovered. If they could do it, we could do it. *Was hope born in me the day I walked into A.A.?*

Meditation for the Day

"He that heareth these sayings and doeth them is like unto a man who built his house upon a rock and the rain descended and the floods came and the wind blew and beat upon that house and it fell not for it was founded upon a rock." When your life is built upon obedience to God and upon doing His will as you understand it, you will be steadfast and unmovable even in the midst of storms. The serene, steadfast, unmovable life—the rock home—is laid stone by stone—foundations, walls and roof—by acts of obedience to the heavenly vision. The daily following of God's guidance and the daily doing of His will, builds your house upon a rock.

Prayer for the Day

I pray that my life may be founded upon the rock of faith. I pray that I may be obedient to the heavenly vision.

JUNE 13—A.A. Thought for the Day

In A.A. we have to reeducate our minds. We have to learn to think differently. We have to take a long view of drinking instead of a short view. We have to look through the glass to what lies beyond it. We have to look through the night before to the morning after. No matter how good liquor looks from the short view, we must realize that in the long run it is poison to us. *Have I learned to look through the bottle to the better life that lies ahead?*

Meditation for the Day

If you are honestly trying to live the way you believe God wants you to live, you can get guidance from God in times of quiet communion with Him, provided your thoughts are directed towards God's will and all good things. The attitude of "Thy will, not mine, be done" leads to clear guidance. Act on this guidance and you will be led to better things. Your impulses seem to become less your own and more the leading of God's spirit acting through your thoughts. Obeyed, they will bring you the answers to your prayers.

Prayer for the Day

I pray that I may try to think God's thoughts after Him. I pray that my thoughts may be guided by His thoughts.

JUNE 14—A.A. Thought for the Day

In A.A. we have to learn that drink is our greatest enemy. Although we used to think that liquor was our friend, the time came when it turned against us and became our enemy. We don't know just when this happened, but we know that it did because we began to get into trouble—jails and hospitals. We realize now that liquor is our enemy. *Is it still my main business to keep sober?*

Meditation for the Day

It is not your circumstances that need altering so much as yourself. After you have changed, conditions will naturally change. Spare no effort to become all that God would have you become. Follow every good leading of your conscience. Take each day with no backward look. Face the day's problems with God, and seek God's help and guidance as to what you should do in every situation that may arise. Never look back. Never leave until tomorrow the thing that you are guided to do today.

Prayer for the Day

I pray that God will help me to become all that He would have me be. I pray that I may face today's problems with good grace.

JUNE 15—A.A. Thought for the Day

In A.A. we have three things: fellowship, faith, and service. Fellowship is wonderful, but its wonder lasts just so long. Then some gossip, disillusionment, and boredom may come in. Worry and fear come back at times and we find that fellowship is not the whole story. Then we need faith. When we're alone, with nobody to pat us on the back, we must turn to God for help. *Can I say: "They will be done"—and mean it?*

Meditation for the Day

There is beauty in a God-guided life. There is wonder in the feeling of being led by God. Try to realize God's bounty and goodness more and more. God is planning for you. Wonderful are His ways—they are beyond your knowledge. But God's leading will enter your consciousness more and more and bring you ever more peace and joy. Your life is being planned and blessed by God. You may count all material things as loss if they prevent your winning your way to the consciousness of God's guidance.

Prayer for the Day

I pray that I may earn the rewards of God's power and peace. I pray that I may develop the feeling of being led by God.

JUNE 16—A.A. Thought for the Day

But even faith is not the whole story. There must be service. We must give this thing away if we want to keep it. The Dead Sea has no outlet and it is stagnant and full of salt. The Sea of Galilee is clear and clean and blue, as the Jordan River carries it out to irrigate the desert. To be of service to other people makes our lives worth living. *Does service to others give me a real purpose in life?*

Meditation for the Day

Seek God early in the day, before He gets crowded out by life's problems, difficulties or pleasures. In that early quiet time gain a calm, strong confidence in the goodness and purpose in the universe. Do not seek God only when the world's struggles prove too much and too many for you to bear or face alone. Seek God early, when you can have a consciousness of God's spirit in the world. People often only seek God when their difficulties are too great to be surmounted in any other way, forgetting that if they sought God's companionship before they need it, many of their difficulties would never arise.

Prayer for the Day

I pray that I may not let God be crowded out by the hurly-burly of life. I pray that I may seek God early and often.

JUNE 17—A.A. Thought for the Day

We in A.A. have the privilege of living two lives in one lifetime. One life of drunkenness, failure, and defeat. Then, through A.A., another life of sobriety, peace of mind, and usefulness. We who have recovered our sobriety are modern miracles. And we're living on borrowed time. Some of us might have been dead long ago. But we have been given another chance to live. *Do I owe a debt of gratitude to A.A. that I can never repay as long as I live?*

Meditation for the Day

Thinking about God in love and worship drives away evil. It is the thought before which the hosts of evil flee. The thought of a Power greater than yourself is the call for a life-line to rescue you from temptation. The thought of God banishes loneliness and dispels gloom. It summons help to conquer your faults. Think of God as often as possible. Use the thought prayerfully and purposefully. It will carry your thoughts away from material things and toward the spiritual things that make life worthwhile.

Prayer for the Day

I pray that I may think of God often. I pray that I may rest in peace at the thought of His love and care.

JUNE 18—A.A. Thought for the Day

The A.A. way of living is not an easy one. But it's an adventure in living that is really worthwhile. And it's so much better than our old drunken way of living that there's no comparison. Our lives without A.A. would be worth nothing. With A.A., we have a chance to live reasonably good lives. It's worth the battle, no matter how tough the going is from day to day. *Isn't it worth the battle?*

Meditation for the Day

The spiritual life has two parts. One is the life apart, the life of prayer and quiet communion with God. You spend this part of your life apart with God. Every day your mind can be set in the right direction so that your thoughts will be of the right kind. The other is the life impart—imparting to others what you have learned from your own meditative experience. The victories you have won over yourself through the help of God can be shared with others. You can help them by imparting to them some of the victory and security which you have gained in your life apart.

Prayer for the Day

I pray that I may grow strong from my times apart with God. I pray that I may pass on some of this strength to others.

JUNE 19—A.A. Thought for the Day

We have this choice every day of our lives. We can take the path that leads to insanity and death. And remember, our next drunk could be our last one. Or we can take the path that leads to a reasonably happy and useful life. The choice is ours each day of our lives. God grant that we take the right path. *Have I made my choice today?*

Meditation for the Day

Your real work in life is to grow spiritually. To do this you must follow the path of diligently seeking good. The hidden spiritual wonders are revealed to those who diligently seek this treasure. From one point to the next, you have to follow the way of obedience to God's will until finally you reach greater and greater spiritual heights. Work on the material plane should be secondary to your real life's work. The material things which you need most are those which help you to attain the spiritual.

Prayer for the Day

I pray that I may keep growing spiritually. I pray that I may make this my real life's work.

JUNE 20—A.A. Thought for the Day

You should be ready and willing to carry the A.A. message when called upon to do so. Live for some purpose greater than yourself. Each day you will have something to work for. You have received so much from this program that you should have a vision that gives your life a direction and a purpose that gives meaning to each new day. Let us not slide along through life. Let us have a purpose for each day and let us make that purpose for something greater than just ourselves. *What is my purpose for today?*

Meditation for the Day

To see God with eyes of faith is to cause God's power to manifest itself in the material world. God cannot do His work because of unbelief. In response to your belief, God can work a miracle in your personality. All miracles happen in the realm of personality and all are caused by and based on belief in God's never-failing power. But God's power cannot manifest itself in personalities, unless those personalities make His power available by their faith. We can only see God with the eyes of faith, but this kind of seeing produces a great change in our way of living.

Prayer for the Day

I pray that I may see God with the eyes of faith. I pray that this seeing will produce a change in my personality.

JUNE 21—A.A. Thought for the Day

Intelligent faith in that Power greater than ourselves can be counted on to stabilize our emotions. It has an incomparable capacity to help us look at life in balanced perspective. We look up, around, and away from ourselves, and we see that nine out of ten things which at the moment upset us will shortly disappear. Problems solve themselves, criticism and unkindness vanish as though they had never been. *Have I got the proper perspective toward life?*

Meditation for the Day

A truly spiritual man or woman would like to have a serene mind. The only way to keep calm in this troubled world is to have a serene mind. The calm and sane mind sees spiritual things as the true realities and material things as only temporary and fleeting. That sort of mind you can never obtain by reasoning, because your reasoning powers are limited by space and time. That kind of a mind you can never obtain by reading, because other minds are also limited in the same way. You can only have that mind by an act of faith, by making the venture of belief.

Prayer for the Day

I pray that I may have a calm and sane mind. I pray that I may look up, around, and away from myself.

JUNE 22—A.A. Thought for the Day

If you have any doubt, just ask any of the older members of the A.A. group, and they will readily tell you that since they turned their lives over to the care of God as they understand Him, many of their problems have vanished into the forgotten yesterdays. When you allow yourself to be upset over one thing, you succeed only in opening the door for the coming of hundreds of other upsetting things. *Am I allowing myself to be upset over little things?*

Meditation for the Day

I would do well not to think of the Red Sea of difficulties that lies ahead. I am sure that when I come to that Red Sea, the waters will part and I will be given all the power I need to face and overcome many difficulties and meet what is in store for me with courage. I believe that I will pass through that Red Sea to the promised land, the land of the spirit where many souls meet in perfect comradeship. I believe that when that time comes, I will be freed of all the dross of material things and find peace.

Prayer for the Day

I pray that I may face the future with courage. I pray that I may be given strength to face both life and death fearlessly.

JUNE 23—A.A. Thought for the Day

No chain is stronger than its weakest link. Likewise, if you fail in the day by day program, in all probability it will be at your weakest point. Great faith and constant contact with God's power can help you discover, guard, and under-gird your weakest point with a strength not your own. Intelligent faith in God's power can be counted on to help you master your emotions, help you to think kindly of others, and help you with any task that you undertake, no matter how difficult. *Am I master of my emotions?*

Meditation for the Day

You need to be constantly recharged by the power of the spirit of God. Commune with God in quiet times until the life from God, the Divine life, by that very contact, flows into your being and revives your fainting spirit. When weary, take time out and rest. Rest and gain power and strength from God, and then you will be ready to meet whatever opportunities come your way. Rest until every care and worry and fear have gone and then the tide of peace and serenity, love and joy, will flow into your consciousness.

Prayer for the Day

I pray that I may rest and become recharged. I pray that I may pause and wait for the renewing of my strength.

JUNE 24—A.A. Thought for the Day

Alcohol is our weakness. We suffer from mental conflicts from which we look for escape by drowning our problems in drink. We try through drink to push away from the realities of life. But alcohol does not feed, alcohol does not build, it only borrows from the future and it ultimately destroys. We try to drown our feelings in order to escape life's realities, little realizing or caring that in continued drinking we are only multiplying our problems. *Have I got control over my unstable emotions?*

Meditation for the Day

When I let personal piques and resentments interfere with what I know to be my proper conduct, I am on the wrong track and I am undoing all I have built up by doing the right thing. I must never let personal piques interfere with living the way I know God wants me to live. When I have no clear guidance from God, I must go forward quietly along the path of duty. The attitude of quiet faith will receive its reward as surely as acting upon God's direct guidance. I must not weaken my spiritual power by letting personal piques upset me.

Prayer for the Day

I pray that I may not let myself become too upset. I pray that I may go quietly along the path I have chosen.

JUNE 25—A.A. Thought for the Day

One of the most encouraging facts of life is that your weakness can become your greatest asset. Kites and airplanes rise against the wind. In climbing up a high mountain, we need the stony crags and rough places to aid us in our climb. So your weakness can become an asset if you will face it, examine it, and trace it to its origin. Set it in the very center of your mind. No weakness, such as drinking, ever turned into an asset until it was first fairly faced. *Am I making my weakness my greatest asset?*

Meditation for the Day

Whenever we seek to worship God, we think of the great universe that God rules over, of creation, of mighty law and order throughout the universe. Then we feel the awe that precedes worship. I too must feel awe, feel the desire to worship God in wondering amazement. My mind is in a box of space and time and it is so made that I cannot conceive of what is beyond space or time, the limitless and the eternal. But I know that there must be something beyond space and time, and that something must be the limitless and eternal Power behind the universe. I also know that I can experience that Power in my life.

Prayer for the Day

I pray that I may accept the limitless and eternal Spirit. I pray that It may express Itself in my life.

JUNE 26—A.A. Thought for the Day

We must know the nature of our weakness before we can determine how to deal with it. When we are honest about its presence, we may discover that it is imaginary and can be overcome by a change of thinking. We admit that we are alcoholics and we would be foolish if we refused to accept our handicap and do something about it. So by honestly facing our weakness and keeping ever present the knowledge that for us alcoholism is a disease with which we are afflicted, we can take the necessary steps to arrest it. *Have I fully accepted my handicap?*

Meditation for the Day

There is a proper time for everything. I must learn not to do things at the wrong time, that is, before I am ready or before conditions are right. It is always a temptation to do something at once, instead of waiting until the proper time. Timing is important. I must learn, in the little daily situations of life, to delay action until I am sure that I am doing the right thing at the right time. So many lives lack balance and timing. In the momentous decisions and crises of life, they may ask God's guidance, but into the small situations of life, they rush alone.

Prayer for the Day

I pray that I may delay action until I feel that I am doing the right thing. I pray that I may not rush in alone.

JUNE 27—A.A. Thought for the Day

If you can take your troubles as they come, if you can maintain your calm and composure amid pressing duties and unending engagements, if you can rise above the distressing and disturbing circumstances in which you are set down, you have discovered a priceless secret of daily living. Even if you are forced to go through life weighed down by some unescapable misfortune or handicap and yet live each day as it comes with poise and peace of mind, you have succeeded where most people have failed. You have wrought a greater achievement than a person who rules a nation. *Have I achieved poise and peace of mind?*

Meditation for the Day

Take a blessing with you wherever you go. You have been blessed, so bless others. Such stores of blessings are awaiting you in the months and years that lie ahead. Pass on your blessings. Blessing can and does go around the world, passed on from one person to another. Shed a little blessing in the heart of one person. That person is cheered to pass it on, and so, God's vitalizing, joy-giving message travels on. Be a transmitter of God's blessings.

Prayer for the Day

I pray that I may pass on my blessings. I pray that they may flow into the lives of others.

JUNE 28—A.A. Thought for the Day

You can prove to yourself that life is basically and fundamentally an inner attitude. Just try to remember what troubled you most a week ago. You probably will find it difficult to remember. Why then should you unduly worry or fret over the problems that arise today? Your attitude toward them can be changed by putting yourself and your problems in God's hands and trusting Him to see that everything will turn out all right, provided you are trying to do the right thing. Your changed mental attitude toward your problems relieves you of their burden and you can face them without fear. *Has my mental attitude changed?*

Meditation for the Day

You cannot see the future. It's a blessing that you cannot. You could not bear to know all the future. That is why God only reveals it to you day by day. The first step each day is to lay your will before God as an offering, ready for God to do what is best for you. Be sure that, if you trust God, what He does for you will be for the best. The second step is to be confident that God is powerful enough to do anything He wills, and that no miracle in human lives is impossible with Him. Then leave the future to God.

Prayer for the Day

I pray that I may gladly leave my future in God's hands. I pray that I may be confident that good things will happen, as long as I am on the right path.

JUNE 29—A.A. Thought for the Day

The program of Alcoholics Anonymous involves a continuous striving for improvement. There can be no long resting period. We must try to work at it all the time. We must continually keep in mind that it is a program not to be measured in years, because we never fully reach our goals nor are we ever cured. Our alcoholism is only kept in abeyance by daily living of the program. It is a timeless program in every sense. We live it day by day, or more precisely, moment by moment—now. *Am I always striving for improvement?*

Meditation for the Day

Life is all a preparation for something better to come. God has a plan for your life and it will work out, if you try to do His will. God has things planned for you, far beyond what you can imagine now. But you must prepare yourself so that you will be ready for the better things to come. Now is the time for discipline and prayer. The time of expression will come later. Life can be flooded through and through with joy and gladness. So prepare yourself for those better things to come.

Prayer for the Day

I pray that I may prepare myself for better things which God has in store for me. I pray that I may trust God for the future.

JUNE 30—A.A. Thought for the Day

Alcoholics are unable or unwilling, during their addiction to alcohol, to live in the present. The result is that they live in a constant state of remorse and fear because of their unholy past and its morbid attraction, or the uncertain future and its vague forebodings. So the only real hope for the alcoholic is to face the present. Now is the time. Now is ours. The past is beyond recall. The future is as uncertain as life itself. Only the now belongs to us. *Am I living in the now?*

Meditation for the Day

I must forget the past as much as possible. The past is over and gone forever. Nothing can be done about the past, except to make what restitution I can. I must not carry the burden of my past failures. I must go on in faith. The clouds will clear and the way will lighten. The path will become less stony with every forward step I take. God has no reproach for anything that He has healed. I can be made whole and free, even though I have wrecked my life in the past. Remember the saying: "Neither do I condemn thee; go and sin no more."

Prayer for the Day

I pray that I may not carry the burden of the past. I pray that I may cast it off and press on in faith.

In following the A.A. program with its twelve steps, we have the advantage of a better understanding of our problems. Day after day our sobriety results in the formation of new habits, normal habits. As each twenty-four hour period ends, we find that the business of staying sober is a much less trying and fearsome ordeal than it seemed in the beginning. *Do I find it easier as I go along?*

Meditation for the Day

Learn daily the lesson of trust and calm in the midst of the storms of life. Whatever of sorrow or difficulty the day may bring, God's command to you is the same. Be grateful, humble, calm, and loving to all people. Leave each soul the better for having met you or heard you. For all kinds of people, this should be your attitude: a loving desire to help and an infectious spirit of calmness and trust in God. You have the answer to loneliness and fear, which is calm faith in the goodness and purpose in the universe.

Prayer for the Day

I pray that I may be calm in the midst of storms. I pray that I may pass on this calmness to others who are lonely and full of fear.

JULY 2—A.A. Thought for the Day

In the association with members of the A.A. group to which we belong, we have the advantage of sincere friendship and understanding of the other members who, through social and personal contact, take us away from our old haunts and environments and help to remove in large measure the occasions of alcoholic suggestion. We find in this association a sympathy and a willingness on the part of most members to do everything in their power to help us. *Do I appreciate the wonderful fellowship of A.A.?*

Meditation for the Day

"Except ye become as little children, ye cannot enter the kingdom of heaven." In this saying it is urged that all who seek heaven on earth or in the hereafter should become like little children. In seeking things of the spirit and in our faith, we should try to become childlike. Even as we grow older, the years of seeking can give us the attitude of the trusting child. Not only for its simple trust should we have the childlike spirit, but also for its joy in life, its ready laughter, its lack of criticism, and its desire to share. In Charles Dickens' story, *A Christmas Carol*, even old Scrooge changed when he got the child-spirit.

Prayer for the Day

I pray that I may become like a child in faith and hope. I pray that I may, like a child, be friendly and trusting.

JULY 3—A.A. Thought for the Day

In the beginning of Alcoholics Anonymous there were only two persons. Now there are many groups and thousands of members. True, the surface has only been scratched. There are probably ten million or more persons in America alone who need our help. More and more people are making a start in A.A. each day. In the case of individual members, the beginning has been accomplished when they admit they are powerless and turn to a Power greater than themselves, admitting that their lives have become unmanageable. That Higher Power works for good in all things and helps us to accomplish much in individual growth and in the growth of A.A. groups. *Am I doing my part in helping A.A. to grow?*

Meditation for the Day

"Blessed are they that hunger and thirst after righteousness, for they shall be filled." Only in the fullness of faith can the heart-sick and faint and weary be satisfied, healed, and rested. Think of the wonderful spiritual revelations still to be found by those who are trying to live the spiritual life. Much of life is spiritually unexplored country. Only to the consecrated and loving people who walk with God in spirit can these great spiritual discoveries be revealed. Keep going forward and keep growing in righteousness.

Prayer for the Day

I pray that I may not be held back by the material things of the world. I pray that I may let God lead me forward.

JULY 4—A.A. Thought for the Day

In Alcoholics Anonymous there is no thought of individual profit. No greed or gain. No membership fees, no dues. Only voluntary contributions of our money and ourselves. All that we hope for is sobriety and regeneration, so that we can live normal, respectable lives and can be recognized by others as men and women willing to do unto others as we would be done by. These things we accomplish by the help of each other, by following the twelve steps and by the grace of God. *Am I willing to work for A.A. without material gain to myself?*

Meditation for the Day

What is sometimes called by religion as conversion is often only the discovery of God as a friend in need. What is sometimes called religion is often only the experiencing of the help and strength of God's power in our lives. What is sometimes called holiness is often only the invitation of God to be our Friend. As God becomes your friend, you become a friend to others. We experience true human friendship and from this experience we can imagine what kind of a Great Friend God can be. We believe Him to be a tireless, selfless, all conquering, miracle-working Friend. We can reach out to the Great Friend and figuratively take His hand in ours.

Prayer for the Day

I pray that I may think of God as a Great Friend in need. I pray that I may go along with Him.

JULY 5—A.A. Thought for the Day

Until we came into A.A. most of us had tried desperately to stop drinking. We were filled with the delusion that we could drink like our friends. We tried time and again to take it or leave it, but we could do neither. We always lapsed into ceaseless, unhappy drinking. Wives or husbands, families, friends, and employers threw up their hands in hurt bewilderment, in despair, and finally in disgust. We wanted to stop. We realized that every reason for drinking was only a crazy excuse. *Have I given up every excuse for drinking?*

Meditation for the Day

Many things can upset you and you can easily get off the track. But remember that God is near you all the time, ready to help you if you call on Him. You cannot forever stand against God's will for you, nor can you forever upset God's plan for your life, even though God's plan may be postponed by your willfulness and deliberate choice of evil. A whole world of men and women cannot permanently change God's laws nor His purpose for the universe. The sea of life may look very rough to us, but we can believe that our Captain steers the boat on a straight course.

Prayer for the Day

I pray that I may try to steer a straight course. I pray that I may accept God's direction in my life's journey.

JULY 6—A.A. Thought for the Day

We tried to study our alcoholic problem, wondering what was the cause of our strange obsession. Many of us took special treatments, hospitalization, even confinement in institutions. In every case, the relief was only temporary. We tried through crazy excuses to convince ourselves that we knew why we drank, but we went on regardless. Finally drinking had gone far beyond even a habit. We had become alcoholics, men and women who had been destroying themselves against their own will. *Am I completely free from my alcoholic obsession?*

Meditation for the Day

"Ask and ye shall receive." Never let yourself think that you cannot do something useful or that you never will be able to accomplish a useful task. The fact is that you can do practically anything in the field of human relationships, if you are willing to call on God's supply of strength. The supply may not be immediately available, because you may not be entirely ready to receive it. But it will surely come when you are properly prepared for it. As you grow spiritually, a feeling of being plentifully supplied by God's strength will possess you and you will be able to accomplish many useful things.

Prayer for the Day

I pray that I may claim God's supply of strength by my faith in Him. I pray that it shall be given to me according to my faith.

JULY 7—A.A. Thought for the Day

We had become hopelessly sick people, spiritually, emotionally, and physically. The power that controlled us was greater than ourselves—it was John Barleycorn. Many drinkers have said: "I hadn't gone that far; I hadn't lost my job on account of drink; I still had my family; I managed to keep out of jail. True, I took too much sometimes and I guess I managed to make quite an ass of myself when I did, but I still thought I could control my drinking. I didn't really believe that I was an alcoholic." *If I was one of these, have I fully changed my mind?*

Meditation for the Day

Painful as the present time may be, you will one day see the reason for it. You will see that it was not only testing, but also a preparation for the life-work which you are to do. Have faith that your prayers and aspirations will some day be answered. Answered in a way that perhaps seems painful to you but is the only right way. Selfishness and pride often make us want things that are not good for us. They need to be burned out of our natures. We must be rid of the blocks which are holding us back, before we can expect our prayers to be answered.

Prayer for the Day

I pray that I may be willing to go through a time of testing. I pray that I may trust God for the outcome.

JULY 8—A.A. Thought for the Day

A.A. members will tell you that they can look back and clearly see that they were out of control long before they finally admitted it. Every one of us has gone through that stage when we wouldn't admit that we were alcoholics. It takes a lot of punishment to convince us, but one thing is certain. We all know from actual experience that when it comes to dishing out punishment, John Barleycorn has no equal. *Have I any reservations as to my status as an alcoholic?*

Meditation for the Day

There is a force for good in the world and when you are cooperating with that force for good, good things happen to you. You have free-will, the choice to be on the side of right or on the side of wrong. This force for good we call God's will. God has a purpose for the world and He has a purpose for your life. He wants you to bring all your desires into oneness with His desires. He can only work through people. If you try to make God's will your will, you will be guided by Him. You will be in the stream of goodness, carried along by everything that is right. You will be on God's side.

Prayer for the Day

I pray that I may try to make God's will my will. I pray that I may keep in the stream of goodness in the world.

Thought for the Day

...ent and spiritual confusion ...ge. Many of us have cast ...eas without acquiring new ...men and women are creeping through life on their hands and knees, merely because they refuse to rely on any power but themselves. Many of them feel that they are being brave and independent, but actually they are only courting disaster. Anxiety and the inferiority complex have become the greatest of all modern plagues. In A.A. we have the answer to these ills. *Have I ceased to rely on myself only?*

Meditation for the Day

Disillusionment and doubt spoil life. The doubting ones are the disillusioned ones. When you are in doubt, you are on the fence. You are not going anywhere. Doubt poisons all action. "Well, I don't know"—so you don't do anything. You should meet life with a "Yes," an affirmative attitude. There is good in the world and we can follow that good. There is power available to help us to do the right thing; therefore we will accept that power. There are miracles of change in people's lives; therefore we will accept those miracles as evidence of God's power.

Prayer for the Day

I pray that I will not be paralyzed by doubt. I pray that I may go along on the venture of faith.

JULY 10—A.A. Thought for the Day

We in Alcoholics Anonymous do not enter into theological discussions, but in carrying our message we attempt to explain the simple "how" of the spiritual life. How faith in a Higher Power can help you to overcome loneliness, fear, and anxiety. How it can help you get along with other people. How it can make it possible for you to rise above pain, sorrow, and despondency. How it can help you to overcome your desires for the things that destroy. *Have I reached a simple, effective faith?*

Meditation for the Day

Expect miracles of change in people's lives. Do not be held back by unbelief. People can be changed and they are often ready and waiting to be changed. Never believe that human nature cannot be changed. We see changed people every day. Do you have the faith to make those changes possible? Modern miracles happen every day in the lives of people. All miracles are in the realm of personalities. Human nature can be changed and is always being changed. But we must have enough faith so that we can be channels for God's strength into the lives of others.

Prayer for the Day

I pray that I may have the faith to expect miracles. I pray that I may be used by God to help change the lives of others.

JULY 11—A.A. Thought for the Day

We in Alcoholics Anonymous do not try to chart the path for the human soul or try to lay out a blueprint of the workings of faith, as one might plan a charity drive. We do tell the newcomer that we have renewed our faith in a Higher Power. In the telling, our faith is further renewed. We believe that faith is always close at hand, waiting for those who will listen to the heartbeat of the spirit. We believe there is a force for good in the universe and that if we link up with this force, we are carried onward to a new life. *Am I in this stream of goodness?*

Meditation for the Day

God will protect you from the forces of evil, if you will rely on Him. You can face all things through the power of God which strengthens you. Once God has set on you His stamp and seal of ownership, all His strength will serve and protect you. Remember that you are a child of the Father. Realize that the Father's help is always ready and available to all His children, so that they can face anything. God will do all that is necessary for your spiritual well-being, if you will let Him live His way.

Prayer for the Day

I pray that I may rely on God as I go through this day. I pray that I may feel deeply secure, no matter what happens to me.

JULY 12—A.A. Thought for the Day

Today is ours. Let us live today as we believe God wants us to live. Each day will have a new pattern which we cannot foresee. But we can open each day with a quiet period in which we say a little prayer, asking God to help us through the day. Personal contact with God, as we understand Him, will from day to day bring us nearer to an understanding of His will for us. At the close of the day, we offer Him thanks for another day of sobriety. A full, constructive day has been lived and we are grateful. *Am I asking God each day for strength and thanking Him each night?*

Meditation for the Day

If you believe that God's grace has saved you, then you must believe that He is meaning to save you yet more and to keep you in the way that you should go. Even a human rescuer would not save you from drowning only to place you in other deep and dangerous waters. Rather, he would place you on dry land, there to restore you. God, who is your rescuer, would certainly do this and even more. God will complete the task He sets out to do. He will not throw you overboard, if you are depending on Him.

Prayer for the Day

I pray that I may trust God to keep me in the way. I pray that I may rely on Him not to let me go.

JULY 13—A.A. Thought for the Day

Before alcoholics come into A.A., they are "flying blind." But A.A. gives them a directed beam in the A.A. program. As long as they keep on this beam, the signal of sobriety keeps coming through. If they have a slip, the signal is broken. If they swing off course into drunkenness, the signal stops. Unless they regain the A.A. directed beam, they are in danger of crashing against the mountain peak of despair. *Am I on the beam?*

Meditation for the Day

Be expectant. Constantly expect better things. Believe that what God has in store for you is better than anything you ever had before. The way to grow old happily is to expect better things right up to the end of your life and even beyond that. A good life is a growing, expanding life, with ever-widening horizons, an ever-greater circle of friends and acquaintances, and an ever-greater opportunity for usefulness.

Prayer for the Day

I pray that I may await with complete faith for the next good thing in store for me. I pray that I may always keep an expectant attitude toward life.

JULY 14—A.A. Thought for the Day

One of the best things about the A.A. program is the peace of mind and serenity that it can bring us. In our drinking days, we had no peace of mind or serenity. We had the exact opposite, a kind of turmoil and that "quiet desperation" we knew so well. The turmoil of our drinking days was caused partly by our physical suffering, the terrible hangovers, the cold sweats, the shakes and the jitters. But it was caused even more by our mental suffering, the loneliness, the feeling of inferiority, the lying, the remorse that every alcoholic understands. *Have I achieved more peace of mind?*

Meditation for the Day

Try to look for God's leading in all your personal relationships, in all your dealings with other persons. God will help you to take care of all your relationships with people, if you are willing to let Him guide you. Rejoice that God can protect you and keep you from temptation and failure. God can protect you in all situations during the day, if you will rely on His strength and go forward. You should feel that you are entering upon the stage of success in the proper way of living. You should not doubt that better things are ahead for you. Go forward unafraid because you feel deeply safe under God's protection.

Prayer for the Day

I pray that God may protect and keep me as long as I try to serve Him. I pray that I may go forward today unafraid.

JULY 15—A.A. Thought for the Day

After we had sobered up through the A.A. program, we gradually began to get a peace of mind and serenity which we never thought were possible. This peace of mind is based on a feeling that fundamentally all is well. That does not mean that all is well on the surface of things. Little things can keep going wrong and big things can keep on upsetting us. But deep down in our hearts we know that everything is eventually going to be all right, now that we are living sober lives. *Have I achieved a deep down, inner calm?*

Meditation for the Day

You are climbing up the ladder of life, which reaches into eternity. Would God plant your feet upon an insecure ladder? Its supports may be out of sight, hidden in secret places, but if God has asked you to step on and up firmly, then surely He has secured your ladder. Faith gives you the strength to climb steadily this ladder of life. You should leave your security to God and trust Him not to let you fall. He is there to give you all the power you need to keep on climbing.

Prayer for the Day

I pray that I may climb the ladder of life without fear. I pray that I may progress steadily through the rest of my life with faith and confidence.

JULY 16—A.A. Thought for the Day

We can believe that God is in His heaven and that He has a purpose for our lives, which will eventually work out as long as we try to live the way we believe He wants us to live. It has been said that we should "wear the world like a loose garment." That means that nothing should seriously upset us because we have a deep, abiding faith that God will always take care of us. To us that means not to be too upset by the surface wrongness of things, but to feel deeply secure in the fundamental goodness and purpose in the universe. *Do I feel deeply secure?*

Meditation for the Day

Like the shadow of a great rock in a desert land, God is your refuge from the ills of life. The old hymn says: "Rock of ages cleft for me, let me hide myself in Thee." God can be your shelter from the storm. God's power can protect you from every temptation and defeat. Try to feel His divine power—call on it—accept it—and use it. Armed with that power, you can face anything. Each day, seek safety in God's secret place, in communion with Him. You cannot be wholly touched or seriously harmed there. God can be your refuge.

Prayer for the Day

I pray that I may find a haven in the thought of God. I pray that I may abide in that Strong Tower, strongly guarded.

JULY 17—A.A. Thought for the Day

The new life of sobriety we are learning to live in A.A. is slowly growing on
us and we are beginning to get some of
that deep peace of mind and serenity
that we never thought were possible.
At first we may have doubted that this
could happen to us, but after any considerable length of time in A.A., looking at the happy faces around us, we
know that somehow it is happening to
us. In fact, it cannot help happening to
anyone who takes the A.A. program
seriously day by day. *Can I see my
own happiness reflected in the faces of
others?*

Meditation for the Day

God does not withhold His presence from you.
He does not refuse to reveal more of His truth
to you. He does not hold back His spirit from
you. He does not withhold the strength that
you need. His presence, His truth, His spirit,
His strength are always immediately available
to you, whenever you are fully willing to
receive them. But they may be blocked off
by selfishness, intellectual pride, fear, greed,
and materialism. We must try to get rid of
these blocks and let God's spirit come in.

Prayer for the Day

I pray that I may remove all blocks that are
keeping me from God. I pray that I may let
God come into my life with power.

JULY 18—A.A. Thought for the Day

Two things can spoil group unity—gossip and criticism. To avoid these divisive things, we must realize that we're all in the same boat. We're like a group of people in a life-boat after the steamer has sunk. If we're going to be saved, we've got to pull together. It's a matter of life or death for us. Gossip and criticism are sure ways of disrupting any A.A. group. We're all in A.A. to keep sober ourselves and to help each other to keep sober. And neither gossip nor criticism helps anyone to stay sober. *Am I often guilty of gossip or criticism?*

Meditation for the Day

We should try to be grateful for all the blessings we have received and which we do not deserve. Gratitude to God for all His blessings will make us humble. Remember that we could do little by ourselves, and now we must rely largely on God's grace in helping ourselves and others. People do not care much for those who are smug and self-satisfied or those who gossip and criticize. But people are impressed by true humility. So we should try to walk humbly at all times. Gratitude to God and true humility are what make us effective.

Prayer for the Day

I pray that I may walk humbly with God. I pray that I may rely on His grace to carry me through.

JULY 19—A.A. Thought for the Day

Gossip about or criticism of personalities has no place in an A.A. clubroom. Every man in A.A. is a brother and every woman is a sister, as long as he or she is a member of A.A. We ought not to gossip about the relationships of any man or woman in the group. And if we say about another member, "I think she or he is taking a few drinks on the side," it's the worst thing we could do to that person. If a woman or a man is not living up to A.A. principles or has a slip, it's up to her or him to stand up in a meeting and say so. If they don't do that, they are only hurting themselves. *Do I talk about other members behind their backs?*

Meditation for the Day

To God, a miracle of change in a person's life is only a natural happening. But it is a natural happening operated by spiritual forces. There is no miracle in personalities too marvelous to be an everyday happening. But miracles happen only to those who are fully guided and strengthened by God. Marvelous changes in people's natures happen so simply, and yet they are free from all other agency than the grace of God. But these miracles have been prepared for by days and months of longing for something better. They are always accompanied by a real desire to conquer self and to surrender one's life to God.

Prayer for the Day

I pray that I may expect miracles in the lives of people. I pray that I may be used to help people change.

JULY 20—A.A. Thought for the Day

We must be loyal to the group and to each member of it. We must never accuse members behind their backs or even to their faces. It's up to them to tell us themselves if anything is wrong. More than that, we must try not to think bad things about any members, because if we do, we're consciously or unconsciously hurting that person. We must be loyal to each other if A.A. is going to be successful. While we're in this lifeboat, trying to save ourselves and each other from alcoholism, we must be truly and sincerely helpful to each other. *Am I a loyal member of my group?*

Meditation for the Day

Carry out God's guidance as best you can. Leave the results to Him. Do this obediently and faithfully with no question that if the working out of the guidance is left in God's hands, the results will be all right. Believe that the guidance God gives you has already been worked out by God to produce the required results according to your case and in your circumstances. So follow God's guidance according to your conscience. God has knowledge of your individual life and character, your capabilities and your weaknesses.

Prayer for the Day

I pray that I may live according to the dictates of my conscience. I pray that I may leave the results to God.

JULY 21—A.A. Thought for the Day

If we feel the need of saying something to put another member on the right track, we should try to say it with understanding and sympathy, not with a critical attitude. We should keep everything out in the open and aboveboard. The A.A. program is wonderful, but we must really follow it. We must all pull together or we'll all be sunk. We enjoy the privilege of being associated with A.A. and we are entitled to all its benefits. But gossip and criticism are not tolerance, and tolerance is an A.A. principle that is absolutely necessary to group unity. *Am I truly tolerant of all my group's members?*

Meditation for the Day

"Faith can move mountains." That expression means that faith can change any situation in the field of personal relationships. If you trust Him, God shows you the way to "move mountains." If you are humble enough to know that you can do little by yourself to change a situation, if you have enough faith to ask God to give you the power you need, and if you are grateful enough for the grace He gives you, you can "move mountains." Situations will be changed for the better by your presence.

Prayer for the Day

I pray that I may have enough faith to make me really effective. I pray that I may learn to depend less on myself and more on God.

One of the finest things abou...
is the diversity of its membership.
come from all walks and stations o...
life. All types and classes of people
are represented in an A.A. group. Being different from each other in certain
ways, we can each make a different
contribution to the whole. Some of us
are weak in one respect, but strong in
another. A.A. can use the strong points
of all its members and can disregard
their weaknesses. A.A. is strong, not
only because we all have the same
problem, but also because of the diver-
sified talents of its members. Each can
contribute his part. *Do I recognize the
good points of all my group's members?*

Meditation for the Day

"And greater works than these shall ye do."
Each individual has the ability to do good
works through the power of God's spirit. This
is the wonder of the world, the miracle of the
earth, that God's power goes out to bless the
human race through the agency of so many
people who are actuated by His grace. We
need not be held back by doubt, despondency
and fear. A wonderful future can lie before
any person who depends on God's power, a
future of unlimited power to do good works.

Prayer for the Day

I pray that I may not limit myself by doubting. I pray that I may have confidence that
I can be effective for good.

... member that all A.A.'s ... et." We should not set ... upon a pedestal and mark ... as a perfect A.A. It's not ... erson to be singled out in this fashion, and if the person is wise she or he will not wish it. If the person we single out as an ideal A.A. has a fall, we are in danger of falling, too. Without exception, we are all only one drink away from a drunk, no matter how long we have been in A.A. Nobody is entirely safe. A.A. itself should be our ideal, not any particular member of it. *Am I putting my trust in A.A. principles and not in any one member of the group?*

Meditation for the Day

The inward peace that comes from trust in God truly passes all understanding. That peace no one can take from you. No person has the power to disturb that inner peace. But you must be careful not to let in the world's worries and distractions. You must try not to give entrance to fears and despondency. You must refuse to open the door to the distractions that disturb your inward peace. Make it a point to allow nothing today to disturb your inner peace, your heart-calm.

Prayer for the Day

I pray that I may not allow those about me to spoil my peace of mind. I pray that I may keep a deep inner calm throughout the day.

JULY 24—A.A. Thought for the Day

A.A. is like a dike, holding back the ocean of liquor. If we take one glass of liquor, it is like making a small hole in the dike and once such a hole has been made, the whole ocean of alcohol may rush in upon us. By practicing the A.A. principles we keep the dike strong and in repair. We spot any weakness or crack in that dike and make the necessary repairs before any damage is done. Outside the dike is the whole ocean of alcohol, waiting to engulf us again in despair. *Am I keeping the dike strong?*

Meditation for the Day

Keep as close as you can to the Higher Power. Try to think, act, and live as though you were always in God's presence. Keeping close to a Power greater than yourself is the solution to most of the earth's problems. Try to practice the presence of God in the things you think and do. That is the secret of personal power. It is the thing which influences the lives of others for good. Abide in the Lord and rejoice in His love. Keep close to the Divine Spirit in the universe. Keep God close behind your thoughts.

Prayer for the Day

I pray that I may keep close to the Mind of God. I pray that I may live with Him in my heart and mind.

JULY 25—A.A. Thought for the Day

We are living on borrowed time. We are living today because of A.A. and the grace of God. And what there is left of our lives we owe to A.A. and to God. We should make the best use we can of our borrowed time and in some small measure pay back for that part of our lives which we wasted before we came into A.A. Our lives from now on are not our own. We hold them in trust for God and A.A. And we must do all we can to forward the great movement that has given us a new lease on life. *Am I holding my life in trust for A.A.?*

Meditation for the Day

You should hold your life in trust for God. Think deeply on what that means. Is anything too much to expect from such a life? Do you begin to see how dedicated a life in trust for God can be? In such a life miracles can happen. If you are faithful, you can believe that God has many good things in store for you. God can be Lord of your life, controller of your days, of your present and your future. Try to act as God guides and leave all results to Him. Do not hold back, but go all out for God and the better life. Make good your trust.

Prayer for the Day

I pray that I may hold my life in trust for God. I pray that I may no longer consider my life as all my own.

JULY 26—A.A. Thought for the Day

When we come to the end of our lives on earth, we will take no material thing with us. We will not take one cent in our cold, dead hands. The only things that we may take are the things we have given away. If we have helped others, we may take that with us; if we have given of our time and money for the good of A.A., we may take that with us. Looking back over our lives, what are we proud of? Not what we have gained for ourselves, but what few good deeds we have done. Those are the things that really matter in the long run. *What will I take with me when I go?*

Meditation for the Day

"Hallowed be Thy Name." What does that mean to us? Here "name" is used in the sense of "spirit." The words mean praise to God for His spirit in the world, making us better. We should be especially grateful for God's spirit, which gives us the strength to overcome all that is base in our lives. His spirit is powerful. It can help us to live a conquering, abundant life. So we praise and thank Him for His spirit in our lives and in the lives of others.

Prayer for the Day

I pray that I may be grateful for God's spirit in me. I pray that I may try to live in accordance with it.

JULY 27—A.A. Thought for the Day

To paraphrase the psalm: "We alcoholics declare the power of liquor and drunkenness showeth its handiwork. Day unto day uttereth hangovers and night unto night showeth suffering. The law of A.A. is perfect, converting the drunk. The testimony of A.A. is sure, making wise the simple. The statutes of A.A. are right, rejoicing the heart. The program of A.A. is pure, enlightening the eyes. The fear of the first drink is clean, enduring forever." *Have I any doubt about the power of liquor?*

Meditation for the Day

"Walk humbly with thy Lord." Walking with God means practicing the presence of God in your daily affairs. It means asking God for strength to face each new day. It means turning to Him often during the day in prayer for yourself and for other people. It means thanking Him at night for the blessings you have received during the day. Nothing can seriously upset you if you are "walking with God." You can believe that He is beside you in spirit, to help you and to guide you on your way.

Prayer for the Day

I pray that I may try to walk humbly with God. I pray that I may turn to Him often as to a close friend.

JULY 28—A.A. Thought for the Day

To continue the paraphrase of the psalm: "The judgments of the twelve steps are true and righteous altogether. More to be desired are they than whiskey, yea, than much fine whiskey, sweeter also than wine. Moreover, by them are alcoholics warned and in keeping of them there is great reward. Who can understand our alcoholism? Cleanse us from secret faults. Keep us from presumptuous resentments. Let them not have dominion over us. Then shall we be upright and free of the great transgression." *Am I resolved that liquor will never again have dominion over me?*

Meditation for the Day

God can be your shield. Then no problems of the world can harm you. Between you and all scorn and indignity from others is your trust in God, like a shining shield. Nothing can then have the power to spoil your inward peace. With this shield, you can attain this inward peace quickly, in your surroundings as well as in your heart. With this inward peace, you do not need to resent the person who troubles you. Instead, you can overcome the resentment in your own mind which may have been aroused by that person.

Prayer for the Day

I pray that I may strive for inward peace. I pray that I may not be seriously upset, no matter what happens around me.

JULY 29—A.A. Thought for the Day

There are two days in every week about which we should not worry, two days which should be kept from fear and apprehension. One of these days is yesterday, with its mistakes and cares, its faults and blunders, its aches and pains. Yesterday has passed forever beyond our control. All the money in the world cannot bring back yesterday. We cannot undo a single act we performed. We cannot erase a single word we said. Yesterday is gone beyond recall. *Do I still worry about what happened yesterday?*

Meditation for the Day

"God will not suffer you to be tempted above what you are able, but with the temptation He will also find a way of escape, that you may be able to bear it." If you have enough faith and trust in God, He will give you all the strength you need to face every temptation and to overcome it. Nothing will prove too hard for you to bear. You can face any situation. "Be of good cheer, I have overcome the world." You can overcome any temptation with God's help. So fear nothing.

Prayer for the Day

I pray that I may face every situation without fear. I pray that nothing will prove too hard for me to bear.

JULY 30—A.A. Thought for the Day

The other day we should not worry about is tomorrow, with its possible adversities, its burdens, its large promise, and perhaps its poor performance. Tomorrow is also beyond our immediate control. Tomorrow's sun will rise, either in splendor or behind a mask of clouds, but it will rise. Until it does, we have no stake in tomorrow, for it is as yet unborn. *Do I still worry too much about tomorrow?*

Meditation for the Day

"Faith is the substance of things hoped for, the evidence of things not seen." Faith is not seeing, but believing. Down through the ages, there have always been those who obeyed the heavenly vision, not seeing but believing in God. And their faith was rewarded. So shall it be to you. Good things will happen to you. You cannot see God, but you can see the results of faith in human lives, changing them from defeat to victory. God's grace is available to all who have faith—not seeing, but believing. With faith, life can be victorious and happy.

Prayer for the Day

I pray that I may have faith enough to believe without seeing. I pray that I may be content with the results of my faith.

JULY 31—A.A. Thought for the Day

This leaves only one day—today. Any one can fight the battles of just one day. It is only when you and I add the burden of those two awful eternities, yesterday and tomorrow, that we break down. It is not the experience of today that drives us mad. It is the remorse or bitterness for something which happened yesterday or the dread of what tomorrow may bring. Let us therefore do our best to live but one day at a time. *Am I living one day at a time?*

Meditation for the Day

Give God the gift of a thankful heart. Try to see causes of thankfulness in your everyday life. When life seems hard and troubles crowd, then look for some reasons for thankfulness. There is nearly always something you can be thankful for. The offering of thanksgiving is indeed a sweet incense going up to God throughout a busy day. Seek diligently for something to be glad and thankful about. You will acquire in time the habit of being constantly grateful to God for all His blessings. Each new day some new cause for joy and gratitude will spring to your mind and you will thank God sincerely.

Prayer for the Day

I pray for a truly thankful heart. I pray that I may be constantly reminded of causes for sincere gratitude.

AUGUST 1—A.A. Thought for the Day

The Alcoholics Anonymous program has borrowed from medicine, psychiatry, and religion. It has taken from these what it wanted and combined them into the program which it considers best suited to the alcoholic mind and which will best help the alcoholic to recover. The results have been very satisfactory. We do not try to improve on the A.A. program. Its value has been proved by the success it has had in helping thousands of alcoholics to recover. It has everything we alcoholics need to arrest our illness. *Do I try to follow the A.A. program just as it is?*

Meditation for the Day

You should strive for a union between your purposes in life and the purposes of the Divine Principle directing the universe. There is no bond of union on earth to compare with the union between a human soul and God. Priceless beyond all earth's rewards is that union. In merging your heart and mind with the heart and mind of the Higher Power, a oneness of purpose results, which only those who experience it can even dimly realize. That oneness of purpose puts you in harmony with God and with all others who are trying to do His will.

Prayer for the Day

I pray that I may become attuned to the will of God. I pray that I may be in harmony with the music of the spheres.

AUGUST 2—A.A. Thought for the Day

Alcoholics Anonymous has no quarrel with medicine, psychiatry, or religion. We have great respect for the methods of each. And we are glad for any success they may have had with alcoholics. We are desirous always of cooperating with them in every way. The more doctors, the more psychiatrists, the more clergymen and rabbis we can get to work with us, the better we like it. We have many who take a real interest in our program and we would like many more. *Am I ready to cooperate with those who take a sincere interest in A.A.?*

Meditation for the Day

God is always ready to pour His blessings into our hearts in generous measure. But like the seed-sowing, the ground must be prepared before the seed is dropped in. It is our task to prepare the soil. It is God's to drop the seed. This preparation of the soil means many days of right living, choosing the right and avoiding the wrong. As you go along, each day you are better prepared for God's planting, until you reach the time of harvest. Then you share the harvest with God—the harvest of a useful and more abundant life.

Prayer for the Day

I pray that my way of living may be properly prepared day by day. I pray that I may strive to make myself ready for the harvest which God has planted in my heart.

AUGUST 3—A.A. Thought for the Day

We in A.A. must remember that we are offering something intangible. We are offering a psychological and spiritual program. We are not offering a medical program. If people need medical treatment, we call in a doctor. If they need a medical prescription, we let the doctor prescribe for them. If they need hospital treatment, we let the hospital take care of them. Our vital A.A. work begins when a person is physically able to receive it. *Am I willing to leave medical care to the doctors?*

Meditation for the Day

Each moment of your day which you devote to this new way of life is a gift to God. The gift of the moments. Even when your desire to serve God is sincere, it is not an easy thing to give Him many of these moments: the daily things you had planned to do, given up gladly so that you can perform a good service or say a kind word. If you can see God's purpose in many situations, it will be easier to give Him many moments of your day. Every situation has two interpretations—your own and God's. Try to handle each situation in the way you believe God would have it handled.

Prayer for the Day

I pray that I may make my day count somewhat for God. I pray that I may not spend it all selfishly.

AUGUST 4—A.A. Thought for the Day

We in A.A. are offering a kind of psychological program as well as a spiritual one. First, people must be mentally able to receive it. They must have made up their minds that they want to quit drinking, and they must be willing to do something about it. Their confidence must be obtained. We must show them that we are their friends and really desire to help them. When we have their confidence, they will listen to us. Then the A.A. fellowship is a kind of group therapy. Newcomers need the fellowship of other alcoholics who understand their problem because they have had it themselves. Individuals must learn to re-educate their mind. They must learn to think differently. *Do I do my best to give mental help?*

Meditation for the Day

"And this is life eternal, that they may know Thee." It is the flow of the life eternal through spirit, mind, and body that cleanses, heals, restores, and renews. Seek conscious contact with God more and more each day. Make God an abiding presence during the day. Be conscious of His spirit helping you. All that is done without God's spirit is passing. All that is done with God's spirit is life eternal.

Prayer for the Day

I pray that I may be in the stream of eternal life. I pray that I may be cleansed and healed by the Eternal Spirit.

AUGUST 5—A.A. Thought for the Day

We in A.A. are offering a spiritual program. The fundamental basis of A.A. is belief in some Power greater than ourselves. This belief takes us off the center of the universe and allows us to transfer our problems to some power outside of ourselves. We turn to this Power for the strength we need to get sober and stay sober. We put our drink problem in God's hands and leave it there. We stop trying to run our own life and seek to let God run it for us. *Do I do my best to give spiritual help?*

Meditation for the Day

God is your healer and your strength. You do not have to ask Him to come to you. He is always with you in spirit. At your moment of need He is there to help you. Could you know God's love and His desire to help you, you would know that He needs no pleading for help. Your need is God's opportunity. You must learn to rely on God's strength whenever you need it. Whenever you feel inadequate to any situation, you should realize that the feeling of inadequacy is disloyalty to God. Just say to yourself: I know that God is with me and will help me to think and say and do the right thing.

Prayer for the Day

I pray that I may never feel inadequate to any situation. I pray that I may be buoyed up by the feeling that God is with me.

AUGUST 6—A.A. Thought for the Day

Psychologists are turning to religion because just knowing about ourselves is not enough. We need the added dynamic of faith in a power outside of ourselves on which we can rely. Books on psychology and psychiatric treatments are not enough without the strength that comes from faith in God. And clergymen and rabbis are turning to psychology because faith is an act of the mind and will. Religion must be presented in psychological terms to some extent in order to satisfy the modern person. Faith must be built largely on our own psychological experience. *Have I taken what I need from both psychology and religion when I live the A.A. way?*

Meditation for the Day

Refilling with the spirit is something you need every day. For this refilling with the spirit, you need these times of quiet communion, away, alone, without noise, without activity. You need this dwelling apart, this shutting yourself away in the very secret place of your being, away alone with your Maker. From these times of communion you come forth with new power. This refilling is the best preparation for effective work. When you are spiritually filled, there is no work too hard for you.

Prayer for the Day

I pray that I may be daily refilled with the right spirit. I pray that I may be full of the joy of true living.

AUGUST 7—A.A. Thought for the Day

We in A.A. are offering an intangible thing, a psychological and spiritual program. It's a wonderful program. When we learn to turn to a Higher Power, with faith that that Power can give us the strength we need, we find peace of mind. When we reeducate our minds by learning to think differently, we find new interests that make life worthwhile. We who have achieved sobriety through faith in God and mental reeducation are modern miracles. It is the function of our A.A. program to produce modern miracles. *Do I consider the change in my life a modern miracle?*

Meditation for the Day

You should never doubt that God's spirit is always with you, wherever you are, to keep you on the right path. God's keeping power is never at fault, only your realization of it. You must try to believe in God's nearness and the availability of His grace. It is not a question of whether God can provide a shelter from the storm, but of whether or not you seek the security of that shelter. Every fear, worry or doubt is disloyalty to God. You must endeavor to trust God wholly. Practice saying: "All is going to be well." Say it to yourself until you feel it deeply.

Prayer for the Day

I pray that I may feel deeply that all is well. I pray that nothing will be able to move me from that deep conviction.

AUGUST 8—A.A. Thought for the Day

For awhile, we are going back to the big book, *Alcoholics Anonymous*, and pick out passages here and there, so that they may become fixed in our minds, a little at a time, day by day, as we go along. There is no substitute for reading the Big Book. It is our "bible." We should study it thoroughly and make it a part of ourselves. We should not try to change any of it. Within its covers is the full exposition of the A.A. program. There is no substitute for it. We should study it often. *Have I studied the Big Book faithfully?*

Meditation for the Day

All of life is a fluctuation between effort and rest. You need both every day. But effort is not truly effective until first you have had the proper preparation for it, by resting in a time of quiet meditation. This daily time of rest and meditation gives you the power necessary to make your best effort. There are days when you are called on for much effort and then comes a time when you need much rest. It is not good to rest too long and it is not good to carry on great effort too long without rest. The successful life is a proper balance between the two.

Prayer for the Day

I pray that I may be ready to make the proper effort. I pray that I may also recognize the need for relaxation.

AUGUST 9—A.A. Thought for the Day

"We have an allergy to alcohol. The action of alcohol on chronic alcoholics is a manifestation of an allergy. We allergic types can never safely use alcohol in any form at all. We cannot be reconciled to a life without alcohol, unless we can experience an entire psychic change. Once this psychic change has occurred, we who seemed doomed, we who had so many problems that we despaired of ever solving them, find ourselves able to control our desire for alcohol." *Have I had a psychic change?*

Meditation for the Day

Ask God in daily prayer to give you the strength to change. When you ask God to change you, you must at the same time fully trust Him. If you do not fully trust Him, God may answer your prayer as a rescuer does that of a drowning person who is putting up too much of a struggle. The rescuer must first render the person still more helpless, until he or she is wholly at the rescuer's mercy. Just so must we be wholly at God's mercy before we can be rescued.

Prayer for the Day

I pray that I may be daily willing to be changed. I pray that I may put myself wholly at the mercy of God.

AUGUST 10—A.A. Thought for the Day

"The tremendous fact for every one of us is that we have discovered a common solution. We who have found this solution to our alcoholic problem, who are properly armed with the facts about ourselves, can generally win the entire confidence of another alcoholic. We who are making the approach to new prospects have had the same difficulty they have had. We obviously know what we are talking about. Our whole deportment shouts at new prospects that we are people with a real answer." *Am I a person with the real answer to the alcoholic problems of others?*

Meditation for the Day

For straying from the right way there is no cure except to keep so close to the thought of God that nothing, no other interest, can seriously come between you and God. Sure of that, you can stay on God's side. Knowing the way, nothing can prevent your staying in the way and nothing can cause you to seriously stray from it. God has promised peace if you stay close to Him, but not leisure. You still have to carry on in the world. He has promised heart-rest and comfort, but not pleasure in the ordinary sense. Peace and comfort bring real inward happiness.

Prayer for the Day

I pray that I may keep my feet on the way. I pray that I may stay on God's side.

AUGUST 11—A.A. Thought for the Day

"While alcoholics keep strictly away from drink, they react to life much like other people. But the first drink sets the terrible cycle in motion. Alcoholics usually have no idea why they take the first drink. Some drinkers have excuses with which they are satisfied, but in their hearts they really do not know why they do it. The truth is that at some point in their drinking they have passed into a state where the most powerful desire to stop drinking is of no avail." *Am I satisfied that I have passed my tolerance point for alcohol?*

Meditation for the Day

He who made the ordered world out of chaos and set the stars in their courses and made each plant to know its season, He can bring peace and order out of your private chaos if you will let Him. God is watching over you, too, to bless you and care for you. Out of the darkness He is leading you to light, out of unrest to rest, out of disorder to order, out of faults and failure to success. You belong to God and your affairs are His affairs and can be ordered by Him if you are willing.

Prayer for the Day

I pray that I may be led out of disorder into order. I pray that I may be led out of failure into success.

AUGUST 12—A.A. Thought for the Day

"There was nothing left for us but to pick up the simple kit of spiritual tools laid at our feet by Alcoholics Anonymous. By doing so, we have a spiritual experience which revolutionizes our whole attitude toward life, toward others and toward God's universe. The central fact of our lives today is the absolute certainty that our Creator has entered into our hearts and lives there in a way which is indeed miraculous. He has commenced to accomplish those things for us which we could never do for ourselves." *Have I let God come into my life?*

Meditation for the Day

The moment a thing seems wrong to you or a person's actions to be not what you think they should be, at that moment begins your obligation and responsibility to pray for those wrongs to be righted or that person to be changed. What is wrong in your surroundings or in the people you know? Think about these things and make these matters your responsibility. Not to interfere or be a busybody, but to pray that a change may come through your influence. You may see lives altered and evils banished in time. You can become a force for good wherever you are.

Prayer for the Day

I pray that I may be a co-worker with God. I pray that I may help people by my example.

AUGUST 13—A.A. Thought for the Day

"We had but two alternatives; one was to go on to the bitter end, blotting out the consciousness of our intolerable situation as best we could, and the other was to accept spiritual help. We became willing to maintain a certain simple attitude toward life. What seemed at first a flimsy reed has proved to be the loving and powerful hand of God. A new life has been given us, a design for living that really works. All of us establish in our own individual way our personal relationship with God." *Have I established my own relationship with God?*

Meditation for the Day

Make it a daily practice to review your character. Take your character in relation to your daily life, to your dear ones, your friends, your acquaintances, and your work. Each day try to see where God wants you to change. Plan how best each fault can be eradicated or each mistake be corrected. Never be satisfied with a comparison with those around you. Strive toward a better life as your ultimate goal. God is your helper through weakness to power, through danger to security, through fear and worry to peace and serenity.

Prayer for the Day

I pray that I may make real progress toward a better life. I pray that I may never be satisfied with my present state.

AUGUST 14—A.A. Thought for the Day

"None of us like to think that we are bodily and mentally different from others. Our drinking careers have been characterized by countless vain attempts to prove that we could drink like other people. This delusion that we are like other people has to be smashed. It has been definitely proved that no real alcoholic has ever recovered control. Over any considerable period we get worse, never better. There is no such thing as making a normal drinker out of an alcoholic." *Am I convinced that I can never drink again normally?*

Meditation for the Day

We should have life and have it more abundantly—spiritual, mental, physical, abundant life—joyous, powerful life. These we can have if we follow the right way. Not all people will accept from God the gift of an abundant life, a gift held out free to all. Not all people care to stretch out a hand and take it. God's gift, the richest He has to offer, is the precious gift of abundant life. People often turn away from it, reject it, and will have none of it. Do not let this be true of you.

Prayer for the Day

I pray that I may hasten to accept the gift of abundant spiritual life. I pray that I may live the good life to the best of my ability.

AUGUST 15—A.A. Thought for the Day

"Once an alcoholic, always an alcoholic. Commencing to drink after a period of sobriety, we are in a short time as bad as ever. If we have admitted we are alcoholics, we must have no reservations of any kind, nor any lurking notion that some day we will be immune to alcohol. What sort of thinking dominates an alcoholic who repeats time after time the desperate experiment of the first drink? Parallel with sound reasoning, there inevitably runs some insanely trivial excuse for taking the first drink. There is little thought of what the terrific consequences may be." *Have I given up all excuses for taking a drink?*

Meditation for the Day

"Where two or three are banded together, I will be there in the midst of them." When God finds two or three people in union, who only want His will to be done, who want only to serve Him, He has a plan that can be revealed to them. The grace of God can come to people who are together in one place with one accord. A union like this is miracle-working. God is able to use such people. Only good can come through such consecrated people, brought together in unified groups for a single purpose and of a single mind.

Prayer for the Day

I pray that I may be part of a unified group. I pray that I may contribute my share to its consecrated purpose.

AUGUST 16—A.A. Thought for the Day

"The alcoholic is absolutely unable to stop drinking on the basis of self-knowledge. We must admit we can do nothing about it ourselves. Will power and self-knowledge will never help in the strange mental blank spots when we are tempted to drink. An alcoholic mentally is in a very sick condition. The last flicker of conviction that we can do the job ourselves must be snuffed out. The spiritual answer and the program of action are the only hope. Only spiritual principles will solve our problems. We are completely helpless apart from Divine help. Our defense against drinking must come from a Higher Power." *Have I accepted the spiritual answer and the program of action?*

Meditation for the Day

Rest now until life, eternal life, flowing through your veins and heart and mind, bids you to bestir yourself. Then glad work will follow. Tired work is never effective. The strength of God's spirit is always available to the tired mind and body. He is your physician and your healer. Look to these quiet times of communion with God for rest, for peace, for cure. Then rise refreshed in spirit and go out to work, knowing that your strength is able to meet any problems because it is reinforced by God's power.

Prayer for the Day

I pray that the peace I have found will make me effective. I pray that I may be relieved of all strain during this day.

AUGUST 17—A.A. Thought for the Day

"To one who feels he is an atheist or agnostic, a spiritual experience seems impossible, but to continue as he is means disaster. To be doomed to an alcoholic death or to live on a spiritual basis are not always easy alternatives to face. But we have to face the fact that we must find a spiritual basis of life—or else. Lack of power is our dilemma. We have to find a power by which we can live, and it has to be a power greater than ourselves." *Have I found that power by which I can live?*

Meditation for the Day

Sunshine is the laughter of nature. Live out in the sunshine. The sun and air are good medicine. Nature is a good nurse for tired bodies. Let her have her way with you. God's grace is like the sunshine. Let your whole being be enwrapped in the Divine spirit. Faith is the soul's breathing in of the Divine spirit. It makes glad the hearts of human beings. The Divine spirit heals and cures the mind. Let it have its way and all will be well.

Prayer for the Day

I pray that I may live in the sunshine of God's spirit. I pray that my mind and soul may be energized by it.

AUGUST 18—A.A. Thought for the Day

"We of agnostic temperament have found that as soon as we were able to lay aside prejudice and express a willingness to believe in a Power greater than ourselves, we commenced to get results, even though it was impossible for any of us to fully define or comprehend that Power, which we call God. As soon as you can say that you do believe or are willing to believe, you are on your way. Upon this simple cornerstone a wonderfully effective spiritual structure can be built." *Am I willing to depend on a Power that I cannot fully define or comprehend?*

Meditation for the Day

We seek God's presence and "they who seek shall find." It is not a question of searching so much as an inner consciousness of the Divine spirit in your heart. To realize God's presence you must surrender to His will in the small as well as in the big things of life. This makes God's guidance possible. Some things separate you from God—a false word, a fear-inspired failure, a harsh criticism, a stubborn resentment. These are the things that put a distance between your mind and God. A word of love, a selfless reconciliation, a kind act of helpfulness—these bring God closer.

Prayer for the Day

I pray that I may think and say and do the things that bring God closer to me. I pray that I may find Him in a sincere prayer, a kind word, or an unselfish deed.

AUGUST 19—A.A. Thought for the Day

"People of faith have a logical idea of what life is all about. There is a wide variation in the way each one of us approaches and conceives of the Power greater than ourself. Whether we agree with a particular approach or conception seems to make little difference. There are questions for each of us to settle for ourselves. But in each case the belief in a Higher Power has accomplished the miraculous, the humanly impossible. There has come a revolutionary change in their way of living and thinking." *Has there been a revolutionary change in me?*

Meditation for the Day

Worship is consciousness of God's divine majesty. As you pause to worship, God will help you to raise your humanity to His divinity. The earth is a material temple to enclose God's divinity. God brings to those who worship Him a divine power, a divine love and a divine healing. You only have to open your mind to Him and try to absorb some of His divine spirit. Pausing quietly in the spirit of worship, turn your inward thoughts upward and realize that His divine power may be yours, that you can experience His love and healing.

Prayer for the Day

I pray that I may worship God by sensing the eternal Spirit. I pray that I may experience a new power in my life.

AUGUST 20—A.A. Thought for the Day

"When many hundreds of people are able to say that the consciousness of the presence of God is today the most important fact of their lives, they present a powerful reason why one should have faith. When we see others solve their problems by simple reliance upon some Spirit of the universe, we have to stop doubting the power of God. Our ideas did not work, but the God-idea does. Deep down in every man, woman, and child is the fundamental idea of God. Faith in a Power greater than ourselves and miraculous demonstrations of that power in our lives are facts as old as the human race." *Am I willing to rely on the Spirit of the universe?*

Meditation for the Day

You should not dwell too much on the mistakes, faults, and failures of the past. Be done with shame and remorse and contempt for yourself. With God's help, develop a new self-respect. Unless you respect yourself, others will not respect you. You ran a race, you stumbled and fell, you have risen again, and now you press on toward the goal of a better life. Do not stay to examine the spot where you fell, only feel sorry for the delay, the shortsightedness that prevented you from seeing the real goal sooner.

Prayer for the Day

I pray that I may not look back. I pray that I may keep picking myself up and making a fresh start each day.

AUGUST 21—A.A. Thought for the Day

"Who are you to say there is no God? This challenge comes to all of us. Are we capable of denying that there is a design and purpose in all of life as we know it? Or are we willing to admit that faith in some kind of Divine Principle is a part of our make-up, just as much as the feeling we have for a friend? We find a great Reality deep down within us, if we face ourselves as we really are. In the last analysis, it is only there that God may be found. When we find this Reality within us, we are restored to our right minds." *Have I found the great Reality?*

Meditation for the Day

"Behold, I make all things new." When you change to a new way of life, you leave many things behind you. It is only the earth-bound spirit that cannot soar. Loosen somewhat the strands that tie you to the earth. It is only the earthly desires that bind you. Your new freedom will depend on your ability to rise above earthly things. Clipped wings can grow again. Broken wings can regain a strength and beauty unknown before. If you will, you can be released and free.

Prayer for the Day

I pray that I may be freed from things that hold me down. I pray that my spirit may soar in freedom.

AUGUST 22—A.A. Thought for the Day

"Those who do not recover are people who are constitutionally incapable of being honest with themselves. There are such unfortunates. They are not at fault. They seem to be born that way. They are naturally incapable of grasping and developing a manner of living which demands rigorous honesty. Their chances are less than average. There are those, too, who suffer from grave emotional and mental disorders, but many of them do recover, if they have the capacity to be honest." *Am I completely honest with myself and with other people?*

Meditation for the Day

You can make use of your mistakes, failures, losses, and sufferings. It is not what happens to you so much as what use you make of it. Take your sufferings, difficulties, and hardships and make use of them to help some unfortunate soul who is faced with the same troubles. Then something good will come out of your suffering and the world will be a better place because of it. The good you do each day will live on, after the trouble and distress have gone, after the difficulty and the pain have passed away.

Prayer for the Day

I pray that I may make good use of my mistakes and failures. I pray that some good may result from my painful experiences.

AUGUST 23—A.A. Thought for the Day

"We who have accepted the A.A. principles have been faced with the necessity for a thorough personal housecleaning. We must face and be rid of the things in ourselves which have been blocking us. We therefore take a personal inventory. We take stock honestly. We search out the flaws in our make-up which caused our failure. Resentment is the number one offender. Life which includes deep resentment leads only to futility and unhappiness. If we are to live, we must be free of anger." *Am I free of resentment and anger?*

Meditation for the Day

Keep in mind the goal you are striving for, the good life you are trying to attain. Do not let little things divert you from the path. Do not be overcome by the small trials and vexations of each day. Try to see the purpose and plan to which all is leading. If, when climbing a mountain, you keep your eyes on each stony or difficult place, how weary is your climb. But if you think of each step as leading to the summit of achievement from which a glorious landscape will open out before you, then your climb will be endurable and you will achieve your goal.

Prayer for the Day

I pray that I may realize that life without a goal is futile. I pray that I may find the good life worth striving for.

AUGUST 24—A.A. Thought for the Day

"When we saw our faults, we listed them. We placed them before us in black and white. We admitted our wrongs honestly and we were willing to set these matters straight. We reviewed our fears thoroughly. We asked God to remove our fears and we commenced to outgrow fear. Many of us needed an overhauling in regard to sex. We came to believe that sex powers were God-given and therefore good, if used properly. Sex is never to be used lightly or selfishly, nor is it to be despised or loathed. If sex is troublesome, we throw ourselves the harder into helping others, and so take our minds off ourselves." *Am I facing my sex problems in the proper way?*

Meditation for the Day

Cling to the belief that all things are possible with God. If this belief is truly accepted, it is the ladder upon which a human soul can climb from the lowest pit of despair to the sublimest heights of peace of mind. It is possible for God to change your way of living. When you see the change in another person through the grace of God, you cannot doubt that all things are possible in the lives of people through the strength that comes from faith in Him who rules us all.

Prayer for the Day

I pray that I may live expectantly. I pray that I may believe deeply that all things are possible with God.

AUGUST 25—A.A. Thought for the Day

"Unless we discuss our defects with another person, we do not acquire enough humility, fearlessness, and honesty to really get the program. We must be entirely honest with somebody, if we expect to live happily in this world. We must be hard on ourselves, but always considerate of others. We pocket our pride and go to it, illuminating every twist of character and every dark cranny of the past. Once we have taken this step, withholding nothing, we can look the world in the eyes." *Have I discussed all my defects with another person?*

Meditation for the Day

Never yield to weariness of the spirit. At times, the world's cares and distractions will intrude and the spirit will become weak. At times like this, carry on and soon the spirit will become strong again. God's spirit is always with you, to replenish and renew. None ever sincerely sought God's help in vain. Physical weariness and exhaustion make a time of rest and communion with God more necessary. When you are overcome by temporary conditions which you cannot control, keep quiet and wait for the power of the spirit to flow back.

Prayer for the Day

I pray that I may not speak or act in the midst of emotional upheaval. I pray that I may wait until the tempest is past.

AUGUST 26—A.A. Thought for the Day

"If we are still clinging to something that we will not let go, we must sincerely ask God to help us to be willing to let even that go, too. We cannot divide our lives into compartments and keep some for ourselves. We must give all the compartments to God. We must say: 'My Creator, I am now willing that you should have all of me, good and bad. I pray that you now remove from me every single defect of character which stands in the way of my usefulness to you and my friends.'" *Am I still clinging to something that I will not let go?*

Meditation for the Day

The laws of nature cannot be changed and must be obeyed if you are to stay healthy. No exceptions will be made in your case. Submit to the laws of nature or they will finally break you. And in the realm of the spirit, in all human relationships, submit to the moral laws and to the will of God. If you continue to break the laws of honesty, purity, unselfishness, and love, you will be broken to some extent yourself. The moral and spiritual laws of God, like the laws of nature, are unbreakable without some disaster. If you are dishonest, impure, selfish, and unloving, you will not be living according to the laws of the spirit and you will suffer the consequences.

Prayer for the Day

I pray that I may submit to the laws of nature and to the laws of God. I pray that I may live in harmony with all the laws of life.

AUGUST 27—A.A. Thought for the Day

"We must be willing to make amends to all the people we have harmed. We must do the best we can to repair the damage done in the past. When we make amends, when we say: 'I'm sorry,' the person is sure at least to be impressed by our sincere desire to set right the wrong. Sometimes people we are making amends to admit their own faults, so feuds of long standing melt away. Our most ruthless creditors will sometimes surprise us. In general, we must be willing to do the right thing, no matter what the consequences may be for us." *Have I made a sincere effort to make amends to the people I have harmed?*

Meditation for the Day

The grace of God cures disharmony and disorder in human relationships. Directly you put your affairs, with their confusion and their difficulties, into God's hands, He begins to effect a cure of all the disharmony and disorder. You can believe that He will cause you no more pain in the doing of it than a physician, who plans and knows that he can effect a cure, would cause his patient. You can have faith that God will do all that is necessary as painlessly as possible. But you must be willing to submit to His treatment, even if you cannot now see the meaning or purpose of it.

Prayer for the Day

I pray that I may willingly submit to whatever spiritual discipline is necessary. I pray that I may accept whatever it takes to live a better life.

AUGUST 28—A.A. Thought for the Day

"We must continue to take personal inventory and continue to set right any new mistakes as we go along. We should grow in understanding and effectiveness. This is not an overnight matter; it should continue for our life time. Continue to watch for selfishness, dishonesty, resentment, and fear. When these crop up, we ask God at once to remove them. We must not rest on our laurels. We are headed for trouble if we do. We are not cured of alcoholism. What we really have is a daily reprieve, contingent on the maintenance of our spiritual condition." *Am I checking my spiritual condition daily?*

Meditation for the Day

Happiness cannot be sought directly; it is a by-product of love and service. Service is a law of our being. With love in your heart, there is always some service to other people. A life of power and joy and satisfaction is built on love and service. Persons who hate or are selfish are going against the law of their own being. They are cutting themselves off from God and other people. Little acts of love and encouragement, of service and help, erase the rough places of life and help to make the path smooth. If we do these things, we cannot help having our share of happiness.

Prayer for the Day

I pray that I may give my share of love and service. I pray that I may not grow weary in my attempts to do the right thing.

AUGUST 29—A.A. Thought for the Day

"We cannot get along without prayer and meditation. On awakening, let us think about the twenty-four hours ahead. We consider our plans for the day. Before we begin, we ask God to direct our thinking. Our thought lives will be placed on a much higher plane when we start the day with prayer and meditation. We conclude this period of meditation with a prayer that we will be shown through the day what our next step is to be. The basis of all our prayers is: Thy will be done in me and through me today." *Am I sincere in my desire to do God's will today?*

Meditation for the Day

Breathe in the inspiration of goodness and truth. It is the spirit of honesty, purity, unselfishness, and love. It is readily available if we are willing to accept it wholeheartedly. God has given us two things—His spirit and the power of choice—to accept or not, as we will. We have the gift of free will. When we choose the path of selfishness and greed and pride, we are refusing to accept God's spirit. When we choose the path of love and service, we accept God's spirit and it flows into us and makes all things new.

Prayer for the Day

I pray that I may choose the right way. I pray that I may try to follow it to the end.

AUGUST 30—A.A. Thought for the Day

"Practical experience shows that nothing will so much insure immunity from drinking as extensive work with other alcoholics. Carry the message to other alcoholics. You can help when no one else can. You can secure their confidence when others fail. Life will take on a new meaning for you. To watch people recover, to see them help others in turn, to watch loneliness vanish, to see a fellowship grow about you, to have a host of friends, this is an experience you must not miss." *Am I always ready and willing to help other alcoholics?*

Meditation for the Day

One secret of abundant living is the art of giving. The paradox of life is that the more you give, the more you have. If you lose your life in the service of others, you will save it. You can give abundantly and so live abundantly. You are rich in one respect—you have a spirit that is inexhaustible. Let no mean or selfish thought keep you from sharing this spirit. Of love, of help, of understanding, and of sympathy, give and keep giving. Give your personal ease and comfort, your time, your money, and most of all, yourself. And you will be living abundantly.

Prayer for the Day

I pray that I may live to give. I pray that I may learn this secret of abundant living.

AUGUST 31—A.A. Thought for the Day

"Call on new prospects while they are still jittery. They may be more receptive when depressed. See them alone if possible. Tell them enough about your drinking habits and experiences to encourage them to speak of themselves. If they wish to talk, let them do so. If they are not communicative, talk about the troubles liquor has caused you, being careful not to moralize or lecture. When they see you know all about the drinking game, commence to describe yourself as an alcoholic and tell them how you learned you were sick." *Am I ready to talk about myself to new prospects?*

Meditation for the Day

Try not to give way to criticism, blame, scorn, or judgment of others, when you are trying to help them. Effectiveness in helping others depends on controlling yourself. You may be swept away by a temporary natural urge to criticize or blame, unless you keep a tight rein on your emotions. You should have a firm foundation of spiritual living which makes you truly humble, if you are going to really help other people. Go easy on them and be hard on yourself. That is the way you can be used most to uplift a despairing spirit. And seek no personal recognition for what you are used by God to accomplish.

Prayer for the Day

I pray that I may try to avoid judgment and criticism. I pray that I may always try to build up others instead of tearing them down.

SEPT. 1—A.A. Thought for the Day

"Be careful not to brand new prospects as alcoholics. Let them draw their own conclusion. But talk to them about the hopelessness of alcoholism. Tell them exactly what happened to you and how you recovered. Stress the spiritual feature freely. If they are agnostics or atheists, make it emphatic that they do not have to agree with your conception of God. They can choose any conception they like, provided it makes sense to them. The main thing is that they be willing to believe in a Power greater than themselves and that they live by spiritual principles." *Do I hold back too much in speaking of the spiritual principles of the program?*

Meditation for the Day

"I will never leave nor forsake thee." Down through the centuries, thousands have believed in God's constancy, untiringness, and unfailing love. God has love. Then forever you are sure of His love. God has power. Then forever you are sure, in every difficulty and temptation, of His strength. God has patience. Then always there is One who can never tire. God has understanding. Then always you will understand and be understood. Unless you want Him to go, God will never leave you. He is always ready with power.

Prayer for the Day

I pray that I may feel that God's love will never fail. I pray that I may have confidence in His unfailing power.

SEPT. 2—A.A. Thought for the Day

"Outline the program of action to new prospects, explaining how you made a self-appraisal, how you straightened out your past, and why you are now endeavoring to help them. It is important for them to realize that your attempt to pass this on to them plays a vital part in your own recovery. The more hopeless they feel, the better. They will be more likely to follow your suggestions. Tell them about the fellowship of A.A. and if they show interest, lend them a copy of the book." *Can I get over the A.A. story to another alcoholic?*

Meditation for the Day

You should try to stand aside and let God work through you. You should try not to block Him off by your own efforts, or prevent His spirit working through you. God desires your obedient service and your loyalty to the ideals of the new life you are seeking. If you are loyal to God, He will give you protection against mistakes. His spirit will plan for you and secure for you a sufficiency of all spiritual help. You will have true victory and real success, if you will put yourself in the background and let God work through you.

Prayer for the Day

I pray that I may not interfere with the working of God's spirit in me and through me. I pray that I may give it full rein.

SEPT. 3—A.A. Thought for the Day

"Offer new prospects friendship and fellowship. Tell them that if they want to get well you will do anything to help. Burn the idea into the consciousness of new prospects that they can get well, regardless of anyone else. Job or no job, spouse or no spouse, they cannot stop drinking as long as they place dependence on other people ahead of dependence on God. Let no alcoholic say they cannot recover unless they have their family back. This just isn't so. Their recovery is not dependent upon other people. It is dependent on their own relationship to God." *Can I recognize all excuses made by a prospect?*

Meditation for the Day

The spiritual life depends upon the Unseen. To live the spiritual life, you must believe in the Unseen. Try not to lose the consciousness of God's spirit in you and in others. As a child in its mother's arms, stay sheltered in the understanding and love of God. God will relieve you of the weight of worry and care, misery and depression, want and woe, faintness and heartache, if you will let Him. Lift up your eyes from earth's troubles and view the glory of the unseen God. Each day try to see more good in people, more of the Unseen in the seen.

Prayer for the Day

I pray that I may rest and abide in the presence of the unseen God. I pray that I may leave my burdens in His care.

SEPT. 4—A.A. Thought for the Day

"We must be careful never to show intolerance or hatred of drinking as an institution. Experience shows that such an attitude is not helpful to anyone. We are not fanatics or intolerant of people who can drink normally. Prospects are relieved when they find we are not witch burners. Temperate drinking is okay, but we alcoholics can't get away with it. And no alcoholic likes to be told about alcohol by anyone who hates it. We shall be of little use if our attitude is one of bitterness or hostility." *Do I have tolerance for those who can drink normally?*

Meditation for the Day

Do not become encumbered by petty annoyances. Never respond to emotional upsets by emotional upset. Try to keep calm in all circumstances. Try not to fight back. Call on the grace of God to calm you when you feel like retaliating. Look to God for the inner strength to drop those resentments that drag you down. If you are burdened by annoyances, you will lose your inward peace and the spirit of God will be shut out. Try to keep peaceful within.

Prayer for the Day

I pray that I may do the things that make for peace. I pray that I may have a mission of conciliation.

SEPT. 5—A.A. Thought for the Day

One of the mottoes of A.A. is "First Things First." This means that we should always keep in mind that alcohol is our number one problem. We must never let any other problem, whether of family, business, friends, or anything else take precedence in our minds over our alcoholic problem. As we go along in A.A., we learn to recognize the things that may upset us emotionally. When we find ourselves getting upset over something, we must realize that it's a luxury we alcoholics can't afford. Anything that makes us forget our number one problem is dangerous to us. *Am I keeping sobriety in first place in my mind?*

Meditation for the Day

Spiritual progress is the law of your being. Try to see around you more and more of beauty and truth, knowledge and power. Today try to be stronger, braver, more loving as a result of what you did yesterday. This law of spiritual progress gives meaning and purpose to your life. Always expect better things ahead. You can accomplish much good through the strength of God's spirit in you. Never be too discouraged. The world is sure to get better, in spite of setbacks of war, hate, and greed. Be part of the cure of the world's ills, rather than part of the disease.

Prayer for the Day

I pray that I may keep progressing in the better life. I pray that I may be a part of the forces for good in the world.

SEPT. 6—A.A. Thought for the Day

Another of the mottoes of A.A. is "Live and Let Live." This, of course, means tolerance of people who think differently than we do, whether they are in A.A. or outside of A.A. We cannot afford the luxury of being intolerant or critical of other people. We do not try to impose our wills on those who differ from us. We are not "holier than thou." We do not have all the answers. We are not better than other good people. We live the best way we can and we allow others to do likewise. *Am I willing to live and let live?*

Meditation for the Day

"And this is life eternal, that we may know Thee, the only true God." Learning to know God as best you can draws the eternal life nearer to you. Freed from some of the limitations of humanity, you can grow in the things that are eternal. You can strive for what is real and of eternal value. The more you try to live in the consciousness of the unseen world, the gentler will be your passing into it when the time comes for you to go. This life on earth should be largely a preparation for the eternal life to come.

Prayer for the Day

I pray that I may live each day as though it were my last. I pray that I may live my life as though it were everlasting.

SEPT. 7—A.A. Thought for the Day

Another of the mottoes of A.A. is "Easy Does It." This means that we just go along in A.A. doing the best we can and not getting steamed up over problems that arise in A.A. or outside of it. We alcoholics are emotional people and we have gone to excess in almost everything we have done. We have not been moderate in many things. We have not known how to relax. Faith in a Higher Power can help us to learn to take it easy. We are not running the world. I am only one among many. We are resolved to live normal, regular lives. From our A.A. experience we learn that "easy does it." *Have I learned to take it easy?*

Meditation for the Day

"The eternal God is thy refuge and underneath are the everlasting arms." Sheltering arms express the loving protection of God's spirit. Human beings, in their troubles and difficulties need nothing so much as a refuge, a place to relax where they can lay down their burdens and get relief from cares. Say to yourself: "God is my refuge." Say it until its truth sinks into your very soul. Say it until you know it and are sure of it. Nothing can seriously upset you or make you afraid, if God is truly your refuge.

Prayer for the Day

I pray that I may go each day to God as a refuge until fear goes and peace and security come. I pray that I may feel deeply secure in the Haven of His spirit.

SEPT. 8—A.A. Thought for the Day

Another of the mottoes of A.A. is "But for the Grace of God." Once we have fully accepted the program we become humble about our achievement. We do not take too much credit for our sobriety. When we see another suffering alcoholic in the throes of alcoholism, we say to ourselves: "But for the grace of God, there go I." We do not forget the kind of people we were. We remember those we left behind us. And we are very grateful to the grace of God which has given us another chance. *Am I truly grateful for the grace of God?*

Meditation for the Day

A consciousness of God's presence as One who loves you makes all life different. The consciousness of God's love promotes the opening of your whole being to God. It brings wonderful relief from the cares and worries of our daily lives. Relief brings peace and peace brings contentment. Try to walk in God's love. You will have that peace which passes all understanding and a contentment that no one can take from you. Feel sure of God's unfailing love and care for you and for all His children. There is freedom and serenity in those who walk in God's love, held safe in His loving care.

Prayer for the Day

I pray that I may walk in God's love. I pray that, as I go, I may feel the spring of God's power in my steps and the joy of His love in my heart.

SEPT. 9—A.A. Thought for the Day

When alcoholics are offered a life of sobriety by following the A.A. program, they will look at the prospect of living without alcohol and they will ask: "Am I to be consigned to a life where I shall be stupid, boring and glum, like some of the righteous people I see? I know I must get along without liquor, but how can I? Have you a sufficient substitute?" *Have I found a more than sufficient substitute for drinking?*

Meditation for the Day

In God's strength you conquer life. Your conquering power is the grace of God. There can be no complete failure with God. Do you want to make the best of life? Then live as near as possible to God, the Master and Giver of all life. Your reward for depending on God's strength will be sure. Sometimes the reward will be renewed power to face life, sometimes wrong thinking overcome, sometimes people brought to a new way of living. Whatever success comes will not be all your own doing, but largely the working out of the grace of God.

Prayer for the Day

I pray that I may try to rely more fully on the grace of God. I pray that I may live a victorious life.

SEPT. 10—A.A. Thought for the Day

Here are answers to the question of how a person can live without liquor and be happy: "The things we put in place of drinking are more than substitutes for it. One is the fellowship of Alcoholics Anonymous. In this company, you find release from care, boredom, and worry. Your imagination will be fired. Life will mean something at last. The most satisfactory years of your existence lie ahead. Among other A.A.s you will make lifelong friends. You will be bound to them with new and wonderful ties." *Does life mean something to me now?*

Meditation for the Day

Do you want the full and complete satisfaction that you find in serving God and all the satisfactions of the world also? It is not easy to serve both God and the world. It is difficult to claim the rewards of both. If you work for God, you will still have great rewards in the world. But you must be prepared to sometimes stand apart from the world. You cannot always turn to the world and expect all the rewards which life has to offer. If you are trying sincerely to serve God, you will have other and greater rewards than the world has to offer.

Prayer for the Day

I pray that I may not expect too much from the world. I pray that I may also be content with the rewards that come from serving God.

SEPT. 11—A.A. Thought for the Day

Continuing the answers to the question of how a person can live without liquor and be happy, we say: "You will be bound to the other A.A.s with new and wonderful ties, for you and they will escape disaster together and all will commence shoulder to shoulder the common journey to a better and more satisfactory life. You will know what it means to give of yourself that others may survive and rediscover life. You will become happy, respected, and useful once more. Since these things have happened to us, they can happen to you." *Have these things happened to me?*

Meditation for the Day

God manifests Himself in human lives as strength to overcome evil and power to resist temptation. The grace of God is that power which enables a human being to change from a useless, hopeless individual to a useful, normal person. God also manifests Himself as love—love for other people, compassion for their problems, and a real willingness to help them. The grace of God also manifests itself as peace of mind and serenity of character. We can have plenty of power, love, and serenity in our lives if we are willing to ask God for these things each day.

Prayer for the Day

I pray that I may see God's grace in the strength I receive, the love I know, and the peace I have. I pray that I may be grateful for the things I have received through the grace of God.

SEPT. 12—A.A. Thought for the Day

"What draws newcomers to A.A. and gives them hope? They hear the stories of men and women whose experiences tally with their own. The expressions on the faces of the women, that undefinable something in the eyes of the men, the stimulating atmosphere of the A.A. clubroom, conspire to let them know that there is haven at last. The very practical approach to their problems, the absence of intolerance of any kind, the informality, the genuine democracy, the uncanny understanding which these people in A.A. have is irresistible." *Have I found a real haven in A.A.?*

Meditation for the Day

"If thine eye be single, thy whole body shall be full of light." The eye of the soul is the will. If your will is to do the will of God, to serve Him with your life, to serve Him by helping others, then truly shall your whole body be full of light. The important thing is to strive that your will be attuned to the will of God, a single eye to God's purpose, desiring nothing less than that His purposes be fulfilled. Try to seek in all things the advance of His kingdom, seek the spiritual values of honesty and purity, unselfishness and love, and earnestly desire spiritual growth. Then your life will emerge from the darkness of futility into the light of victory.

Prayer for the Day

I pray that my eye may be single. I pray that my life may be lived in the light of the best that I know.

SEPT. 13—A.A. Thought for the Day

"No one is too discredited, nor has sunk too low, to be welcomed cordially into A.A., if he or she means business. Social distinctions, petty rivalries and jealousies are laughed out of countenance. Being wrecked in the same vessel, being restored and united under one God, with hearts and minds attuned to the welfare of others, the things which matter so much to some people no longer signify much to us. In A.A., we have true democracy and true brotherhood." *Has A.A. taught me to be truly democratic?*

Meditation for the Day

When you call on God in prayer to help you overcome weakness, sorrow, pain, discord, and conflict, God never fails in some way to answer the appeal. When you are in need of strength for yourself or for the help of some other person, call on God in prayer. The power you need will come simply, naturally, and forcefully. Pray to God not only when you need help, but also just to commune with Him. The spirit of prayer can alter an atmosphere from one of discord to one of reconciliation. It will raise the quality of thought and word and bring order out of chaos.

Prayer for the Day

I pray that I may bring peace where there is discord. I pray that I may bring conciliation where there is conflict.

SEPT. 14—A.A. Thought for the Day

"How does A.A. grow? Some of us sell A.A. as we go about. Little clusters of twos and threes and fives keep springing up in different communities, through contact with the larger centers. Those of us who travel drop in at other groups as often as we can. This practice enables us to lend a hand to new groups which are springing up all over the land. New groups are being started each month. A.A. is even spreading outside the United States and is slowly becoming world-wide. Thus we grow." *Am I doing all I can to spread A.A. wherever I go?*

Meditation for the Day

"Lord we believe. Help Thou our unbelief." This cry of the human heart is an expression of human frailty. It signifies the soul's sincere desire for progress. As a person feels the existence of God and His power, that person believes in Him more and more. At the same time, a person is more conscious of his falling short of absolute trust in God. The soul's progress is an increasing belief, then a cry for more faith, a plea to conquer all unbelief, all lack of trust. We can believe that that cry is heard by God and that prayer is answered in due time. And so our faith grows, little by little, day by day.

Prayer for the Day

I pray that with more power in my life will come more faith. I pray that I may come to trust God more each day.

SEPT. 15—A.A. Thought for the Day

"We all realize that we know only a little. God will constantly disclose more to all of us. Ask Him in your morning meditations what you can do today for the person who is still sick. The answers will come, if your own house is in order. See to it that your relationship with God is right and great events will come to pass for you and countless others. Give freely of what you find in A.A. But, obviously, you cannot transmit something which you haven't got. So make a life-study of A.A." *Am I always looking for ways of presenting the A.A. program?*

Meditation for the Day

"In quietness and confidence shall be your strength." Confidence means to have faith in something. We could not live without confidence in others. When you have confidence in God's grace, you can face whatever comes. When you have confidence in God's love, you can be serene and at peace. You can rest in the faith that God will take care of you. Try to rest in God's presence until His life-power flows through you. Be still and in that stillness the still, small Voice will come. It speaks in quietness to the human mind that is attuned to its influence.

Prayer for the Day

I pray that I may find strength today in quietness. I pray that I may be content today that God will take care of me.

SEPT. 16—A.A. Thought for the Day

Today, let us begin a short study of The Twelve Suggested Steps of A.A. These Twelve Suggested Steps seem to embody five principles. The first step is the membership requirement step. The second, third, and eleventh steps are the spiritual steps of the program. The fourth, fifth, sixth, seventh and tenth steps are the personal inventory steps. The eighth and ninth steps are the restitution steps. The twelfth step is the passing on of the program, or helping others, step. So the five principles are membership requirement, spiritual basis, personal inventory, restitution, and helping others. *Have I made all these steps a part of me?*

Meditation for the Day

We seem to live not only in time but also in eternity. If we abide with God and He abides with us, we may bring forth spiritual fruit which will last for eternity. If we live with God, our lives can flow as some calm river through the dry land of earth. It can cause the trees and flowers of the spiritual life—love and service—to spring forth and yield abundantly. Spiritual work may be done for eternity, not just for now. Even here on earth we can live as though our real lives were eternal.

Prayer for the Day

I pray that I may try to make my life like a cool river in a thirsty land. I pray that I may give freely to all who ask my help.

SEPT. 17—A.A. Thought for the Day

Step One is, "We admitted we were powerless over alcohol—that our lives had become unmanageable." This step states the membership requirement of A.A. We must admit that our lives are disturbed. We must accept the fact that we are helpless before the power of alcohol. We must admit that we are licked as far as drinking is concerned and that we need help. We must be willing to accept the bitter fact that we cannot drink like normal people. And we must make, as gracefully as possible, a surrender to the inevitable fact that we must stop drinking. *Is it difficult for me to admit that I am different from normal drinkers?*

Meditation for the Day

"Show us the way, O Lord, and let us walk in Thy paths." There seems to be a right way to live and a wrong way. You can make a practical test. When you live the right way, things seem to work out well for you. When you live the wrong way, things seem to work out badly for you. You seem to take out of life about what you put into it. If you disobey the laws of nature, the chances are that you will be unhealthy. If you disobey the spiritual and moral laws, the chances are that you will be unhappy. By following the laws of nature and the spiritual laws of honesty, purity, unselfishness, and love, you can expect to be reasonably healthy and happy.

Prayer for the Day

I pray that I may try to live the right way. I pray that I may follow the path that leads to a better life.

SEPT. 18—A.A. Thought for the Day

Step Two is, "Came to believe that a Power greater than ourselves could restore us to sanity." *Step Three* is, "Made a decision to turn our will and our lives over to the care of God *as we understood Him.*" *Step Eleven* is, "Sought through prayer and meditation to improve our conscious contact with God, *as we understood Him,* praying only for knowledge of His will for us and the power to carry that out." The fundamental basis of A.A. is a belief in some Power greater than ourselves. Let us not take this lightly. We cannot fully get the program without this venture of belief. *Have I made the venture of belief in a Power greater than my own?*

Meditation for the Day

"He that dwelleth in the secret place of the Most High, shall abide under the shadow of the Almighty." Dwell for a moment each day in a secret place, the place of communion with God, apart from the world, and thence receive strength to face the world. Material things cannot intrude upon this secret place, they cannot ever find it, because it is outside the realm of material things. When you abide in this secret place, you are under the shadow of the Almighty. God is close to you in this quiet place of communion. Each day, dwell for a while in this secret place.

Prayer for the Day

I pray that I may renew my strength in quietness. I pray that I may find rest in quiet communion with God.

SEPT. 19—A.A. Thought for the Day

Let us continue with *Steps Two, Three, and Eleven.* We must turn to a Higher Power for help, because we are helpless ourselves. When we put our drink problem in God's hands and leave it there, we have made the most important decision of our lives. From then on, we trust God for the strength to keep sober. This takes us off the center of the universe and allows us to transfer our problems to a Power outside ourselves. By prayer and meditation, we seek to improve our conscious contact with God. We try to live each day the way we believe God wants us to live. *Am I trusting God for the strength to stay sober?*

Meditation for the Day

"These things have I spoken unto you, that your joy may be full." Even a partial realization of the spiritual life brings much joy. You feel at home in the world when you are in touch with the Divine Spirit of the universe. Spiritual experience brings a definite satisfaction. Search for the real meaning of life by following spiritual laws. God wants you to have spiritual success and He intends that you have it. If you live your life as much as possible according to spiritual laws, you can expect your share of joy and peace, satisfaction and success.

Prayer for the Day

I pray that I will find happiness in doing the right thing. I pray that I will find satisfaction in obeying spiritual laws.

SEPT. 20—A.A. Thought for the Day

Step Four is, "Made a searching and fearless moral inventory of ourselves." *Step Five* is, "Admitted to God, to ourselves, and to another human being the exact nature of our wrongs." *Step Six* is, "Were entirely ready to have God remove all these defects of character." *Step Seven* is, "Humbly asked Him to remove our shortcomings." *Step Ten* is, "Continued to take personal inventory and when we were wrong, promptly admitted it." In taking a personal inventory, we have to be absolutely honest with ourselves and with other people. *Have I taken an honest inventory of myself?*

Meditation for the Day

God is good. You can often tell whether or not a thing is of God. If it is of God, it must be good. Honesty, purity, unselfishness, and love are all good, unselfish helpfulness is good, and these things all lead to the abundant life. Leave in God's hands the present and the future, knowing only that He is good. The hand that veils the future is the hand of God. He can bring order out of chaos, good out of evil, and peace out of turmoil. We can believe that everything really good comes from God and that He shares His goodness with us.

Prayer for the Day

I pray that I may reach out for the good. I pray that I may try to choose the best in life.

SEPT. 21—A.A. Thought for the Day

Let us continue with *Steps Four, Five, Six, Seven, and Ten.* In taking a personal inventory of ourselves, we have to face facts as they really are. We have to stop running away. We must face reality. We must see ourselves as we really are. We must admit our faults openly and try to correct them. We must try to see where we have been dishonest, impure, selfish, and unloving. We do not do this once and forget it. We do it every day of our lives, as long as we live. We are never done with checking up on ourselves. *Am I taking a daily inventory of myself?*

Meditation for the Day

In improving our personal lives, we have Unseen help. We were not made so that we could see God. That would be too easy for us and there would be no merit in obeying Him. It takes an act of faith, a venture of belief, to realize the Unseen Power. Yet we have much evidence of God's existence in the strength that many people have received from the act of faith, the venture of belief. We are in a box of space and time and we can see neither our souls nor God. God and the human spirit are both outside the limitations of space and time. Yet our Unseen help is effective here and now. That has been proved in thousands of changed lives.

Prayer for the Day

I pray that I may make the great venture of belief. I pray that my vision may not be blocked by intellectual pride.

SEPT. 22—A.A. Thought for the Day

Step Eight is, "Made a list of all persons we had harmed and became willing to make amends to them all." *Step Nine* is, "Made direct amends to such people wherever possible, except when to do so would injure them or others." Making restitution for the wrongs we have done is often very difficult. It hurts our pride. But the rewards are great. When we go to a person and say we are sorry, the reaction we get is almost invariably good. It takes courage to make the plunge, but the results more than justify it. A load is off your chest and often an enemy has been turned into a friend. *Have I done my best to make all the restitution possible?*

Meditation for the Day

There should be joy in living the spiritual life. A faith without joy is not entirely genuine. If you are not happier as a result of your faith, there is probably something wrong with it. Faith in God should bring you a deep feeling of happiness and security, no matter what happens on the surface of your life. Each new day is another opportunity to serve God and improve your relationships with other people. This should bring joy. Life should be abundant and outreaching. It should be glowing and outgoing, in ever widening circles.

Prayer for the Day

I pray that my horizons may grow ever wider. I pray that I may keep reaching out for more service and companionship.

SEPT. 23—A.A. Thought for the Day

Step Twelve is, "Having had a spiritual awakening as the result of these steps, we tried to carry this message to alcoholics, and to practice these principles in all our affairs." Note that the basis of our effectiveness in carrying the message to others is the reality of our own spiritual awakening. If we have not changed, we cannot be used to change others. To keep this program, we must pass it on to others. We cannot hoard it for ourselves. We may lose it unless we give it away. It cannot flow into us and stop; it must continue to flow into us as it flows out to others. *Am I always ready to give away what I have learned in A.A.?*

Meditation for the Day

"Draw nigh unto God and He will draw nigh unto you." When you are faced with a problem beyond your strength, you must turn to God by an act of faith. It is that turning to God in each trying situation that you must cultivate. The turning may be one of glad thankfulness for God's grace in your life. Or your appeal to God may be a prayerful claiming of His strength to face a situation and finding that you have it when the time comes. Not only the power to face trials, but also the comfort and joy of God's nearness and companionship are yours for the asking.

Prayer for the Day

I pray that I may try to draw near to God each day in prayer. I pray that I may feel His nearness and His strength in my life.

SEPT. 24—A.A. Thought for the Day

Let us continue with *Step Twelve*. We must practice these principles in all our affairs. This part of the twelfth step must not be overlooked. It is the carrying on of the whole program. We do not just practice these principles in regard to our drinking problem. We practice them in *all* our affairs. We do not give one compartment of our lives to God and keep the other compartments to ourselves. We give our whole lives to God and we try to do His will in every respect. "Herein lies our growth, herein lies all the promise of the future, an ever-widening horizon." *Do I carry the A.A. principles with me wherever I go?*

Meditation for the Day

"Lord, to whom shall we go but to Thee? Thou hast the words of eternal life." The words of eternal life are the words from God controlling your true being, controlling the real spiritual you. They are the words from God which are heard by you in your heart and mind when these are wide open to His spirit. These are the words of eternal life which express the true way you are to live. They say to you in the stillness of your heart and mind and soul: "Do this and live."

Prayer for the Day

I pray that I may follow the dictates of my conscience. I pray that I may follow the inner urging of my soul.

SEPT. 25—A.A. Thought for the Day

Let us consider the term *"spiritual experience"* as given in Appendix II of the Big Book, *Alcoholics Anonymous*: "A spiritual experience is something that brings about a personality change. By surrendering our lives to God as we understand Him, we are changed. The nature of this change is evident in recovered alcoholics. This personality change is not necessarily in the nature of a sudden and spectacular upheaval. We do not need to acquire an immediate and overwhelming God-consciousness, followed at once by a vast change in feeling and outlook. In most cases, the change is gradual." *Do I see a gradual and continuing change in myself?*

Meditation for the Day

"Come unto me all ye that labor and are heavy laden and I will give you rest." For rest from the care of life, you can turn to God each day in prayer and communion. Real relaxation and serenity come from a deep sense of the fundamental goodness of the universe. God's everlasting arms are underneath all and will support you. Commune with God, not so much for petitions to be granted as for the rest that comes from relying on His will and His purposes for your life. Be sure of God's strength available to you, be conscious of His support, and wait quietly until that true rest from God fills your being.

Prayer for the Day

I pray that I may be conscious of God's support today. I pray that I may rest safe and sure therein.

SEPT. 26—A.A. Thought for the Day

Continuing the consideration of the term "spiritual experience": "The acquiring of an immediate and overwhelming God-consciousness, resulting in a dramatic transformation, though frequent, is by no means the rule. Most of our spiritual experiences are of the educational variety, and they develop slowly over a period of time. Quite often friends of newcomers are aware of the difference long before they are themselves. They finally realize that they have undergone a profound alteration in their reaction to life and that such a change could hardly have been brought about by themselves alone." *Is my outlook on life changing for the better?*

Meditation for the Day

Look at the world as your Father's house. Think of all people you meet as guests in your Father's house, to be treated with love and consideration. Look at yourself as a servant in your Father's house, as a servant of all. Think of no work as beneath you. Be ever ready to do all you can for others who need your help. There is gladness in God's service. There is much satisfaction in serving the highest that you know. Express your love for God in service to all who are living with you in your Father's house.

Prayer for the Day

I pray that I may serve others out of gratitude to God. I pray that my work may be a small repayment for His grace so freely given me.

SEPT. 27—A.A. Thought for the Day

Continuing the consideration of the term "spiritual experience": "What often takes place in a few months could seldom have been accomplished by years of self-discipline. With few exceptions, our members find that they have tapped an unsuspected inner resource which they presently identify with their own conception of a Power greater than themselves. Most of us think this awareness of a Power greater than ourselves the essence of spiritual experience. Some of us call it God-consciousness. In any case, willingness, honesty, and open-mindedness are the essentials of recovery." *Have I tapped that inner resource which can change my life?*

Meditation for the Day

God's power in your life increases as your ability to understand His grace increases. The power of God's grace is only limited by the understanding and will of each individual. God's miracle-working power is only limited in each individual soul by the lack of spiritual vision of that soul. God respects free will, the right of each person to accept or reject His miracle-working power. Only the sincere desire of the soul gives Him the opportunity to bestow it.

Prayer for the Day

I pray that I may not limit God's power by my lack of vision. I pray that I may keep my mind open today to His influence.

SEPT. 28—A.A. Thought for the Day

For the past two months we have been studying passages and steps from the Big Book, *Alcoholics Anonymous*. Now why not read the book itself again? It is essential that the A.A. program become part of us. We must have its essentials at our finger tips. We cannot study the big book too much or too often. The more we read it and study it, the better equipped we are to think A.A., act A.A., and live A.A. We cannot know too much about the program. The chances are that we will never know enough. But we can make as much of it our own as possible. *How much of the Big Book have I thoroughly mastered?*

Meditation for the Day

We need to accept the difficulties and disciplines of life so as to fully share the common life of other people. Many things that we must accept in life are not to be taken so much as being necessary for us personally, as to be experienced in order that we may share in the sufferings and problems of humanity. We need sympathy and understanding. We must share many of the experiences of life, in order to understand and sympathize with others. Unless we have been through the same experiences, we cannot understand other people or their makeup well enough to be able to help them.

Prayer for the Day

I pray that I may accept everything that comes my way as a part of life. I pray that I may make use of it in helping other people.

SEPT. 29—A.A. Thought for the Day

Having got this far, shall we pause and ask ourselves some searching questions? We need to check up on ourselves periodically. Just how good an A.A. am I? Am I attending meetings regularly? Am I doing my share to carry the load? When there is something to be done, do I volunteer? Do I speak at meetings when asked, no matter how nervous I am? Do I accept each opportunity to do twelfth-step work as a challenge? Do I give freely of my time and money? Am I trying to spread A.A. wherever I go? Is my daily life a demonstration of A.A. principles? *Am I a good A.A.?*

Meditation for the Day

How do I get strength to be effective and to accept responsibility? By asking the Higher Power for the strength I need each day. It has been proved in countless lives that for every day I live, the necessary power shall be given me. I must face each challenge that comes to me during the day, sure that God will give me the strength to face it. For every task that is given me, there is also given me all the power necessary for the performance of that task. I do not need to hold back.

Prayer for the Day

I pray that I may accept every task as a challenge. I know I cannot wholly fail if God is with me.

SEPT. 30—A.A. Thought for the Day

There are no leaders in A.A., except as they volunteer to accept responsibility. The work of carrying on A.A.—leading group meetings, serving on committees, speaking before other groups, doing twelfth-step work, spreading A.A. among the alcoholics of the community—all these things are done on a volunteer basis. If I don't volunteer to do something concrete for A.A., the movement is that much less effective. I must do my fair share to carry the load. A.A. depends on all its members to keep it alive and to keep it growing. *Am I doing my share for A.A.?*

Meditation for the Day

When you look to God for strength to face responsibility and are quiet before Him, His healing touch causes the Divine Quiet to flow into your very being. When in weakness you cry to God, His touch brings healing, the renewal of your courage, and the power to meet every situation and be victorious. When you faint by the way or are distracted by feelings of inferiority, then rely on the touch of God's spirit to support you on your way. Then arise and go forth with confidence.

Prayer for the Day

I pray that I may lay myself open today to the healing touch of God. I pray that I may not falter or faint by the wayside, but renew my courage through prayer.

OCT. 1—A.A. Thought for the Day

A.A. will lose some of its effectiveness if I do not do my share. Where am I failing? Are there some things I do not feel like doing? Am I held back by self-consciousness or fear? Self-consciousness is a form of pride. It is a fear that something may happen to you. What happens to you is not very important. The impression you make on others does not depend so much on the kind of a job you do as on your sincerity and honesty of purpose. *Am I holding back because I am afraid of not making a good impression?*

Meditation for the Day

Look to God for the true power that will make you effective. See no other wholly dependable supply of strength. That is the secret of a truly effective life. And you, in your turn, will be used to help many others find effectiveness. Whatever spiritual help you need, whatever spiritual help you desire for others, look to God. Seek that God's will be done in your life and seek that your will conforms to His. Failures come from depending too much on your own strength.

Prayer for the Day

I pray that I may feel that nothing good is too much for me if I look to God for help. I pray that I may be effective through His guidance.

OCT. 2—A.A. Thought for the Day

What makes an effective talk at an A.A. meeting? It is not a fine speech with fine choice of words and an impressive delivery. Often a few simple words direct from the heart are more effective than the most polished speech. There is always a temptation to speak beyond your own experience, in order to make a good impression. This is never effective. What does not come from the heart does not reach the heart. What comes from personal experience and a sincere desire to help the other person reaches the heart. *Do I speak for effect or with a deep desire to help?*

Meditation for the Day

"Thy will be done" must be your oft-repeated prayer. And in the willing of God's will there should be gladness. You should delight to do that will because when you do, all your life goes right and everything tends to work well for you in the long run. When you are honestly trying to do God's will and humbly accepting the results, nothing can seriously hurt you. Those who accept the will of God in their life may not inherit the earth, but they will inherit real peace of mind.

Prayer for the Day

I pray that I may have a yielded will. I pray that my will may be attuned to the will of God.

OCT. 3—A.A. Thought for the Day

How do I talk with new prospects? Am I always trying to dominate the conversation? Do I lay down the law and tell prospects what they will have to do? Do I judge them privately and feel that they have small chance of making the program? Do I belittle them to myself? Or am I willing to bare my soul so as to get them talking about themselves? And, then, am I willing to be a good listener, not interrupting, but hearing them out to the end? Do I feel deeply that they are my brothers or my sisters? *Will I do all I can to help them along the path to sobriety?*

Meditation for the Day

"The work of righteousness shall be peace and the effect of righteousness shall be quietness and assurance forever." Only when the soul attains this calm, can there be true spiritual work done, and mind and soul and body be strong to conquer and bear all things. Peace is the result of righteousness. There is no peace in wrong doing, but if we live the way God wants us to live, quietness and assurance follow. Assurance is that calmness born of a deep certainty of God's strength available to us and in His power to love and guard us from all harm and wrong doing.

Prayer for the Day

I pray that I may attain a state of true calmness. I pray that I may live in quietness and peace.

OCT. 4—A.A. Thought for the Day

Am I critical of other members of A.A. or of new prospects? Do I ever say about other members: "I don't think they're sincere, I think they're bluffing, or I think they're taking a few drinks on the quiet?" Do I realize that my doubtful and skeptical attitude is hurting those members, if only in my attitude toward them, which they cannot help sensing? Do I say about new prospects: "They'll never make the program," or do I say: "They'll only last a few months?" If I take this attitude, I am unconsciously hurting those prospects' chances. *Is my attitude always constructive and never destructive?*

Meditation for the Day

To be attracted toward God and a better life, you must be spirit-guided. There is wonderful illumination of thought given to those who are spirit-guided. To those who are material-guided, there is nothing in God or a finer life to appeal to them or to attract them. But to those who are spirit-guided there is strength and peace and calm to be found in communion with an Unseen Lord. To those who believe in this God they cannot see but whose power they can feel, life has a meaning and purpose. They are children of the Unseen Lord, and all human beings are their brothers and sisters.

Prayer for the Day

I pray that I may be spirit-guided. I pray that I may feel God's presence and power in my life.

OCT. 5—A.A. Thought for the Day

Do I have any hard feelings about other group members or for any other A.A. group? Am I critical of the way a group member thinks or acts? Do I feel that another group is operating in the wrong way and do I broadcast it? Or do I realize that all A.A. members, no matter what their limitations, have something to offer, some good, however little, that they can do for A.A. in spite of their handicaps? Do I believe that there is a place for all kinds of groups in A.A., provided they are following A.A. traditions, and that they can be effective, even if I do not agree with their procedure? *Am I tolerant of people and groups?*

Meditation for the Day

"The Lord shall preserve thy going out and thy coming in, from this time forth and even forever more." All your movements, your goings and comings can be guided by the Unseen Spirit. Every visit to help another, every unselfish effort to assist, can be blessed by that Unseen Spirit. There can be a blessing on all you do, on every interview with one who is suffering. Every meeting of a need may not be a chance meeting, but it may have been planned by the Unseen Spirit. Led by the Spirit of the Lord, you can be tolerant, sympathetic, and understanding of others and so accomplish much.

Prayer for the Day

I pray that I may be led by the spirit of God. I pray that the Lord will preserve my goings and my comings.

OCT. 6—A.A. Thought for the Day

Is it my desire to be a big shot in A.A.? Do I always want to be up front in the limelight? Do I feel that nobody else can do as good a job as I can? Or am I willing to take a seat in the back row once in a while and let somebody else carry the ball? Part of the effectiveness of any A.A. group is the development of new members to carry on, to take over from the older members. Am I reluctant to give up authority? Do I try to carry the load for the whole group? If so, I am not being fair to the newer members. Do I realize that no one person is essential? *Do I know that A.A. could carry on without me, if it had to?*

Meditation for the Day

The Unseen God can help to make us truly grateful and humble. Since we cannot see God, we must believe in Him without seeing. What we can see clearly is the change in a human being, when he sincerely asks God for the strength to change. We should cling to faith in God and in His power to change our ways. Our faith in an Unseen God will be rewarded by a useful and serviceable life. God will not fail to show us the way we should live, when in real gratitude and true humility we turn to Him.

Prayer for the Day

I pray that I may believe that God can change me. I pray that I may be always willing to be changed for the better.

OCT. 7—A.A. Thought for the Day

Do I put too much reliance on any one member of the group? That is, do I make a tin god out of some one person? Do I set that person on a pedestal? If I do, I am building my house on sand. All A.A. members have "clay feet." They are all only one drink away from a drunk, no matter how long they have been in A.A. This has been proved to be true more than once. It's not fair to any member to be singled out as a leader in A.A. and to always quote that member on the A.A. program. If that person should fail, where would I be? *Can I afford to be tipped over by the failure of my ideal?*

Meditation for the Day

You must always remember that you are weak but that God is strong. God knows all about your weakness. He hears every cry for mercy, every sign of weakness, every plea for help, every sorrow over failure, every weakness felt and expressed. We only fail when we trust too much to our own strength. Do not feel bad about your weakness. When you are weak, that is when God is strong to help you. Trust God enough, and your weakness will not matter. God is always strong to save.

Prayer for the Day

I pray that I may learn to lean on God's strength. I pray that I may know that my weakness is God's opportunity.

OCT. 8—A.A. Thought for the Day

There is such a thing as being too loyal to any *one* group. Do I feel put out when another group starts and some members of my group leave it and branch out into new territory? Or do I send them out with my blessing? Do I visit that new offshoot group and help it along? Or do I sulk in my own tent? A.A. grows by the starting of new groups all the time. I must realize that it's a good thing for a large group to split up into smaller ones, even if it means that the large group—my own group—becomes smaller. *Am I always ready to help new groups?*

Meditation for the Day

Pray—and keep praying until it brings peace and serenity and a feeling of communion with One who is near and ready to help. The thought of God is balm for our hates and fears. In praying to God, we find healing for hurt feelings and resentments. In thinking of God, doubts and fears leave us. Instead of those doubts and fears, there will flow into our hearts such faith and love as is beyond the power of material things to give, and such peace as the world can neither give nor take away. And with God, we can have the tolerance to live and let live.

Prayer for the Day

I pray that I may have true tolerance and understanding. I pray that I may keep striving for these difficult things.

OCT. 9—A.A. Thought for the Day

Am I willing to be bored sometimes at meetings? Am I willing to listen to much repetition of A.A. principles? Am I willing to hear the same thing over and over again? Am I willing to listen to a long blow by blow personal story, because it might help some new member? Am I willing to sit quietly and listen to long-winded members go into every detail of their past? Am I willing to take it, because it is doing them good to get it off their chest? My feelings are not too important. The good of A.A. comes first, even if it is not always comfortable for me. *Have I learned to take it?*

Meditation for the Day

God would draw us all closer to Him in the bonds of the spirit. He would have all people drawn closer to each other in the bonds of the spirit. God, the great Spirit of the universe, of which each of our own spirits is a small part, must want unity between Himself and all His children. "Unity of the spirit in the bonds of peace." Each experience of our life, of joy, of sorrow, of danger, of safety, of difficulty, of success, of hardship, of ease, each should be accepted as part of our common lot, in the bonds of the spirit.

Prayer for the Day

I pray that I may welcome the bonds of true fellowship. I pray that I may be brought closer to unity with God and other people.

OCT. 10—A.A. Thought for the Day

When new members come into my A.A. group, do I make a special effort to make them feel at home? Do I put myself out to listen to them, even if their ideas of A.A. are vague? Do I make it a habit to talk to all new members myself, or do I often leave that to someone else? I may not be able to help them, but, then, again it may be something that I might say that would put them on the right track. When I see any members sitting alone, do I put myself out to be nice to them, or do I stay among my own special group of friends and leave them out in the cold? *Are all new A.A.s my responsibility?*

Meditation for the Day

You are God's servant. Serve Him cheerfully and readily. Nobody likes a servant who avoids extra work, who complains about being called from one task to do one less enjoyable. A master would feel that he was being ill served by such a servant. But is that not how you so often serve God? View your day's work in this light. Try to do your day's work the way you believe God wants you to do it, never shirking any responsibility and often going out of your way to be of service.

Prayer for the Day

I pray that I may be a good servant. I pray that I may be willing to go out of my way to be of service.

OCT. 11—A.A. Thought for the Day

How good a sponsor am I? When I bring new members to a meeting, do I feel that my responsibility has ended? Or do I make it my job to stay with them until they have either become good members of A.A. or have found another sponsor? If they don't show up for a meeting, do I say to myself: "Well they've had it put up to them, so if they don't want it, there's nothing more I can do?" Or do I look them up and find out whether there is a reason for their absences or that they don't want A.A.? Do I go out of my way to find out if there is anything more I can do to help? *Am I a good sponsor?*

Meditation for the Day

"First be reconciled to your brother and then come and offer your gift to God." First I must get right with other people and then I can get right with God. If I hold a resentment against someone, which I find it very difficult to overcome, I should try to put something else constructive into my mind. I should pray for the one against whom I hold the resentment. I should put that person in God's hands and let God show him or her the way to live. "If a man say: 'I love God' and hateth his brother, he is a liar, for he that loveth not his brother whom he hath seen, how can he love God whom he hath not seen?"

Prayer for the Day

I pray that I may see something good in every person, even one I dislike, and that I may let God develop the good in that person.

OCT. 12—A.A. Thought for the Day

Am I still on a "free ride" in A.A.? Am I all get and no give? Do I go to meetings and always sit in the back row and let the others do all the work? Do I think it's enough just because I'm sober and can rest on my laurels? If so, I haven't gone very far in the program, nor am I getting nearly enough of what it has to offer. I will be a weak member until I get in there and help carry the load. I must eventually get off the bench and get into the game. I'm not just a spectator; I'm supposed to be one of the team. *Do I go in there and carry the ball?*

Meditation for the Day

Try to be thankful for whatever vision you have. Try to perform, in the little things, faithful service to God and others. Do your small part every day in a spirit of service to God. Be a doer of God's word, not a hearer only. In your daily life try to keep faith with God. Every day brings a new opportunity to be of some use. Even when you are tempted to rest or let things go or to evade the issue, make it a habit to meet the issue squarely as a challenge and not to hold back.

Prayer for the Day

I pray that I may perform each task faithfully. I pray that I may meet each issue of life squarely and not hold back.

OCT. 13—A.A. Thought for the Day

A.A. work is one hundred percent voluntary. It depends on each and every one of our members to volunteer to do his or her share. Newcomers can sit on the sidelines until they have got over their nervousness and confusion. They have a right to be helped by all, until they can stand on their own feet. But the time inevitably comes when they have to speak up and volunteer to do their share in meetings and in twelfth-step work. Until that time comes, they are not a vital part of A.A. They are only in the process of being assimilated. *Has my time come to volunteer?*

Meditation for the Day

God's kingdom on earth is growing slowly, like a seed in the ground. In the growth of His kingdom there is always progress among the few who are out ahead of the crowd. Keep striving for something better and there can be no stagnation in your life. Eternal life, abundant life is yours for the seeking. Do not misspend time over past failures. Count the lessons learned from failures as rungs upon the ladder of progress. Press onward toward the goal.

Prayer for the Day

I pray that I may be willing to grow. I pray that I may keep stepping up on the rungs of the ladder of life.

OCT. 14—A.A. Thought for the Day

How big a part of my life is A.A.? Is it just one of my activities and a small one at that? Do I only go to A.A. meetings now and then and sometimes never go at all? Do I think of A.A. only occasionally? Am I reticent about mentioning the subject of A.A. to people who might need help? Or does A.A. fill a large part of my life? Is it the foundation of my whole life? Where would I be without A.A.? Does everything I have and do depend on my A.A. foundation? *Is A.A. the foundation on which I build my life?*

Meditation for the Day

Lay upon God your failures and mistakes and shortcomings. Do not dwell upon your failures, upon the fact that in the past you have been nearer a beast than an angel. You have a mediator between you and God—your growing faith—which can lift you up from the mire and point you toward the heavens. You can still be reconciled with the spirit of God. You can still regain your harmony with the Divine Principle of the universe.

Prayer for the Day

I pray that I may not let the beast in me hold me back from my spiritual destiny. I pray that I may rise and walk upright.

OCT. 15—A.A. Thought for the Day

Am I deeply grateful to A.A. for what it has done for me in regaining my sobriety and opening up an entirely new life for me? A.A. has made it possible for me to carry on other interests in business and in various other associations with people. It has made a full life possible for me. It would perhaps be wrong if all my activities were limited to A.A. work. It has made a well-rounded life possible for me in work, in play, and in hobbies of various kinds. But will I desert A.A. because of this? Will I accept a diploma and become a graduate of A.A.? *Do I realize that I could have nothing worth while without A.A.?*

Meditation for the Day

There is only one way to get full satisfaction from life and that is to live the way you believe God wants you to live. Live with God in that secret place of the spirit and you will have a feeling of being on the right road. You will have a deep sense of satisfaction. The world will have meaning and you will have a place in the world, work to do that counts in the eternal order of things. Many things will work for you and with you, as long as you feel you are on God's side.

Prayer for the Day

I pray that I may have a sense of the eternal value of the work I do. I pray that I may not only work for now, but also for eternity.

OCT. 16—A.A. Thought for the Day

How seriously do I take my obligations to A.A.? Have I taken all the good I can get out of it and then let my obligations slide? Or do I constantly feel a deep debt of gratitude and a deep sense of loyalty to the whole A.A. movement? Am I not only grateful but also proud to be a part of such a wonderful fellowship, which is doing such marvelous work among alcoholics? Am I glad to be a part of the great work that A.A. is doing and do I feel a deep obligation to carry on that work at every opportunity? *Do I feel that I owe A.A. my loyalty and devotion?*

Meditation for the Day

If your heart is right, your world will be right. The beginning of all reform must be in yourself. It's not what happens to you, it's how you take it. However restricted your circumstances, however little you may be able to remedy financial affairs, you can always turn to your inward self and, seeing something not in order there, seek to right it. And as all reform is from within outward, you will always find that the outward is improved as the inward is improved. As you improve yourself, your outward circumstances will change for the better. The power released from within yourself will change your outward life.

Prayer for the Day

I pray that the hidden power within me may be released. I pray that I may not imprison the spirit that is within me.

OCT. 17—A.A. Thought for the Day

What am I going to do *today* for A.A.? Is there someone I should call up on the telephone or someone I should go to see? Is there a letter I should write? Is there an opportunity somewhere to advance the work of A.A. which I have been putting off or neglecting? If so, will I do it *today*? Will I be done with procrastination and do what I have to do today? Tomorrow may be too late. How do I know there will be a tomorrow for me? How about getting out of my easy chair and getting going? *Do I feel that A.A. depends partly on me today?*

Meditation for the Day

Today look upward toward God, not downward toward yourself. Look away from unpleasant surroundings, from lack of beauty, from the imperfections in yourself and in those around you. In your unrest, behold God's calmness; in your impatience, God's patience; in your limitations, God's perfection. Looking upward toward God, your spirit will begin to grow. Then others will see something in you that they also want. As you grow in the spiritual life, you will be enabled to do many things that seemed too hard for you before.

Prayer for the Day

I pray that I may keep my eyes trained above the horizon of myself. I pray that I may see infinite possibilities for spiritual growth.

OCT. 18—A.A. Thought for the Day

Have I got over most of my sensitiveness, my feelings which are too easily hurt, and my just plain laziness and self-satisfaction? Am I willing to go all out for A.A. at no matter what cost to my precious self? Is my own comfort more important to me than doing the things that need to be done? Have I got to the point where what happens to me is not so important? Can I face up to things that are embarrassing or uncomfortable if they are the right things to do for the good of A.A.? Have I given A.A. just a small piece of myself? *Am I willing to give all of myself whenever necessary?*

Meditation for the Day

Not until you have failed can you learn true humility. Humility arises from a deep sense of gratitude to God for giving you the strength to rise above past failures. Humility is not inconsistent with self-respect. The true person has self-respect and the respect of others and yet is humble. The humble person is tolerant of others' failings, and does not have a critical attitude toward the foibles of others. Humble people are hard on themselves and easy on others.

Prayer for the Day

I pray that I may be truly humble and yet have self-respect. I pray that I may see the good in myself as well as the bad.

OCT. 19—A.A. Thought for the Day

Do I realize that I do not know how much time I have left? It may be later than I think. Am I going to do the things that I know I should do before my time runs out? By the way, what is my purpose for the rest of my life? Do I realize all I have to make up for in my past wasted life? Do I know that I am living on borrowed time and that I would not have even this much time left without A.A. and the grace of God? *Am I going to make what time I have left count for A.A.?*

Meditation for the Day

We can believe that somehow the cry of the human soul is never unheard by God. It may be that God hears the cry, even if we fail to notice God's response to it. The human cry for help must always evoke a response of some sort from God. It may be that our failure to discern properly keeps us unaware of the response. But one thing we can believe is that the grace of God is always available for every human being who sincerely calls for help. Many changed lives are living proofs of this fact.

Prayer for the Day

I pray that I may trust God to answer my prayer as He sees fit. I pray that I may be content with whatever form that answer may take.

OCT. 20—A.A. Thought for the Day

For the past few weeks we have been asking ourselves some searching questions. We have not been able to answer them all as we would like. But on the right answers to these questions will depend the usefulness and effectiveness of our lives and to some extent the usefulness and effectiveness of the whole A.A. movement. It all boils down to this: I owe a deep debt to A.A. and to grace of God. Am I going to do all I can to repay that debt? Let us search our souls, make our decisions, and act accordingly. Any real success we have in life will depend on that. Now is the time to put our conclusions into effect. *What am I going to do about it?*

Meditation for the Day

"Our Lord and our God, be it done unto us according to Thy will." Simple acceptance of God's will in whatever happens is the key to abundant living. We must continue to pray. "Not my will but Thy will be done." It may not turn out the way you want it to, but it will be the best way in the long run, because it is God's way. If you decide to accept whatever happens as God's will for yourself, whatever it may be, your burdens will be lighter. Try to see in all things some fulfillment of the Divine Intent.

Prayer for the Day

I pray that I may see the working out of God's will in my life. I pray that I may be content with whatever He wills for me.

OCT. 21—A.A. Thought for the Day

Now that we have considered the obligations of real, working members of A.A., let us examine what the rewards are that have come to us as a result of our new way of living. First, I understand myself more than I ever did before. I have learned what was the matter with me and I know now a lot of what makes me tick. I will never be alone again. I am just one of many who have the illness of alcoholism and one of many who have learned what to do about it. I am not an odd fish or a square peg in a round hole. I seem to have found my right place in the world. *Am I beginning to understand myself?*

Meditation for the Day

"Behold, I stand at the door and knock. If any man hear my voice and open the door, I will come in to him and will remain with him and him with me." The knocking of God's spirit, asking to come into your life, is due to no merit of yours, though it is in response to the longing of your heart. Keep a listening ear, an ear bent to catch the sound of the gentle knocking at the door of your heart by the spirit of God. Then open the door of your heart and let God's spirit come in.

Prayer for the Day

I pray that I may let God's spirit come into my heart. I pray that it may fill me with an abiding peace.

OCT. 22—A.A. Thought for the Day

Second, I am content to face the rest of my life without alcohol. I have made the great decision once and for all. I have surrendered as gracefully as possible to the inevitable. I hope I have no more reservations. I hope that nothing can happen to me now that would justify my taking a drink. No death of a dear one. No great calamity in any area of my life should justify me in drinking. Even if I were on some desert isle, far from the rest of the world, but not far from God, should I ever feel it right to drink. For me, alcohol is out—period. I will always be safe unless I take that first drink. *Am I fully resigned to this fact?*

Meditation for the Day

Day by day we should slowly build up an unshakable faith in a Higher Power and in that Power's ability to give us all the help we need. By having these quiet times each morning, we start each day with a renewing of our faith, until it becomes almost a part of us and is a strong habit. We should keep furnishing the quiet places of our souls with all the furniture of faith. We should try to fill our thoughts each day with all that is harmonious and good, beautiful, and enduring.

Prayer for the Day

I pray that I may build a house in my soul for the spirit of God to dwell in. I pray that I may come at last to an unshakable faith.

OCT. 23—A.A. Thought for the Day

Third, I have learned how to be honest.
What a relief! No more ducking or
dodging. No more tall tales. No more
pretending to be what I am not. My
cards are on the table, for all the
world to see. "I am what I am," as Pop-
eye used to say in the comics. I have
had an unsavory past. I am sorry, yes.
But it cannot be changed now. All that
is yesterday and is done. But now my
life is an open book. Come and look at
it, if you want to. I'm trying to do the
best I can. I will fail often, but I won't
make excuses. I will face things as they
are and not run away. *Am I really
honest?*

Meditation for the Day

Though it may seem a paradox, we must believe
in spiritual forces which we cannot see more than
in material things which we can see, if we are
going to truly live. In the last analysis, the universe consists more of thought or mathematical
formulas than it does of matter as we understand
it. Between one human being and another only
spiritual forces will suffice to keep them in
harmony. These spiritual forces we know, because we can see their results although we cannot
see them. A changed life—a new personality—
results from the power of unseen spiritual forces
working in us and through us.

Prayer for the Day

I pray that I may believe in the Unseen. I pray
that I may be convinced by the results of the
Unseen which I do see.

OCT. 24—A.A. Thought for the Day

Fourth, I have turned to a Power greater than myself. Thank God, I am no longer at the center of the universe. All the world does not revolve around me any longer. I am only one among many. I have a Father in heaven and I am only one of His children and a small one at that. But I can depend on Him to show me what to do and to give me the strength to do it. I am on the Way and the whole power of the universe is behind me when I do the right thing. I do not have to depend entirely on myself any longer. With God, I can face anything. *Is my life in the hands of God?*

Meditation for the Day

The grace of God is an assurance against all evil. It holds out security to the believing soul. The grace of God means safety in the midst of evil. You can be kept unspotted by the world through the power of His grace. You can have a new life of power. But only in close contact with the grace of God is its power realized. In order to realize it and benefit from it, you must have daily quiet communion with God, so that the power of His grace will come unhindered into your soul.

Prayer for the Day

I pray that I may be kept from evil by the grace of God. I pray that henceforth I will try to keep myself more unspotted by the world.

OCT. 25—A.A. Thought for the Day

Fifth, I have learned to live one day at a time. I have finally realized the great fact that all I have is *now*. This sweeps away all vain regret and it makes my thoughts of the future free of fear. Now is mine. I can do what I want with it. I own it, for better or worse. What I do now, in this present moment, is what makes up my life. My whole life is only a succession of nows. I will take this moment, which has been given to me by the grace of God, and I will do something with it. What I do with each now, will make me or break me. *Am I living in the now?*

Meditation for the Day

We should work at overcoming ourselves, our selfish desires and our self-centeredness. This can never be fully accomplished. We can never become entirely unselfish. But we can come to realize that we are not at the center of the universe and that everything does not revolve around us at the center. I am only one cell in a vast network of human cells. I can at least make the effort to conquer the self-life and seek daily to obtain more and more of this self-conquest. "He that overcomes himself is greater than he who conquers a city."

Prayer for the Day

I pray that I may strive to overcome my selfishness. I pray that I may achieve the right perspective of my position in the world.

OCT. 26—A.A. Thought for the Day

Sixth, I have A.A. meetings to go to, thank God. Where would I go without them? Where would I be without them? Where would I find the sympathy, the understanding, the fellowship, the companionship? Nowhere else in the world. I have come home. I have found the place where I belong. I no longer wander alone over the face of the earth. I am at peace and at rest. What a great gift has been given me by A.A.! I do not deserve it. But it is nevertheless mine. I have a home at last. I am content. *Do I thank God every day for the A.A. fellowship?*

Meditation for the Day

Walk all the way with another person and with God. Do not go part of the way and then stop. Do not push God so far into the background that He has no effect on your life. Walk all the way with Him. Make a good companion of God, by praying to Him often during the day. Do not let your contact with Him be broken for too long a period. Work all the way with God and with other people, along the path of life, wherever it may lead you.

Prayer for the Day

I pray that I may walk in companionship with God along the way. I pray that I may keep my feet upon the path that leads upward.

Seventh, I can help other alcoholics. I am of some use in the world. I have a purpose in life. I am worth something at last. My life has a direction and a meaning. All that feeling of futility is gone. I can do something worthwhile. God has given me a new lease on life so that I can help other alcoholics. He has let me live through all the hazards of my alcoholic life to bring me at last to a place of real usefulness in the world. He has let me live for this. This is my opportunity and my destiny. I am worth something! *Will I give as much of my life as I can to A.A.?*

Meditation for the Day

All of us have our own battle to win, the battle between the material view of life and the spiritual view. Something must guide our lives. Will it be wealth, pride, selfishness, greed or will it be faith, honesty, purity, unselfishness, love, and service? Each one has a choice. We can choose good or evil. We cannot choose both. Are we going to keep striving until we win the battle? If we win the victory, we can believe that even God in His heaven will rejoice.

Prayer for the Day

I pray that I may choose the good and resist the evil. I pray that I will not be a loser in the battle for righteousness.

OCT. 28—A.A. Thought for the Day

What other rewards have come to me as a result of my new way of living? Each one of us can answer this question in many ways. My relationship with my husband or my wife is on an entirely new plane. The total selfishness is gone and more cooperation has taken its place. My home is a home again. Understanding has taken the place of misunderstanding, recriminations, bickering, and resentment. A new companionship has developed which bodes well for the future. "There are homes where fires burn and there is bread, lamps are lit and prayers are said. Though people falter through the dark and nations grope, with God Himself back of these little homes, we still can hope." *Have I come home?*

Meditation for the Day

We can bow to God's will in anticipation of the thing happening which will, in the long run, be the best for all concerned. It may not always seem the best thing at the present time, but we cannot see as far ahead as God can. We do not know how His plans are laid, we only need to believe that if we trust Him and accept whatever happens as His will in a spirit of faith, everything will work out for the best in the end.

Prayer for the Day

I pray that I may not ask to see the distant scene. I pray that one step may be enough for me.

OCT. 29—A.A. Thought for the Day

My relationships with my children have greatly improved. Those children who saw me drunk and were ashamed, those children who turned away in fear and even loathing have seen me sober and like me, have turned to me in confidence and trust and have forgotten the past as best they could. They have given me a chance for companionship that I had completely missed. I am their father or their mother now. Not just "that person that Mom or Dad married and God knows why." I am a part of my home now. *Have I found something that I had lost?*

Meditation for the Day

Our true measure of success in life is the measure of spiritual progress that we have revealed in our lives. Others should be able to see a demonstration of God's will in our lives. The measure of His will that those around us have seen worked out in our daily living is the measure of our true success. We can do our best to be a demonstration each day of the power of God in human lives, an example of the working out of the grace of God in the hearts of men and women.

Prayer for the Day

I pray that I may so live that others will see in me something of the working out of the will of God. I pray that my life may be a demonstration of what the grace of God can do.

OCT. 30—A.A. Thought for the Day

I have real friends, where I had none before. My drinking companions could hardly be called my real friends, though when drunk we seemed to have the closest kind of friendship. My idea of friendship has changed. Friends are no longer people whom I can use for my own pleasure or profit. Friends are now people who understand me and I them, whom I can help and who can help me to live a better life. I have learned not to hold back and wait for friends to come to me, but to go half way and to be met half way, openly and freely. *Does friendship have a new meaning for me?*

Meditation for the Day

There is a time for everything. We should learn to wait patiently until the right time comes. Easy does it. We waste our energies in trying to get things before we are ready to have them, before we have earned the right to receive them. A great lesson we have to learn is how to wait with patience. We can believe that all our life is a preparation for something better to come when we have earned the right to it. We can believe that God has a plan for our lives and that this plan will work out in the fullness of time.

Prayer for the Day

I pray that I may learn the lesson of waiting patiently. I pray that I may not expect things until I have earned the right to have them.

OCT. 31—A.A. Thought for the Day

I have more peace and contentment. Life has fallen into place. The pieces of the jigsaw puzzle have found their correct position. Life is whole, all of one piece. I am not cast hither and yon on every wind of circumstance or fancy. I am no longer a dry leaf cast up and away by the breeze. I have found my place of rest, my place where I belong. I am content. I do not vainly wish for things I cannot have. I have "the serenity to accept the things I cannot change, courage to change the things I can, and wisdom to know the difference." *Have I found contentment in A.A.?*

Meditation for the Day

In all of us there is an inner consciousness that tells of God, an inner voice that speaks to our hearts. It is a voice that speaks to us intimately, personally, in a time of quiet meditation. It is like a lamp unto our feet and a light unto our path. We can reach out into the darkness and figuratively touch the hand of God. As the Big Book puts it: "Deep down in every man, woman and child is the fundamental idea of God. We can find the Great Reality deep down within us. And when we find it, it changes our whole attitude toward life."

Prayer for the Day

I pray that I may follow the leading of the inner voice. I pray that I may not turn a deaf ear to the urging of my conscience.

NOV. 1—A.A. Thought for the Day

I have hope. That magic thing that I
had lost or misplaced. The future looks
dark no more. I do not even look at it,
except when necessary to make plans.
I try to let the future take care of itself. The future will be made up of
todays and todays, stretching out as
short as now and as long as eternity.
Hope is justified by many right nows,
by the rightness of the present. Nothing
can happen to me that God does not
will for me. I can hope for the best, as
long as I have what I have and it is
good. *Have I hope?*

Meditation for the Day

Faith is the messenger that bears your prayers
to God. Prayer can be like incense, rising
ever higher and higher. The prayer of faith
is the prayer of trust that feels the presence
of God which it rises to meet. It can be sure
of some response from God. We can say
a prayer of thanks to God every day for
His grace, which has kept us on the right
way and allowed us to start living the good
life. So we should pray to God with faith
and trust and gratitude.

Prayer for the Day

I pray that I may feel sure of some response
to my prayers. I pray that I may be content
with whatever form that response takes.

NOV. 2—A.A. Thought for the Day

I have faith. That thing that makes the world seem right. That thing that makes sense at last. That awareness of the Divine Principle in the universe which holds it all together and gives it unity and purpose and goodness and meaning. Life is no longer ashes in my mouth or bitter to the taste. It is all one glorious whole, because God is holding it together. Faith—that leap into the unknown, the venture into what lies beyond our ken, that which brings untold rewards of peace and serenity. *Have I faith?*

Meditation for the Day

Keep yourself like an empty vessel for God to fill. Keep pouring out yourself to help others so that God can keep filling you up with His spirit. The more you give, the more you will have for yourself. God will see that you are kept filled as long as you are giving to others. But if you selfishly try to keep all for yourself, you are soon blocked off from God, your source of supply, and you will become stagnant. To be clear, a lake must have an inflow and an outflow.

Prayer for the Day

I pray that I may keep pouring out what I receive. I pray that I may keep the stream clear and flowing.

NOV. 3—A.A. Thought for the Day

I have charity, another word for love. That right kind of love which is not selfish passion but an unselfish, outgoing desire to help other people. To do what is best for the other person, to put what is best for him or her above my own desires. To put God first, the other person second, and myself last. Charity is gentle, kind, understanding, long-suffering, and full of desire to serve. A.A. has given me this. What I do for myself is lost; what I do for others may be written somewhere in eternity. *Have I charity?*

Meditation for the Day

"Ask what you will and it shall be done unto you." God has unlimited power. There is no limit to what His power can do in human hearts. But we must will to have God's power and we must ask God for it. God's power is blocked off from us by our indifference to it. We can go along our own selfish way without calling on God's help and we get no power. But when we trust in God, we can will to have the power we need. When we sincerely ask God for it, we get it abundantly.

Prayer for the Day

I pray that I may will to have God's power. I pray that I may keep praying for the strength I need.

NOV. 4—A.A. Thought for the Day

I can do things that I never did before. Liquor took away my initiative and my ambition. I couldn't get up the steam to start anything. I let things slide. When I was drunk, I was too inert to even comb my hair. Now I can sit down and do something. I can write letters that need to be written. I can make telephone calls that should be made. I can work in my garden. I can pursue my hobbies. I have the urge to create something, that creative urge that was completely stifled by alcohol. I am free to achieve again. *Have I recovered my initiative?*

Meditation for the Day

"In Thy presence is fullness of joy. At Thy right hand are pleasures forever." We cannot find true happiness by looking for it. Seeking pleasure does not bring happiness in the long run, only disillusionment. Do not seek to have this fullness of joy by seeking pleasure. It cannot be done that way. Happiness is a by-product of living the right kind of a life. True happiness comes as a result of living in all respects the way you believe God wants you to live, with regard to yourself and to other people.

Prayer for the Day

I pray that I may not always seek pleasure as a goal. I pray that I may be content with the happiness that comes when I do the right thing.

NOV. 5—A.A. Thought for the Day

During our thoughts about the rewards that have come to us as a result of our new way of living, we find that we have new kinds of homes, new relationships with our husbands or wives and our children. Also peace, contentment, hope, faith, charity, and new ambition. What are some of the things we have lost? Each one of us can answer this question in many ways. I have lost much of my fear. It used to control me; it was my master. It paralyzed my efforts. Fear always got me down. It made me an introvert, an ingrown person. When fear was replaced by faith, I got well. *Have I lost some of my fears?*

Meditation for the Day

The world would sooner be brought close to God, His will would sooner be done on earth, if all who acknowledge Him gave themselves unreservedly to being used by Him. God can use every human being as a channel for divine love and power. What delays the bringing of the world closer to God is the backwardness of His followers. If each one lived each day for God and allowed God to work through Him, then the world would soon be drawn much closer to God, its Founder and Preserver.

Prayer for the Day

I pray that I may be used as a channel to express the Divine Love. I pray that I may so live as to bring God's spirit closer to the world.

NOV. 6—A.A. Thought for the Day

Fear and worry had me down. They were increased by my drinking. I worried about what I had done when I was drunk. I was afraid of what the consequences might be. I was afraid to face people because of the fear of being found out. Fear kept me in hot water all the time. I was a nervous wreck from fear and worry. I was a tied-up bundle of nerves. I had a fear of failure, of the future, of growing old, of sickness, of hangovers, of suicide. I had a wrong set of ideas and attitudes. When A.A. told me to surrender these fears and worries to a Higher Power, I did so. I now try to think faith instead of fear. *Have I put faith in place of fear?*

Meditation for the Day

Spiritual power is God in action. God can only act through human beings. Whenever you, however weak you may be, allow God to act through you, then all you think and say and do is spiritually powerful. It is not you alone who produces a change in the lives of others! It is also the Divine Spirit in you and working through you. Power is God in action. God can use you as a tool to accomplish miracles in people's lives.

Prayer for the Day

I pray that I may try to let God's power act through me today. I pray that I may get rid of those blocks which keep His power from me.

NOV. 7—A.A. Thought for the Day

I have lost many of my resentments. I have found that getting even with people doesn't do any good. When we try to get revenge, instead of making us feel better, it leaves us frustrated and cheated. Instead of punishing our enemies, we've only hurt our own peace of mind. It does not pay to nurse a grudge, it hurts us more than anyone else. Hate causes frustration, inner conflict, and neurosis. If we give out hate, we will become hateful. If we are resentful, we will be resented. If we do not like people, we will not be liked by people. Revengefulness is a powerful poison in our systems. *Have I lost my resentments?*

Meditation for the Day

It is not so much you, as the grace of God that is in you, that helps those around you. If you would help even those you dislike, you have to see that there is nothing in you to block the way, to keep God's grace from using you. Your own pride and selfishness are the greatest blocks. Keep those out of the way and God's grace will flow through you into the lives of others. Then all who come in contact with you can be helped in some way. Keep the channel open, free from those things that make your life futile and ineffective.

Prayer for the Day

I pray that all who come in contact with me will feel better for it. I pray that I may be careful not to harbor those things in my heart that put people off.

NOV. 8—A.A. Thought for the Day

I have lost much of my inferiority complex. I was always trying to escape from life. I did not want to face reality. I was full of self-pity. I was constantly sorry for myself. I tried to avoid all responsibilities. I did not feel that I would handle the responsibilities of my family or my work. Owing to my inferiority complex, I was eager to be free of all responsibilities. I wanted to drift; I wanted to be "on the beach." A.A. showed me how to get over my feeling of inferiority. It made me want to accept responsibility again. *Have I lost my inferiority complex?*

Meditation for the Day

"One thing I do, forgetting those things which are behind, and reaching forth unto those things that are before, I press onward toward the goal." We should forget those things which are behind us and press onward toward something better. We can believe that God has forgiven us for all our past sins, provided we are honestly trying to live today the way we believe He wants us to live. We can wipe clean the slate of the past. We can start today with a clean slate and go forward with confidence toward the goal that has been set before us.

Prayer for the Day

I pray that I may drop off the load of the past. I pray that I may start today with a light heart and a new confidence.

NOV. 9—A.A. Thought for the Day

I have learned to be less negative and more positive. I used to take a negative view of almost everything. Most people, in my estimation, were bluffing. There seemed to be very little good in the world, but lots of hypocrisy and sham. People could not be trusted. They would "take you" if they could. All church-goers were partly hypocrites. It seemed I should take everything "with a grain of salt." That was my general attitude toward life. Now I am more positive. I believe in people and in their capabilities. There is much love and truth and honesty in the world. I try not to run people down. Life now seems worthwhile and it is good to live. *Am I less negative and more positive?*

Meditation for the Day

Think of God as a Great Friend and try to realize the wonder of that friendship. When you give God not only worship, obedience, and allegiance, but also close companionship, then He becomes your friend, even as you are His. You can feel that He and you are working together. He can do things for you and you can do things for Him. Your prayers become more real to you when you feel that God counts on your friendship and you count on His.

Prayer for the Day

I pray that I may think of God as my Friend. I pray that I may feel that I am working for Him and with Him.

NOV. 10—A.A. Thought for the Day

I am less self-centered. The world used to revolve around me at the center. I cared more about myself, my own needs and desires, my own pleasure, my own way, than I did about the whole rest of the world. What happened to me was more important than anything else I could think of. I was selfishly trying to be happy and therefore I was unhappy most of the time. I have found that selfishly seeking pleasure does not bring true happiness. Thinking of myself all the time cut me off from the best in life. A.A. taught me to care less about myself and more about the other person. *Am I less self-centered?*

Meditation for the Day

When something happens to upset you and you are discouraged, try to feel that life's difficulties and troubles are not intended to arrest your progress in the spiritual life, but to test your strength and to increase your determination to keep going. Whatever it is that must be met, you are to either overcome it or use it. Nothing should daunt you for long, nor should any difficulty entirely overcome or conquer you. God's strength will always be there, waiting for you to use it. Nothing can be too great to be overcome, or if not overcome, then used.

Prayer for the Day

I pray that I may know that there can be no failure with God. I pray that with His help I may live a more victorious life.

NOV. 11—A.A. Thought for the Day

When I think of all who have gone before me, I realize that I am only one, not very important, person. What happens to me is not so very important after all. And A.A. has taught me to be more outgoing, to seek friendship by going at least half way, to have a sincere desire to help. I have more self-respect now that I have less sensitiveness. I have found that the only way to live comfortably with myself is to take a real interest in others. *Do I realize that I am not so important after all?*

Meditation for the Day

As you look back over your life, it is not too difficult to believe that what you went through was for a purpose, to prepare you for some valuable work in life. Everything in your life may well have been planned by God to make you of some use in the world. Each person's life is like the pattern of a mosaic. Each thing that happened to you is like one tiny stone in the mosaic, and each tiny stone fits into the perfected pattern of the mosaic of your life, which has been designed by God.

Prayer for the Day

I pray that I may not need to see the whole design of my life. I pray that I may trust the Designer.

NOV. 12—A.A. Thought for the Day

I am less critical of other people, inside and outside of A.A. I used to run people down all the time. I realize now that it was because I wanted unconsciously to build myself up. I was envious of people who lived normal lives. I couldn't understand why I couldn't be like them. And so I ran them down. I called them sissies or hypocrites. I was always looking for faults in the other person. I loved to tear down what I called "a stuffed shirt" or "a snob." I have found that I can never make a person any better by criticism. A.A. has taught me this. *Am I less critical of people?*

Meditation for the Day

You must admit your helplessness before your prayer for help will be heard by God. Your own need must be recognized before you can ask God for the strength to meet that need. But once that need is recognized, your prayer is heard above all the music of heaven. It is not theological arguments that solve the problems of the questing soul, but the sincere cry of that soul to God for strength and the certainty of that soul that the cry will be heard and answered.

Prayer for the Day

I pray that I may send my voiceless cry for help out into the void. I pray that I may feel certain that it will be heard somewhere, somehow.

NOV. 13—A.A. Thought for the Day

Who am I to judge other people? Have I proved by my great success in life that I know all the answers? Exactly the opposite. Until I came into A.A., my life could be called a failure. I made all the mistakes one could make. I took all the wrong roads there were to take. On the basis of my record, am I a fit person to be a judge of other people? Hardly. In A.A. I have learned not to judge people. I am so often wrong. Let the results of what they do judge them. It's not up to me. *Am I less harsh in my judgment of people?*

Meditation for the Day

In our time of meditation, we again seem to hear: "Come unto me, all ye that are weary and heavy laden, and I will give you rest." Again and again we seem to hear God saying this to us. "Come unto me" for the solution of every problem, for the overcoming of every temptation, for the calming of every fear, for all our need, physical, mental, or spiritual, but mostly "come unto me" for the strength we need to live with peace of mind and the power to be useful and effective.

Prayer for the Day

I pray that I may go to God today for those things which I need to help me live. I pray that I may find real peace of mind.

NOV. 14—A.A. Thought for the Day

A better way than judging people is to look for all the good in them. If you look hard enough and long enough, you ought to be able to find some good in every person. In A.A. I learned that my job was to try to bring out the good, not criticize the bad. Every alcoholic is used to being judged and criticized. That has never helped anyone to get sober. In A.A. we tell people they can change. We try to bring out the best in them. We encourage their good points and ignore their bad points. People are not converted by criticism. *Do I look for the good in people?*

Meditation for the Day

There must be a design for the world in the mind of God. We believe His design for the world is a universal fellowship of men and women under the fatherhood of God. The plan for your life must also be in the mind of God. In times of quiet meditation you can seek for God's guidance, for the revealing of God's plan for your day. Then you can live this day according to that guidance. Many people are not making of their lives what God meant them to be, and so they are unhappy. They have missed the design for their lives.

Prayer for the Day

I pray that I may try to follow God's design for today. I pray that I may have the sense of Divine Intent in what I do today.

NOV. 15—A.A. Thought for the Day

I am less sensitive and my feelings are less easily hurt. I no longer take myself so seriously. It didn't use to take much to insult me, to feel that I had been slighted or left on the outside. What happens to me now is not so important. One cause of our drinking was that we couldn't take it, so we escaped the unpleasant situation. We have learned to take it on the chin if necessary and smile. When I am all wrapped up in A.A., I do not notice the personal slights so much. They do not seem to matter so much. I have learned to laugh at self-pity because it's so child-ish. *Am I less sensitive?*

Meditation for the Day

God's miracle-working power is as manifest today as it was in the past. It still works miracles of change in lives and miracles of healing in twisted minds. When a person trusts wholly in God and leaves to Him the choosing of the day and hour, there is God's miracle-working power becoming manifest in that person's life. So we can trust in God and have boundless faith in His power to make us whole again, whenever He chooses.

Prayer for the Day

I pray that I may feel sure that there is nothing that God cannot accomplish in chang-ing my life. I pray that I may have faith in His miracle-working power.

NOV. 16—A.A. Thought for the Day

I have got rid of most of my inner conflicts. I was always at war with myself. I was doing things that I did not want to do. I was waking up in strange places and wondering how I got there. I was full of recklessness when I was drunk and full of remorse when I was sober. My life didn't make sense. It was full of broken resolves and frustrated hopes and plans. I was getting nowhere fast. No wonder my nerves were all shot. I was bumping up against a blank wall and I was dizzy from it. A.A. taught me how to get organized and to stop fighting against myself. *Have I got rid of inner conflicts?*

Meditation for the Day

"When two or three are gathered together in My name, there am I in the midst of them." The spirit of God comes upon His followers when they are all together at one time, in one place, and with one accord. When two or three consecrated souls are together at a meeting place, the spirit of God is there to help and guide them. Where any sincere group of people are together, reverently seeking the help of God, His power and His spirit are there to inspire them.

Prayer for the Day

I pray that I may be in accord with the members of my group. I pray that I may feel the strength of a consecrated group.

NOV. 17—A.A. Thought for the Day

Everyone has two personalities, a good and a bad. We are all dual personalities to some extent. When we were drinking, the bad personality was in control. We did things when we were drunk that we would never do when we were sober. When we sober up, we are different people. Then we wonder how we could have done the things we did. But we drink again, and again our bad side comes out. So we are back and forth, always in conflict with our other selves, always in a stew. This division of our selves is not good; we must somehow become unified. We do this by giving ourselves wholeheartedly to A.A. and to sobriety. *Have I become unified?*

Meditation for the Day

"Well done, thou good and faithful servant. Enter into the joy of Thy Lord." These words are for many ordinary people whom the world may pass by, unrecognizing. Not to the world-famed, the proud, the wealthy, are these words spoken, but to the quiet followers who serve God unobtrusively yet faithfully, who bear their crosses bravely and put a smiling face to the world. "Enter into the joy of Thy Lord." Pass into that fuller spiritual life, which is a life of joy and peace.

Prayer for the Day

I pray that I may not desire the world's applause. I pray that I may not seek rewards for doing what I believe is right.

NOV. 18—A.A. Thought for the Day

I have got over my procrastination. I was always putting things off till tomorrow and as a result they never got done. "There is always another day" was my motto instead of "Do it now." Under the influence of alcohol, I had grandiose plans. When I was sober I was too busy getting over my drunk to start anything. "Some day I'll do that" —but I never did it. In A.A. I have learned that it's better to make a mistake once in a while than to never do anything at all. We learn by trial and error. But we must act now and not put it off until tomorrow. *Have I learned to do it now?*

Meditation for the Day

"Do not hide your light under a bushel. Arise and shine, for the light has come and the glory of the Lord is risen in thee." The glory of the Lord shines in the beauty of your character. It is risen in you, even though you can realize it only in part. "Now you see as in a glass darkly, but later you will see face to face." The glory of the Lord is too dazzling for mortals to see fully on earth. But some of this glory is risen in you when you try to reflect that light in your life.

Prayer for the Day

I pray that I may try to be a reflection of the Divine Light. I pray that some of its rays may shine in my life.

NOV. 19—A.A. Thought for the Day

In A.A. we do not speak much of sex. And yet putting sex in its proper place in our lives is one of the rewards that has come to us as a result of our new way of living. The Big Book says that many of us needed an overhauling there. It also says that we subjected each sex relation to this test—was it selfish or not? "We remembered always that our sex powers were God-given and therefore good, neither to be used lightly or selfishly, nor to be despised or loathed." We can ask God to mold our ideals and to help us to live up to them. We can act accordingly. *Have I got my sex life under proper control?*

Meditation for the Day

"I will lift up my eyes unto the heights whence cometh my help." Try to raise your thoughts from the depths of the sordid and mean and impure things of the earth to the heights of goodness and decency and beauty. Train your insight by trying to take the higher view. Train it more and more until distant heights become more familiar. The heights of the Lord, whence cometh your help, will become nearer and dearer and the false values of the earth will seem farther away.

Prayer for the Day

I pray that I may not keep my eyes forever downcast. I pray that I may set my sights on higher things.

NOV. 20—A.A. Thought for the Day

I no longer try to escape life through alcoholism. Drinking built up an unreal world for me and I tried to live in it. But in the morning light the real life was back again and facing it was harder than ever, because I had less resources with which to meet it. Each attempt at escape weakened my personality by the very attempt. Everyone knows that alcohol, by relaxing inhibitions, permits a flight from reality. Alcohol deadens the brain cells that preside over our highest faculties and we are off to the unreal world of drunkenness. A.A. taught me not to run away, but to face reality. *Have I given up trying to escape life?*

Meditation for the Day

In these times of quiet meditation, try more and more to set your hopes on the grace of God. Know that whatever the future may hold, it will hold more and more of good. Do not set all your hopes and desires on material things. There is weariness in an abundance of things. Set your hopes on spiritual things so that you may grow spiritually. Learn to rely on God's power more and more and in that reliance you will have an insight into the greater value of the things of the spirit.

Prayer for the Day

I pray that I may not be overwhelmed by material things. I pray that I may realize the higher value of spiritual things.

NOV. 21—A.A. Thought for the Day

I no longer waste money, but try to put it to good use. Like all of us, when I was drunk, I threw money around like I really had it. It gave me a feeling of importance—a millionaire for a day. But the morning after, with an empty wallet and perhaps also some undecipherable checks, was a sad awakening. How could I have been such a fool? How will I ever make it up? Thoughts like these get you down. When we are sober, we spend our hard-earned money as it should be spent. Although perhaps some of us could be more generous in our A.A. giving, at least we do not throw it away. *Am I making good use of my money?*

Meditation for the Day

You were meant to be at home and comfortable in the world. Yet some people live a life of quiet desperation. This is the opposite of being at home and at peace in the world. Let your peace of mind be evident to those around you. Let others see that you are comfortable, and seeing it, know that it springs from your trust in a Higher Power. The dull, hard way of resignation is not God's way. Faith takes the sting out of the winds of adversity and brings peace even in the midst of struggle.

Prayer for the Day

I pray that I may be more comfortable in my way of living. I pray that I may feel more at home and at peace within myself.

NOV. 22—A.A. Thought for the Day

I have got rid of most of my boredom. One of the hardest things that a new member of A.A. has to understand is how to stay sober and not be bored. Drinking was always the answer to all kinds of boring people or boring situations. But once you have taken up the interest of A.A., once you have given it your time and enthusiasm, boredom should not be a problem to you. A new life opens up before you that can be always interesting. Sobriety should give you so many new interests in life that you shouldn't have time to be bored. *Have I got rid of the fear of being bored?*

Meditation for the Day

"If I have not charity, I am become as sounding brass or a tinkling cymbal." Charity means to care enough about other people to really want to do something for them. A smile, a word of encouragement, a word of love, goes winged on its way, simple though it may seem, while the mighty words of an orator fall on deaf ears. Use up the odd moments of your day in trying to do some little thing to cheer up another person. Boredom comes from thinking too much about yourself.

Prayer for the Day

I pray that my day may be brightened by some little act of charity. I pray that I may try today to overcome the self-centeredness that makes me bored.

NOV. 23—A.A. Thought for the Day

I no longer refuse to do anything because I cannot do it to perfection. Many of us alcoholics use the excuse of not being able to do something perfectly to enable us to do nothing at all. We pretend to be perfectionists. We are good at telling people how a thing should be done, but when we come to the effort of doing it ourselves, we balk. We say to ourselves: "I might make a mistake, so I'd better let the whole thing slide." In A.A. we set our goals high, but that does not prevent us from trying. The mere fact that we will never fully reach these goals does not prevent us from doing the best we can. *Have I stopped hiding behind the smoke-screen of perfectionism?*

Meditation for the Day

"In the world ye shall have tribulation. But be of good cheer. I have overcome the world." Keep an undaunted spirit. Keep your spirit free and unconquered. You can be undefeated and untouched by failure and all its power, by letting your spirit overcome the world; rise above earth's turmoil into the secret chamber of perfect peace and confidence. When a challenge comes to you, remember you have God's help and nothing can wholly defeat you.

Prayer for the Day

I pray that I may have confidence and be of good cheer. I pray that I may not fear the power of failure.

NOV. 24—A.A. Thought for the Day

Instead of pretending to be perfection-ists, in A.A. we are content if we are making progress. The main thing is to be growing. We realize that perfection-ism is only a result of false pride and an excuse to save our faces. In A.A. we are willing to make mistakes and to stumble, provided we are always stumbling forward. We are not so interested in what we are as in what we are be-coming. We are on the way, not at the goal. And we will be on the way as long as we live. No A.A. has ever "arrived." But we are getting better. *Am I making progress?*

Meditation for the Day

Each new day brings an opportunity to do some little thing that will help to make a better world, that will bring God's kingdom a little nearer to being realized on earth. Take each day's happenings as opportunities for some-thing you can do for God. In that spirit, a bless-ing will attend all that you do. Offering this day's service to God, you are sharing in His work. You do not have to do great things.

Prayer for the Day

I pray that today I may do the next thing, the unselfish thing, the loving thing. I pray that I may be content with doing small things as long as they are right.

NOV. 25—A.A. Thought for the Day

I am not so envious of other people, nor am I so jealous of other people's possessions and talents. When I was drinking, I was secretly full of jealousy and envy of those people who could drink normally, who had the love and respect of their families, who lived a normal life and were accepted as equals by their friends. I pretended to myself that I was as good as they were, but I knew it wasn't so. Now I don't have to be envious any more. I try not to want what I don't deserve. I'm content with what I have earned by my efforts to live the right way. More power to those who have what I have not. At least, I'm trying. *Have I got rid of the poison of envy?*

Meditation for the Day

"My soul is restless till it finds its rest in Thee." A river flows on, until it loses itself in the sea. Our spirits long for rest in the Spirit of God. We yearn to realize a peace, a rest, a satisfaction that we have never found in the world or its pursuits. Some are not conscious of their need, and shut the doors of their spirits against the spirit of God. They are unable to have true peace.

Prayer for the Day

I pray that I may feel the divine unrest. I pray that my soul may find its rest in God.

NOV. 26—A.A. Thought for the Day

Continuing our thoughts about the rewards that have come to us as a result of our new way of living, we have found that we have got rid of many of our fears, resentments, inferiority complexes, negative points of view, self-centeredness, criticism of others, oversensitiveness, inner conflicts, the habits of procrastination, undisciplined sex, wasting money, boredom, false perfectionism, jealousy, and envy of others. We are glad to be rid of our drinking, and we are also very glad to be rid of these other things. We can now go forward in the new way of life, as shown us by A.A. *Am I ready to go forward in the new life?*

Meditation for the Day

"He that has eyes to see, let him see." To the seeing eye, the world is good. Pray for a seeing eye, to see the purpose of God in everything good. Pray for enough faith to see God's care in His dealings with you. Try to see how He has brought you safely through your past life so that now you can be of use in the world. With the eyes of faith you can see God's care and purpose everywhere.

Prayer for the Day

I pray that I may have a seeing eye. I pray that with the eye of faith I may see God's purpose everywhere.

NOV. 27—A.A. Thought for the Day

The way of A.A. is the way of sobriety, fellowship, service, and faith. Let us take up each one of these things and see if our feet are truly on the way. The first and greatest to us is sobriety. The others are built on sobriety as a foundation. We could not have the others if we did not have sobriety. We all come to A.A. to get sober, and we stay to help others get sober. We are looking for sobriety first, last, and all the time. We cannot build any decent kind of a life unless we stay sober. *Am I on the A.A. way?*

Meditation for the Day

To truly desire to do God's will, therein lies happiness for a human being. We start out wanting our own way. We want our wills to be satisfied. We take and we do not give. Gradually we find that we are not happy when we are selfish, so we begin to make allowances for other peoples' wills. But this again does not give us full happiness, and we begin to see that the only way to be truly happy is to try to do God's will. In these times of meditation, we seek to get guidance so that we can find God's will for us.

Prayer for the Day

I pray that I may subordinate my will to the will of God. I pray that I may be guided today to find His will for me.

NOV. 28—A.A. Thought for the Day

The A.A. way is the way of sobriety. A.A. is known everywhere as a method that has been successful with alcoholics. Doctors, psychiatrists, and clergymen have had some success. Some men and women have got sober all by themselves. We believe that A.A. is the most successful and happiest way to sobriety. And yet A.A. is, of course, not wholly successful. Some are unable to achieve sobriety and some slip back into alcoholism after they have had some measure of sobriety. *Am I deeply grateful to have found A.A.?*

Meditation for the Day

Gratitude to God is the theme of Thanksgiving Day. The pilgrims gathered to give thanks to God for their harvest which was pitifully small. When we look around at all the things we have today, how can we help being grateful to God? Our families, our homes, our friends, our A.A. fellowship: all these things are free gifts of God to us. "But for the grace of God," we would not have them.

Prayer for the Day

I pray that I may be very grateful today. I pray that I may not forget where I might be but for the grace of God.

NOV. 29—A.A. Thought for the Day

The A.A. way is the way of sobriety, and yet there are slips. Why do these slips occur? Why don't we all accept A.A. and stay sober from then on? There are many reasons, but it has been proved without exception that once we have become alcoholics we can never drink successfully again. This has never been disproved by any case we know of. Many alcoholics have tried drinking after a period of sobriety from a few days to a few years and no one that we know of has been successful in becoming a normal drinker. *Could I be the only exception to this rule?*

Meditation for the Day

"We are gathered together in Thy name." First, we are gathered together, bound by a common loyalty to God and to each other. Then, when this condition has been fulfilled, God is present with us. Then, when God is there and one with us, we voice a common prayer. Then it follows that our prayer will be answered according to God's will. Then, when our prayer is answered, we are bound together in a lasting fellowship of the spirit.

Prayer for the Day

I pray that I may be loyal to God and to others. I pray that my life today may be lived close to His and to theirs.

NOV. 30—A.A. Thought for the Day

We have slips in A.A. It has been said these are not slips but premeditated drunks, because we have to think about taking a drink before we actually take one. The thought always comes before the act. It is suggested that people should always get in touch with an A.A. before taking that first drink. The failure to do so makes it probable that they had decided to take the drink anyway. And yet the thoughts that come before taking a drink are often largely subconscious. People usually don't know consciously what made them do it. Therefore, the common practice is to call these things slips. *Am I on guard against wrong thinking?*

Meditation for the Day

"The eternal God is thy refuge." He is a sanctuary, a refuge from the cares of life. You can get away from the misunderstanding of others by retiring into your own place of meditation. But from yourself, from your sense of failure, your weakness, your shortcomings, whither can you flee? Only to the eternal God, your refuge, until the immensity of His spirit envelopes your spirit and it loses its smallness and weakness and comes into harmony again with His.

Prayer for the Day

I pray that I may lose my limitations in the immensity of God's love. I pray that my spirit may be in harmony with His spirit.

DEC. 1—A.A. Thought for the Day

The thoughts that come before having a slip are often largely subconscious. It is a question whether or not our subconscious minds ever become entirely free from alcoholic thoughts as long as we live. For instance, some of us dream about being drunk when we are asleep, even after several years of sobriety in A.A. During the period of our drinking days, our subconscious minds have been thoroughly conditioned by our alcoholic way of thinking and it is doubtful if they ever become entirely free of such thoughts during our lifetime. But when our conscious minds are fully conditioned against drinking, we can stay sober and our subconscious minds do not often bother us. *Am I still conditioning my conscious mind?*

Meditation for the Day

Having sympathy and compassion for all who are in temptation, a condition which we are sometimes in, we have a responsibility towards them. Sympathy always includes responsibility. Pity is useless because it does not have a remedy for the need. But wherever our sympathy goes, our responsibility goes too. When we are moved with compassion, we should go to the one in need and bind up his wounds as best we can.

Prayer for the Day

I pray that I may have sympathy for those in temptation. I pray that I may have compassion for others' trials.

DEC. 2—A.A. Thought for the Day

The thoughts that come before having a slip seem to be partly subconscious. And yet it is likely that at least part of these thoughts get into our consciousness. An idle thought connected with drinking casually pops into our mind. That is the crucial moment. Will I harbor that thought even for one minute or will I banish it from my mind at once? If I let it stay, it may develop into a daydream. I may begin to see a cool glass of beer or a Manhattan cocktail in my mind's eye. If I allow the daydream to stay in my mind, it may lead to a decision, however unconscious, to take a drink. Then I am headed for a slip. *Do I let myself daydream?*

Meditation for the Day

Many of us have a sort of vision of the kind of person God wants us to be. We must be true to that vision, whatever it is, and we must try to live up to it, by living the way we believe we should live. We can all believe that God has a vision of what he wants us to be like. In all people there is the good person which God sees in us, the person we could be and that God would like us to be. But many a person fails to fulfill that promise and God's disappointments must be many.

Prayer for the Day

I pray that I may strive to be the kind of a person that God would have me be. I pray that I may try to fulfill God's vision of what I could be.

DEC. 3—A.A. Thought for the Day

There is some alcoholic thought, conscious or unconscious, that comes before every slip. As long as we live, we must be on the lookout for such thoughts and guard against them. In fact, our A.A. training is mostly to prepare us, to make us ready to recognize such thoughts at once and to reject them at once. The slip comes when we allow such thoughts to remain in our minds, even before we actually go through the motions of lifting the glass to our lips. The A.A. program is largely one of mental training. *How well is my mind prepared?*

Meditation for the Day

Fret not your mind with puzzles that you cannot solve. The solutions may never be shown to you until you have left this life. The loss of dear ones, the inequality of life, the deformed and the maimed, and many other puzzling things may not be known to you until you reach the life beyond. "I have yet many things to say unto you, but ye cannot bear them now." Only step by step, stage by stage, can you proceed in your journey into greater knowledge and understanding.

Prayer for the Day

I pray that I may be content that things which I now see darkly will some day be made clear. I pray that I may have faith that someday I will see face to face.

DEC. 4—A.A. Thought for the Day

If we allow an alcoholic thought to lodge in our minds for any length of time, we are in danger of having a slip. Therefore we must dispel such thoughts at once, by refusing their admittance and by immediately putting constructive thoughts in their place. Remember that alcohol is poison to you. Remember that it is impossible for you to drink normally. Remember that one drink will lead to others and you will eventually be drunk. Remember what happened to you in the past as a result of your drinking. Think of every reason you have learned in A.A. for not taking that drink. Fill your mind with constructive thoughts. *Am I keeping my thoughts constructive?*

Meditation for the Day

Always seek to set aside the valuations of the world which seem wrong and try to judge only by those valuations which seem right to you. Do not seek the praise and notice of the world. Be one of those who, though sometimes scoffed at, have a serenity and peace of mind which the scoffers never know. Be one of that band who feel the Divine Principle in the universe, though He be often rejected because He cannot be seen.

Prayer for the Day

I pray that I may not heed too much the judgement of the world. I pray that I may test things by what seems right to me.

DEC. 5—A.A. Thought for the Day

In spite of all we have learned in A.A., our old way of thinking comes back on us, sometimes with overwhelming force, and occasionally some of us have slips. We forget or refuse to call on the Higher Power for help. We seem to deliberately make our minds a blank so far as A.A. training goes, and we take a drink. We eventually get drunk. We are temporarily right back where we started from. Those who have had slips say unanimously that they were no fun. They say A.A. had taken all the pleasure out of drinking. They knew they were doing the wrong thing. The old mental conflict was back in full force. They were disgusted with themselves. *Am I convinced that I can never get anything more out of drinking?*

Meditation for the Day

Give something to those who are having trouble, to those whose thoughts are confused, something of your sympathy, your prayers, your time, your love, your thought, your self. Then give of your own confidence, as you have had it given to you by the grace of God. Give of yourself and of your loving sympathy. Give your best to those who need it and will accept it. Give according to need, never according to deserts. Remember that the giving of advice can never take the place of giving of your self.

Prayer for the Day

I pray that as I have received, so may I give. I pray that I may have the right answer to those who are confused.

DEC. 6—A.A. Thought for the Day

People who have had a slip are ashamed of themselves—sometimes so ashamed that they fear to go back to A.A. They develop the old inferiority complex and tell themselves that they are no good, that they have let down their friends in A.A., that they are hopeless, and that they can never make it. This state of mind is perhaps worse than it was originally. They have probably been somewhat weakened by their slip. But their A.A. training cannot ever be entirely lost. They always know they can go back if they want to. They know there is still God's help for them if they will again ask for it. *Do I believe that I can never entirely lose what I have learned in A.A.?*

Meditation for the Day

Nobody entirely escapes temptation. You must expect it and be ready for it when it comes. None of us is entirely safe. You must try to keep your defenses up by daily thought and prayer. That is why we have these daily meditations. You must be able to recognize temptation when it comes. The first step toward conquering temptation always is to see it clearly as temptation and not to harbor it in your mind. Dissociate yourself from it, put it out of your mind as soon as it appears. Do not think of excuses for yielding to it. Turn at once to the Higher Power for help.

Prayer for the Day

I pray that I may be prepared for whatever temptation may come to me. I pray that I may see it clearly and avoid it with the help of God.

DEC. 7—A.A. Thought for the Day

When people come back to A.A. after having a slip, the temptation is strong to say nothing about it. No other A.A. member should force them to declare themselves. It is entirely up to them. If they are well-grounded in A.A., they will realize that it's up to them to speak up at the next meeting and tell about their slip. There is no possible evasion of this duty, if they are thoroughly honest and really desirous of living the A.A. way again. When they have done it, their old confidence returns. They are home again. Their slip should not be mentioned again by others. They are again a good member of A.A. *Am I tolerant of other peoples' mistakes?*

Meditation for the Day

It is in the union of a soul with God that strength, new life, and spiritual power come. Bread sustains the body but we cannot live by bread alone. To try to do the will of God is the meat and support of true living. We feed on that spiritual food. Soul starvation comes from failing to do so. The world talks about bodies that are undernourished. What of the souls that are undernourished? Strength and peace come from partaking of spiritual food.

Prayer for the Day

I pray that I may not try to live by bread alone. I pray that my spirit may live by trying to do the will of God as I understand it.

DEC. 8—A.A. Thought for the Day

The length of time of our sobriety is not as important as its quality. A person who has been in A.A. for a number of years may not be in as good mental condition as a person who has only been in a few months. It is a great satisfaction to have been an A.A. member for a long time and we often mention it. It may sometimes help the newer members, because they may say to themselves, "If they can do it, I can do it." And yet the older members must realize that as long as they live, they are only one drink away from a drunk. *What is the quality of my sobriety?*

Meditation for the Day

"And greater works than this shall ye do." We can do greater works when we have more experience of the new way of life. We can have all the power we need from the Unseen God. We can have His grace, His spirit, to make us effective as we go along each day. Opportunities for a better world are all around us. Greater works can we do. But we do not work alone. The power of God is behind all good works.

Prayer for the Day

I pray that I may find a rightful place in the world. I pray that my work may be made more effective by the grace of God.

DEC. 9—A.A. Thought for the Day

The way of A.A. is the way of fellowship. We have read a good deal about fellowship and yet it is such an important part of the A.A. program that it seems we cannot think too much about it. Human beings were not meant to live alone. A hermit's life is not a normal or natural one. We all need to be by ourselves at times, but we cannot really live without the companionship of others. Our natures demand it. Our lives depend largely upon it. The fellowship of A.A. seems to us to be the best in the world. *Do I fully appreciate what the fellowship of A.A. means to me?*

Meditation for the Day

We are all seeking something, but many do not know what they want in life. They are seeking something because they are restless and dissatisfied, without realizing that faith in God can give an objective and a purpose to their lives. Many of us are at least subconsciously seeking for a Power greater than ourselves because that would give a meaning to our existence. If you have found that Higher Power, you can be the means of leading others aright, by showing them that their search for a meaning to life will end when they find faith and trust in God as the answer.

Prayer for the Day

I pray that my soul will lose its restlessness by finding rest in God. I pray that I may find peace of mind in the thought of God and His purpose for my life.

DEC. 10—A.A. Thought for the Day

Our drinking fellowship was a substitute one, for lack of something better. At the time, we did not realize what real fellowship could be. Drinking fellowship has a fatal fault. It is not based on a firm foundation. Most of it is on the surface. It is based mostly on the desire to use your companions for your own pleasure, and using others is a false foundation. Drinking fellowship has been praised in song and story. The "cup that cheers" has become famous as a means of companionship. But we realize that the higher centers of our brains are dulled by alcohol and such fellowship cannot be on the highest plane. It is at best only a substitute. *Do I see my drinking fellowship in its proper light?*

Meditation for the Day

Set for yourself the task of growing daily more and more into the consciousness of a Higher Power. We must keep trying to improve our conscious contact with God. This is done by prayer, quiet times, and communion. Often all you need to do is sit silent before God and let Him speak to you through your thought. Try to think God's thoughts after Him. When the guidance comes, you must not hesitate, but go out and follow that guidance in your daily work, doing what you believe to be the right thing.

Prayer for the Day

I pray that I may be still and know that God is with me. I pray that I may open my mind to the leading of the Divine Mind.

DEC. 11—A.A. Thought for the Day

Doctors think of the A.A. fellowship as group therapy. This is a very narrow conception of the depth of the A.A. fellowship. Looking at it purely as a means of acquiring and holding sobriety, it is right as far as it goes. But it doesn't go far enough. Group therapy is directed toward the help that the individual receives from it. It is essentially selfish. It is using the companionship of other alcoholics only in order to stay sober ourselves. But this is only the beginning of real A.A. fellowship. *Do I deeply feel the true A.A. fellowship?*

Meditation for the Day

Most of us have had to live through the dark part of our lives, the time of failure, the nighttime of our lives, when we were full of struggle and care, worry and remorse, when we felt deeply the tragedy of life. But with our daily surrender to a Higher Power, come a peace and joy that makes all things new. We can now take each day as a joyous sunrise-gift from God to use for Him and for other people. The night of the past is gone, this day is ours.

Prayer for the Day

I pray that I may take this day as a gift from God. I pray that I may thank God for this day and be glad in it.

DEC. 12—A.A. Thought for the Day

Clergymen speak of the spiritual fellowship of the church. This is much closer to the A.A. way than mere group therapy. Such a fellowship is based on a common belief in God and a common effort to live a spiritual life. We try to do this in A.A. We also try to get down to the real problems in each others' lives. We try to open up to each other. We have a real desire to be of service to each other. We try to go deep down into the personal lives of our members. *Do I appreciate the deep personal fellowship of A.A.?*

Meditation for the Day

Love and fear cannot dwell together. By their very natures, they cannot exist side by side. Fear is a very strong force. And therefore a weak and vacillating love can soon be routed by fear. But a strong love, a love that trusts in God, is sure eventually to conquer fear. The only sure way to dispel fear is to have the love of God more and more in your heart and soul.

Prayer for the Day

I pray that love will drive out the fear in my life. I pray that my fear will flee before the power of the love of God.

DEC. 13—A.A. Thought for the Day

We come now to A.A. fellowship. It is partly group therapy. It is partly spiritual fellowship. But it is even more. It is based on a common illness, a common failure, a common problem. It goes deep down into our personal lives and our personal needs. It requires a full opening up to each other of our inmost thoughts and most secret problems. All barriers between us are swept aside. They have to be. Then we try to help each other get well. The A.A. fellowship is based on a sincere desire to help the other person. In A.A. we can be sure of sympathy, understanding and real help. These things make the A.A. fellowship the best that we know. *Do I fully appreciate the depth of the A.A. fellowship?*

Meditation for the Day

The Higher Power can guide us to the right decisions if we pray about them. We can believe that many details of our lives are planned by God and planned with a wealth of forgiving love for the mistakes we have made. We can pray today to be shown the right way. We can choose the good, and when we choose it, we can feel that the whole power of the universe is behind us. We can achieve a real harmony with God's purpose for our lives.

Prayer for the Day

I pray that I may choose aright today. I pray that I may be shown the right way to live today.

DEC. 14—A.A. Thought for the Day

The way of A.A. is the way of service. Without that, it would not work. We have been "on the wagon" and hated it. We have taken the pledge and waited for the time to be up with impatience. We have tried in all manner of ways to help ourselves. But not until we begin to help other people do we get full relief. It is an axiom that the A.A. program has to be given away in order to be kept. A river flows into the Dead Sea and stops. A river flows into a clear pool and flows out again. We get and then we give. If we do not give, we do not keep. *Have I given up all ideas of holding A.A. for myself alone?*

Meditation for the Day

Try to see the life of the spirit as a calm place, shut away from the turmoil of the world. Think of your spiritual home as a place full of peace, serenity, and contentment. Go to this quiet, meditative place for the strength to carry you through today's duties and problems. Keep coming back here for refreshment when you are weary of the hubbub of the outside world. From this quietness and communion comes our strength.

Prayer for the Day

I pray that I may keep this resting place where I can commune with God. I pray that I may find refreshment in meditation on the Eternal.

DEC. 15—A.A. Thought for the Day

Service to others makes the world a good place. Civilization would cease if all of us were always and only for ourselves. We alcoholics have a wonderful opportunity to contribute to the well-being of the world. We have a common problem. We find a common answer. We are uniquely equipped to help others with the same problem. What a wonderful world it would be if everybody took his own greatest problem and found the answer to it and spent the rest of his life helping others with the same problem in his spare time. Soon we would have the right kind of a world. *Do I appreciate my unique opportunity to be of service?*

Meditation for the Day

Today can be lived in the consciousness of God's contact, upholding you in all good thoughts, words, and deeds. If sometimes there seems to be a shadow on your life and you feel out of sorts, remember that this is not the withdrawl of God's presence, but only your own temporary unwillingness to realize it. The quiet gray days are the days for doing what you must do, but know that the consciousness of God's nearness will return and be with you again, when the gray days are past.

Prayer for the Day

I pray that I may face the dull days with courage. I pray that I may have faith that the bright days will return.

DEC. 16—A.A. Thought for the Day

The way of A.A. is the way of faith. We don't get the full benefit of the program until we surrender our lives to some Power greater than ourselves and trust that Power to give us the strength we need. There is no better way for us. We can get sober without it. We can stay sober for some time without it. But if we are going to truly live, we must take the way of faith in God. That is the path for us. We must follow it. *Have I taken the way of faith?*

Meditation for the Day

Life is not a search for happiness. Happiness is a by-product of living the right kind of a life, of doing the right thing. Do not search for happiness, search for right living and happiness will be your reward. Life is sometimes a march of duty during dull, dark days. But happiness will come again, as God's smile of recognition of your faithfulness. True happiness is always the by-product of a life well lived.

Prayer for the Day

I pray that I may not seek happiness but seek to do right. I pray that I may not seek pleasure so much as the things that bring true happiness.

DEC. 17—A.A. Thought for the Day

The way of faith is, of course, not confined to A.A. It is the way for everybody who really wants to live. But many people can go through life without much of it. Many are doing so, to their own sorrow. The world is full of lack of faith. Many people have lost confidence in any meaning in the universe. Many are wondering if it has any meaning at all. Many are at loose ends. Life has no goal for many. They are strangers in the land. They are not at home. But for us in A.A., the way of faith is the way of life. We have proved by our past lives that we could not live without it. *Do I think I could live happily without faith?*

Meditation for the Day

"He maketh His sun to rise on the evil and the good, and sends the rain on the just and the unjust." God does not interfere with the working of natural laws. The laws of nature are unchangeable, otherwise we could not depend on them. As far as natural laws are concerned, God makes no distinction between good and bad people. Sickness or death may strike anywhere. But spiritual laws are also made to be obeyed. On our choice of good or evil depends whether we go upward to true success and victory in life or downward to loss and defeat.

Prayer for the Day

I pray that I may choose today the way of the spiritual life. I pray that I may live today with faith and hope and love.

DEC. 18—A.A. Thought for the Day

Unless we have the key of faith to un-lock the meaning of life, we are lost. We do not choose faith because it is one way for us, but because it is the only way. Many have failed and will fail. For we cannot live victoriously without faith; we are at sea without a rudder or an anchor, drifting on the sea of life. Wayfarers without a home. Our souls are restless until they find rest in God. Without faith, our lives are a meaning-less succession of unrelated happen-ings, without rhyme or reason. *Have I come to rest in faith?*

Meditation for the Day

This vast universe around us, including this won-derful earth on which we live, was once perhaps only a thought in the mind of God. The nearer the astronomers and the physicists get to the ultimate composition of all things, the nearer the universe approaches a mathematical formula, which is thought. The universe may be the thought of the Great Thinker. We must try to think God's thoughts after Him. We must try to get guidance from the Divine Mind as to what His intention is for the world and what part we can have in carrying out that intention.

Prayer for the Day

I pray that I may not worry over the limitations of my human mind. I pray that I may live as though my mind were a reflection of the Divine Mind.

DEC. 19—A.A. Thought for the Day

The skeptic and the agnostic say it is impossible for us to find the answer to life. Many have tried and failed. But many more have put aside intellectual pride and have said to themselves: Who am I to say there is no God? Who am I to say there is no purpose in life? The atheist makes a declaration: "The world originated in a cipher and aimlessly rushes nowhere." Others live for the moment and do not even think about why they are here or where they are going. They might as well be clams on the bottom of the ocean, protected by their hard shells of indifference. They are going nowhere and they do not care. *Do I care where I am going?*

Meditation for the Day

We may consider the material world as the clay which the artist works with, to make of it something beautiful or ugly. We need not fear material things, which are neither good nor bad in the moral sense. There seems to be no active force for evil—outside of human beings themselves. Humans alone can have either evil intentions—resentments, malevolence, hate and revenge—or good intentions—love and good will. They can make something ugly or something beautiful out of the clay of their lives.

Prayer for the Day

I pray that I may make something good out of my life. I pray that I may be a good artisan of the materials which I have been given to use.

DEC. 20—A.A. Thought for the Day

Our faith should control the whole of our life. We alcoholics were living a divided life. We had to find a way to make it whole. When we were drinking, our lives were made up of a lot of scattered and unrelated pieces. We must pick up our lives and put them together again. We do it by recovering faith in a Divine Principle in the universe which holds us together and holds the whole universe together and gives it meaning and purpose. We surrender our disorganized lives to that Power, we get into harmony with the Divine Spirit, and our lives are made whole again. *Is my life whole again?*

Meditation for the Day

Avoid fear as you would a plague. Fear, even the smallest fear, is a hacking at the cords of faith that bind you to God. However small the fraying, in time those cords will wear thin, and then one disappointment or shock will make them snap. But for the little fears, the cords of faith would have held firm. Avoid depression, which is allied to fear. Remember that all fear is disloyalty to God. It is a denial of His care and protection.

Prayer for the Day

I pray that I may have such trust in God today that I will not fear anything too greatly. I pray that I may have assurance that God will take care of me in the long run.

DEC. 21—A.A. Thought for the Day

Have I ceased being inwardly defeated, at war with myself? Have I given myself freely to A.A. and to the Higher Power? Have I got over being sick inside? Am I still wandering mentally or am I "on the beam?" I can face anything if I am sure I am on the way. When I am sure, I should bet my life on A.A. I have learned how the program works. Now will I follow it with all I have, with all I can give, with all my might, with all my life? *Am I going to let A.A. principles guide the rest of my life?*

Meditation for the Day

In this time of quiet meditation, follow the pressure of the Lord's leading. In all decisions to be made today, yield to the gentle pressure of your conscience. Stay or go as that pressure indicates. Take the events of today as part of God's planning and ordering. He may lead you to a right decision. Wait quietly until you have an inner urge, a leading, a feeling that a thing is right, a pressure on your will by the spirit of God.

Prayer for the Day

I pray that today I may try to follow the inner pressure of God's leading. I pray that I may try to follow my conscience and do what seems right today.

DEC. 22—A.A. Thought for the Day

As we look back over our drinking careers, we must realize that our lives were a mess because we were a mess inside. The trouble was in us, not in life itself. Life itself was good enough, but we were looking at it the wrong way. We were looking at life through the bottom of a whiskey glass, and it was distorted. We could not see all the beauty and goodness and purpose in the world because our vision was blurred. We were in a house with one-way glass in the windows. People could see us but we could not look out and see them and see what life meant to them and should mean to us. We were blind then, but now we can see. *Can I now look at life as it really is?*

Meditation for the Day

Fear no evil, because the power of God can conquer evil. Evil has power to seriously hurt only those who do not place themselves under the protection of the Higher Power. This is not a question of feeling, it is an assured fact of our experience. Say to yourself with assurance that whatever it is, no evil can seriously harm you as long as you depend on the Higher Power. Be sure of the protection of God's grace.

Prayer for the Day

I pray that fear of evil will not get me down. I pray that I may try to place myself today under the protection of God's grace.

DEC. 23—A.A. Thought for the Day

We have definitely left that dream world behind. It was only a sham. It was a world of our own making and it was not the real world. We are sorry for the past, yes, but we learned a lot from it. We can put it down to experience, valuable experience, as we see it now, because it has given us the knowledge necessary to face the world as it really is. We had to become alcoholics in order to find the A.A. program. We would not have got it any other way. In a way, it was worth it. *Do I look at my past as valuable experience?*

Meditation for the Day

Shed peace, not discord, wherever you go. Try to be part of the cure of every situation, not part of the problem. Try to ignore evil, rather than to actively combat it. Always try to build up, never to tear down. Show others by your example that happiness comes from living the right way. The power of your example is greater than the power of what you say.

Prayer for the Day

I pray that I may try to bring something good into every situation today. I pray that I may be constructive in the way I think and speak and act today.

DEC. 24—A.A. Thought for the Day

We have been given a new life just because we happened to become alcoholics. We certainly don't deserve the new life that has been given us. There is little in our past to warrant the life we have now. Many people live good lives from their youth on, not getting into serious trouble, being well adjusted to life, and yet they have not found all that we drunks have found. We had the good fortune to find Alcoholics Anonymous and with it a new life. We are among the lucky few in the world who have learned a new way to live. *Am I deeply grateful for the new life that I have learned in A.A.?*

Meditation for the Day

A deep gratitude to the Higher Power for all the blessings which we have and which we don't deserve has come to us. We thank God and mean it. Then comes service to other people, out of gratitude for what we have received. This entails some sacrifice of ourselves and our own affairs. But we are glad to do it. Gratitude, service, and then sacrifice are the steps that lead to good A.A. work. They open the door to a new life for us.

Prayer for the Day

I pray that I may gladly serve others out of deep gratitude for what I have received. I pray that I may keep a deep sense of obligation.

DEC. 25—A.A. Thought for the Day

Many alcoholics will be saying today: "This is a good Christmas for me." They will be looking back over past Christmases which were not like this one. They will be thanking God for their sobriety and their new found life. They will be thinking about how their lives were changed when they came into A.A. They will be thinking that perhaps God let them live through all the hazards of their drinking careers, when they were perhaps often close to death, in order that they might be used by Him in the great work of A.A. *Is this a happy Christmas for me?*

Meditation for the Day

The kingdom of heaven is also for the lowly, the sinners, the repentant. "And they presented unto him gifts—gold, frankincense, and myrrh." Bring your gifts of gold—your money and material possessions. Bring your frankincense—the consecration of your life to a worthy cause. Bring your myrrh—your sympathy and understanding and help. Lay them all at the feet of God and let Him have full use of them.

Prayer for the Day

I pray that I may be truly thankful on this Christmas Day. I pray that I may bring my gifts and lay them on the altar.

DEC. 26—A.A. Thought for the Day

I am glad to be a part of A.A., of that great fellowship that is spreading over the United States and all over the world. I am only one of the many A.A.s, but I am one. I am grateful to be living at this time, when I can help A.A. to grow, when it needs me to put my shoulder to the wheel and help keep the movement going. I am glad to be able to be useful, to have a reason for living, a purpose in life. I want to lose my life in this great cause and so find it again. *Am I grateful to be an A.A.?*

Meditation for the Day

These meditations can teach us how to relax. We can be of service to other people in a small way, at least. And we can be happy while doing it. We should not worry too much about people we cannot help. We can make it a habit to leave the outcome of the things we do to the Higher Power. We can go along through life doing the best we can, but without a feeling of urgency or strain. We can enjoy all the good things and the beauty of life, but at the same time depend deeply on God.

Prayer for the Day

I pray that I may give my life to this worth-while cause. I pray that I may enjoy the satisfaction that comes from good work well done.

DEC. 27—A.A. Thought for the Day

I need the A.A. principles for the development of the buried life within me, that good life, which I had misplaced, but which I found again in this fellowship. This life within me is developing slowly but surely, with many set-backs, many mistakes, many failures, but still developing. As long as I stick close to A.A., my life will go on developing, and I cannot yet know what it will be, but I know that it will be good. That's all I want to know. It will be good. *Am I thanking God for A.A.?*

Meditation for the Day

Build your life on the firm foundation of true gratitude to God for all His blessings and true humility because of your unworthiness of these blessings. Build the frame of your life out of self-discipline; never let yourself get selfish or lazy or contented with yourself. Build the walls of your life out of service to others, helping them to find the way to live. Build the roof of your life out of prayer and quiet times, waiting for God's guidance from above. Build a garden around your life out of peace of mind and serenity and a sure faith.

Prayer for the Day

I pray that I may build my life on A.A. principles. I pray that it may be a good building when my work is finished.

DEC. 28—A.A. Thought for the Day

A.A. may be human in its organization, but it is divine in its purpose. The purpose is to point me toward God and the good life. My feet have been set upon the right path. I feel it in the depths of my being. I am going in the right direction. The future can be safely left to God. Whatever the future holds, it cannot be too much for me to bear. I have the Divine Power with me to carry me through everything that may happen. *Am I pointed toward God and the good life?*

Meditation for the Day

Although unseen, the Lord is always near to those who believe in Him and trust Him and depend on Him for the strength to meet the challenges of life. Although veiled from mortal sight, the Higher Power is always available to us whenever we humbly ask for it. The feeling that God is with us should not depend on any passing mood of ours; we should try to be always conscious of His power and love in the background of our lives.

Prayer for the Day

I pray that I may feel that God is not too far away to depend on for help. I pray that I may feel confident of His readiness to give me the power that I need.

DEC. 29—A.A. Thought for the Day

Participating in the privileges of the movement, I shall share in the responsibilities, taking it upon myself to carry my fair share of the load, not grudgingly but joyfully. I am deeply grateful for the privileges I enjoy because of my membership in this great movement. They put an obligation upon me which I will not shirk. I will gladly carry my fair share of the burdens. Because of the joy of doing them, they will no longer be burdens, but opportunities. *Will I accept every opportunity gladly?*

Meditation for the Day

Work and prayer are the two forces which are gradually making a better world. We must work for the betterment of ourselves and other people. Faith without works is dead. But all work with people should be based on prayer. If we say a little prayer before we speak or try to help, it will make us more effective. Prayer is the force behind the work. Prayer is based on faith that God is working with us and through us. We can believe that nothing is impossible in human relationships, if we depend on the help of God.

Prayer for the Day

I pray that my life may be balanced between prayer and work. I pray that I may not work without prayer or pray without work.

DEC. 30—A.A. Thought for the Day

To the extent that I fail in my responsibilities, A.A. fails. To the extent that I succeed, A.A. succeeds. Every failure of mine will set back A.A. work to that extent. Every success of mine will put A.A. ahead to that extent. I shall not wait to be drafted for service to others, but I shall volunteer. I shall accept every opportunity to work for A.A. as a challenge, and I shall do my best to accept every challenge and perform my task as best I can. *Will I accept every challenge gladly?*

Meditation for the Day

People are failures in the deepest sense when they seek to live without God's sustaining power. Many people try to be self-sufficient and seek selfish pleasure and find that it does not work too well. No matter how much material wealth they acquire, no matter how much fame and material power, the time of disillusionment and futility usually comes. Death is ahead, and they cannot take any material thing with them when they go. What matters it if I have gained the whole world, but lost my own soul?

Prayer for the Day

I pray that I will not come empty to the end of my life. I pray that I may so live that I will not be afraid to die.

DEC. 31—A.A. Thought for the Day

I shall be loyal in my attendance, generous in my giving, kind in my criticism, creative in my suggestions, loving in my attitudes. I shall give A.A. my interest, my enthusiasm, my devotion, and most of all, myself. The Lord's Prayer has become part of my A.A. thoughts for each day: "Our Father who art in heaven, hallowed be Thy name. Thy kingdom come. Thy will be done, on earth as it is in heaven. Give us this day our daily bread. And forgive us our trespasses as we forgive those who trespass against us. Lead us not into temptation, but deliver us from evil." *Have I given myself?*

Meditation for the Day

As we look back over the year just gone, it has been a good year to the extent that we have put good thoughts, good words, and good deeds into it. None of what we have thought, said, or done need be wasted. Both the good and the bad experiences can be profited by. In a sense, the past is not entirely gone. The result of it, for good or evil, is with us at the present moment. We can only learn by experience and none of our experience is completely wasted. We can humbly thank God for the good things of the year that has gone.

Prayer for the Day

I pray that I may carry good things into the year ahead. I pray that I may carry on with faith, with prayer, and with hope.

THE TWELVE STEPS OF A.A.

1. We admitted we were powerless over alcohol—that our lives had become unmanageable.

2. Came to believe that a Power greater than ourselves could restore us to sanity.

3. Made a decision to turn our will and our lives over to the care of God as we understood Him.

4. Made a searching and fearless moral inventory of ourselves.

5. Admitted to God, to ourselves, and to another human being, the exact nature of our wrongs.

6. Were entirely ready to have God remove all these defects of character.

7. Humbly asked Him to remove our shortcomings.

8. Made a list of all persons we had harmed, and became willing to make amends to them all.

9. Made direct amends to such people wherever possible, except when to do so would injure them or others.

10. Continued to take personal inventory and when we were wrong promptly admitted it.

11. Sought through prayer and meditation to improve our conscious contact with God as we understood Him, praying only for knowledge of His will for us and the power to carry that out.

12. Having had a spiritual awakening as the result of these steps, we tried to carry this message to alcoholics, and to practice these principles in all our affairs.

The Twelve Traditions of A.A.

1. Our common welfare should come first; personal recovery depends upon A.A. unity.

2. For our group purpose there is but one ultimate authority—a loving God as He may express Himself in our group conscience. Our leaders are but trusted servants—they do not govern.

3. The only requirement for A.A. membership is a desire to stop drinking.

4. Each group should be autonomous, except in matters affecting other groups or A.A. as a whole.

5. Each group has but one primary purpose —to carry its message to the alcoholic who still suffers.

6. An A.A. group ought never endorse, finance, or lend the A.A. name to any related facility or outside enterprise lest problems of money, property and prestige divert us from our primary spiritual aim.

7. Every A.A. group ought to be fully self-supporting, declining outside contributions.

8. Alcoholics Anonymous should remain forever non-professional, but our service centers may employ special workers.

9. A.A., as such, ought never to be organized, but we may create service boards or committees directly responsible to those they serve.

10. Alcoholics Anonymous has no opinion on outside issues, hence the A.A. name ought never be drawn into public controversy.

11. Our public relations policy is based on attraction rather than promotion; we need always maintain personal anonymity at the level of press, radio, television and films.

12. Anonymity is the spiritual foundation of all our traditions, ever reminding us to place principles above personalities.

THE SERENITY PRAYER

God grant me the serenity
To accept the things I cannot change,
The courage to change the things I can,
And the wisdom to know the difference.

Compiled by
a member of the
Group at Daytona Beach, Fla.

NOTES

NOTES

NOTES

NOTES

NOTES

516
741-2468

M. 12-2 Corpus Christi
Willis Ave.